Shelby Foote

THE CIVIL WAR

A NARRATIVE

A NARRATIVE

5

★ ★ ★

FREDERICKSBURG
TO STEELE BAYOU

10th Anniversary Edition

BY SHELBY FOOTE
AND THE EDITORS OF TIME-LIFE BOOKS,
ALEXANDRIA, VIRGINIA

*All these were honoured in their generations,
and were the glory of their times.*

*There be of them,
that have left a name behind them,
that their praises might be reported.*

*And some there be, which have no memorial;
who are perished, as though they had never been;
and are become as though they had never been born;
and their children after them.*

*But these were merciful men,
whose righteousness hath not been forgotten.*

*With their seed shall continually remain
a good inheritance,
and their children are within the covenant.*

*Their seed standeth fast,
and their children for their sakes.*

*Their seed shall remain for ever,
and their glory shall not be blotted out.*

*Their bodies are buried in peace;
but their name liveth for evermore.*

— ECCLESIASTICUS XLIV

Contents

★ ★ ★

PROLOGUE 6

1 Davis, Westward and Return   8

2 Fredericksburg   30

3 Prairie Grove; Port Hudson;
    Galveston   64

4 Parker's Crossroads; Holly Springs;
    Walnut Hills   84

5 Murfreesboro: Bragg Retreats   110

6 Lincoln; Mud March; Hooker   146

7 Arkansas Post; Transmississippi;
    Grant   180

8 "Shoddy"; Erlanger; Richmond
    Bread Riot   200

9 Rosecrans; Johnston; Streight's Raid 228

10 Vicksburg — Seven Failures   254

EPILOGUE 296

PICTURE CREDITS 298

INDEX 299

★

Prologue

———— ⌘ ————

★ ★ ★ **A**fter celebrating its second victory along Bull Run near Manassas, Virginia, in August 1862, the Confederacy abandoned its defensive strategy in the late summer and fall and struck boldly into northern territory. In both the East and the West, the invasions were partially successful. They took the pressure off the southern home front by allowing its harvests to supply much-needed foodstuffs for the rebel armies. They frightened Union forces into reacting defensively, postponing or abandoning their own plans of attack. And they exacted a bloody toll. But these partial successes were also partial failures.

The advance of Lee's Army of Northern Virginia into Maryland had been stopped by McClellan's Army of the Potomac at Sharpsburg, Maryland. The single bloodiest day in American history had ended in a draw, but McClellan held the field along Antietam Creek while Lee withdrew across the Potomac River into Virginia and abandoned recently captured Harpers Ferry. Out West, Braxton Bragg and Edmund Kirby Smith had launched their forces north into Kentucky to threaten Louisville and perhaps Cincinnati but were battered severely at Perryville and forced to return south into Tennessee. Neither of these offensives convinced Europeans to recognize the Confederacy.

These rebel incursions had scarcely altered the lines drawn between the warring factions, but following Antietam, Lincoln promulgated a Proclamation of Emancipation that would soon alter the social and moral underpinnings of the strife.

Stalemated in the past few months, both Lincoln and Davis sought strategies, commanders, and combinations that might turn the tide in their favor. Lincoln replaced McClellan — the general who had "the slows" — with General Burnside — the general for whom a bloody stone bridge near Sharpsburg had been named — hoping the latter would launch a rapid drive south. In the West, Sherman, sent by Grant to probe the defenses north of Vicksburg, was stopped by Confederate forces under Stephen D. Lee at Walnut Hills.

From early December 1862 to early January 1863, Davis traveled in the West to confer with his generals and to see first-hand what might be done. During his trip, Lee's army repulsed Burnside's forces at Fredericksburg, Virginia; Earl Van Dorn smashed Grant's supply depot at Holly Springs, Mississippi; John Hunt Morgan mangled Rosecrans' supply lines in Kentucky and Tennessee; Confederate forces retook Galveston; Hindman's rebel infantry had

★

marched on Prairie Grove, Arkansas; and Bragg had marched north to fight Rosecrans' Federals at Murfreesboro. There, as at Antietam, the bloody struggle ended in a draw, but Bragg, like Lee before him, chose to abandon the field.

When Davis returned to a warm welcome in Richmond on January 5, he felt weary but reassured. He believed the Confederacy to be strong and his troops' morale high. But he had little time to enjoy this notion. He was soon confronted by unsettling events. In late January Burnside moved to strike a blow at Fredericksburg's flank but was stopped again, this time not by massed Confederate fire but by a horrendous winter storm. The Southern economy, already crippled by war damage, the Union blockade, and shrinking revenues, suffered another blow in the guise of a disastrous bond issue floated by French bankers that benefited the French far more than it did the Confederacy. The inability to transport and distribute the few goods that were available, coupled with high inflation, had seriously begun to affect daily life in the Confederacy, and its people began to express their frustration. Beginning in Easter week, a series of riots — the first in Richmond itself — resulted in looting, burned stores, and ransacked supply depots.

The North on the other hand was enjoying a boom. Industry was expanding at a phenomenal rate, fueled and lubricated by greatly increased oil production and manned by thousands of fresh European immigrants. Newly manufactured goods, bumper crops of grain, and tons of wool swelled the holds of ever larger numbers of merchantmen bound overseas. While the poor were not necessarily getting poorer, the rich were certainly getting richer. The Yankees were also expecting good things to happen on the war front. Grant was beginning a number of ambitious expeditions — cutting levees, digging canals, and floating and marching men and equipment through the Mississippi bayou country — to by-pass or incircle Vicksburg, the Gibraltar of the West. But these would yield little result, and Grant would again be accused of bungling and of drinking on the job. The greater hope seemed to reside in Fighting Joe Hooker, who had been named to replace Burnside in the East. Perhaps now the North could move again on Richmond.

★ ★ ★

★

Well-accoutered western Union cavalrymen like these faired poorly against their less well equipped Confederate adversaries under Wheeler, Morgan, and Forrest.

Davis, Westward and Return

1862 ★ ★ ★ ★ ★ ★ fter an absence of nearly two years," Jefferson Davis told the legislators assembled under the golden dome of his home-state capitol on the day after Christmas, 1862 — twenty months and two weeks, to the day, since the guns of Charleston opened fire on Sumter to inaugurate the civil war no one could know was not yet halfway over — "I again find myself among those who, from the days of my childhood, have ever been the trusted objects of my affection, those for whose good I have ever striven and whose interests I have sometimes hoped I may have contributed to subserve. . . . I left you to assume the duties which have devolved upon me as the representative of the new Confederacy. The responsibilities of this position have occupied all my time, and have left me no opportunity for mingling with my friends in Mississippi or for sharing in the dangers which have menaced them. But, wherever duty may have called me, my heart has been with you, and the success of the cause in which we are all engaged has been first in my thoughts and prayers."

In February of the year before, he had left for Montgomery, Alabama, to assume his role as President of the newly established provisional government, believing, as he said now, "that the service to which I was called could be but temporary." A West Pointer and an authentic hero of the Mexican War, he had considered his primary talent — or, as he termed it, his "capacity" — to be mili-

★

tary. He had thought to return to the duty he found congenial, that of a line offi-cer in the service of his state, "to lead Mississippians in the field, and to be with them where danger was to be braved and glory won. . . . But it was decided differ-ently. I was called to another sphere of action. How, in that sphere, I have dis-charged the duties and obligations imposed on me, it does not become me to constitute myself the judge. It is for others to decide that question. But, speaking to you with that frankness and that confidence with which I have always spoken to you, and which partakes of the nature of thinking aloud, I can say with my hand upon my heart that whatever I have done has been done with the sincere purpose of promoting the noble cause in which we are engaged. The period which has elapsed since I left you is short; for the time which may appear long in the life of a man is short in the history of a nation. And in that short period remarkable changes have been wrought in all the circumstances by which we are surrounded."

Remarkable changes had indeed been wrought, and of these the most immediately striking to those present, seated row on row beneath him or standing close-packed along the outer aisles, was in the aspect of the man who stood before them, tall and slender, careworn and oracular, in a mote-shot nim-bus of hazy noonday sunlight pouring down from the high windows of the hall. When they had seen him last on this same rostrum, just short of twenty-three months ago this week, he had not appeared to be within a decade of his fifty-two years of age. Now, though, he was fifty-four, and he looked it. The "trou-bles and thorns innumerable" which he foretold on his arrival in Montgomery to take the oath of office, back in the first glad springtime of the nation, had not only come to pass; they had also left their marks — as if the thorns, being more than figurative, had scored his brow and made of him what he had never seemed before, a man of sorrows. The gray eyes, one lustrous, the other sightless, its stone gray pupil covered by a film, were deeply sunken above the jut of the high cheekbones, and the thin upper lip, indicative of an iron will and rigid self-control, was held so tightly against the teeth, even in repose, that you saw their shape behind it. The accustomed geniality was there, the inveterate grace and charm of manner, along with the rich music of the voice, but the symptoms of strain and overwork were all too obvious. These proceeded, it was said, not only from having had to await (as he was awaiting even now) the outcome of battles in which he could have no active part, whatever his inclination, but also, it was added, from a congenital inability to relegate authority, including the minor paperwork which took up such a disproportionate share of his existence.

Other changes there were, too, less physical and therefore less im-mediately obvious, but on closer inspection no less profound. In this case, moreover, the contrast between now and then was emphasized by mutuality, involving others besides Davis. It was two-sided; reciprocal, so to speak. Arriv-ing in Jackson to accept his appointment as commander of Mississippi troops

Lady Liberty holds a portrait of Jefferson Davis in this hand-painted shield cut from the center of the regimental flag of the 14th Mississippi Infantry.

after his farewell to the Senate in January of what had presently turned out to be the first year of the conflict some men had still believed could be avoided, he had been met at the station by Governor J. J. Pettus, whom he advised to push the procurement of arms. "We shall need all and many more than we can get," he said, expressing the conviction that blood would soon be shed. "General, you overrate the risk," the governor protested, and Davis replied: "I only wish I did." So thoroughly had this prediction been fulfilled in the past twenty months — Kentucky and Missouri irretrievably gone, along with most of Tennessee and the northwest quarter of Virginia, New Orleans fallen, Nashville and Memphis occupied, and North Mississippi itself a-swarm with bluecoats — that now it was Governor Pettus who was calling for reassurance, and calling for it urgently, from the man to whom he previously had offered it so blandly.

"You have often visited the army of Virginia," he wired Richmond in early December. "At this critical juncture could you not visit the army of the West? Something must be done to inspire confidence."

By way of reinforcement for this plea there came a letter from Senator James Phelan, whose home lay in the path of the invaders. "The present alarming crisis in this state, so far from arousing the people, seems to have sunk them in listless despondency," he wrote. "The spirit of enlistment is thrice dead. Enthusiasm has expired to a cold pile of damp ashes. Defeats, retreats, sufferings, dangers, magnified by spiritless helplessness and an unchangeable conviction that our army is in the hands of ignorant and feeble commanders, are rapidly producing a sense of settled despair. . . . I imagine but one event that could awaken

★

from its waning spark the enthusiastic hopes and energy of Mississippians. Plant your own foot upon our soil, unfurl your banner at the head of the army, tell your own people that you have come to share with them the perils of this dark hour. . . . If ever your presence was needed as a last refuge from an 'Iliad of woes,' this is the hour. It is not a point to be argued. [Only] you can save us or help us save ourselves from the dread evils now so imminently pending."

Flattering as this was, in part — especially the exhortation to "unfurl your banner," which touched the former hero of Buena Vista where his inclination was strongest and his vanity was most susceptible — the senator's depiction of regional gloom and fears, tossed thus into the balance, added weight to the governor's urgent plea that the Commander in Chief undertake the suggested journey to his homeland and thereby refute in the flesh the growing complaint that the authorities in Richmond were concerned only for the welfare of the soldiers and civilians in Virginia, where if anywhere the war was being won, rather than for those in the western theater, where if anywhere the war was being lost. Not that the danger nearest the national capital was slight. Major General Ambrose Burnside, a month in command of the Army of the Potomac as successor to Major General George McClellan, who had been relieved for a lack of aggressiveness, was menacing the line of the Rappahannock with a mobile force of 150,000 men, backed by another 50,000 in the Washington defenses. To oppose this host General Robert E. Lee had something under 80,000 in the Army of Northern Virginia moving toward a concentration near Fredericksburg, where the threat of a crossing seemed gravest, midway of the direct north-south hundred-mile line connecting the two capitals. That the battle, now obviously at hand, would be fought even closer to the Confederate seat of government appeared likely, for Davis wrote Lee on December 8: "You will know best when it will be proper to make a masked movement to the rear, should circumstances require you to move nearer to Richmond."

Something else he said in this same letter. Hard as it was for him to leave the capital at a time when every day might bring the battle that would perhaps decide his country's fate, he had made up his mind to heed the call that reached him from the West. "I propose to go out there immediately," he told Lee, "with the hope that something may be done to bring out men not heretofore in service, and to arouse all classes to united and desperate resistance." After expressing the hope that "God may bless us, as in other cases seemingly as desperate, with success over our impious foe," he added, by way of apology for not having reviewed the Virginian's army since it marched northward on the eve of Second Manassas: "I have been very anxious to visit you, but feeble health and constant labor have caused me to delay until necessity hurries me in the opposite direction." He sent the letter by special courier that same December 8; then, two days later, he himself was off.

He left incognito, aboard a special car and accompanied by a single military aide, lest his going stir up rumors that the capital was about to be abandoned in the face of the threat to the line of the Rappahannock. His planned itinerary was necessarily roundabout: not only because the only direct east-west route was closed to him by the Federal grip on the final hundred miles of the Memphis & Charleston Railroad, but also because he had decided to combine the attempt to restore morale among the distraught civilians of the region, as suggested by Governor Pettus and Senator Phelan, with a personal inspection of the two main armies charged with the defense of the theater bounded east and west by the Blue Ridge Mountains and the Mississippi River. The Army of Tennessee, the larger of the two, northwest of Chattanooga and covering that city by pretending to threaten Nashville, was under General Braxton Bragg; the other, the Army of Mississippi under Lieutenant General John C. Pemberton, covered Vicksburg. Both were menaced by superior forces, or combinations of forces, under Major Generals William S. Rosecrans and Ulysses S. Grant, and Davis had lately appointed General Joseph E. Johnston to coördinate the efforts of both armies in order to meet the double menace by operating on interior lines, much as Lee had done for the past six months in Virginia, on a smaller scale but with such success as had won for Confederate arms the admiration of the world.

Johnston's was the more difficult task, albeit one on which the survival of the nation was equally dependent. Whether it could be performed — specifically, whether it could be performed by Johnston — remained to be seen. So far, though, the signs had appeared to the general himself to be anything but promising. Pemberton was falling back under pressure from Grant in North Mississippi, and Bragg's preparations for the defense of Middle Tennessee, though they had not yet been tested by Federal pressure, did not meet with the new commander's approval when he inspected them this week. In fact, he found in them full justification for a judgment he had delivered the week before, when he first established headquarters in Chattanooga. "Nobody ever assumed a command under more unfavorable circumstances," he wrote to a friend back East. "If Rosecrans had disposed our troops himself, their disposition could not have been more unfavorable to us."

★ ★ ★ *D*avis did not share the Virginian's gloom; or if he did he did not show it as he left Richmond, December 10, and rode westward through Lynchburg and Wytheville and across the state line to Knoxville, where, beginning his attempt to bolster civilian morale by a show of confidence, he made a speech in which he characterized "the Toryism of East Tennessee" as "greatly exaggerated." Joined by Lieutenant General Edmund Kirby Smith, the department commander whose march north in August and September had cleared the region of bluecoats and delivered

Cumberland Gap, but whose strength had been reduced by considerably more than half in the past month as a result of orders to reinforce Bragg in the adjoining department, the President reached Chattanooga by nightfall and went at once to pay a call on Johnston.

He found him somewhat indisposed, waiting in his quarters. Short of stature, gray and balding, a year older than Davis despite the fact that he had been a year behind him at West Point, the general had a high-colored, wedge-shaped face, fluffed white side whiskers, a grizzled mustache and goatee, eyes that crinkled attractively at their outer corners when he smiled, and a jaunty, gamecock manner. Mrs Johnston, in attendance on her husband, was able to serve their visitor a genuine cup of coffee: the "real Rio," she reported proudly to a friend next day, describing the event. She claimed nonetheless the saddest heart in Chattanooga. Whatever Davis might have accomplished elsewhere on this arduous first day of the journey he had undertaken "to arouse all classes to united and desperate resistance," he obviously had had little success in her direction. "How ill and weary I feel in this desolate land," she added in the letter to her friend in the Old Dominion, which she so much regretted having left, "& how dreary it all looks, & how little prospect there is of my poor husband doing ought than lose his army. Truly a forlorn hope it is."

The general himself was far from well, suffering from a flareup of the wound that had cost him his Virginia command, six months ago at Seven Pines, and from a weariness brought on by his just-completed inspection of the Army of Tennessee. So Davis, postponing their strategy conference until such time as he would be able to see for himself the condition of that army, left next day for Bragg's headquarters at Murfreesboro, ninety miles away and only thirty miles from Nashville.

It was a two-day visit, and unlike Johnston he was heartened by what he saw. Serenaded at his hotel by a large and enthusiastic crowd, he announced that he entertained no fears for the safety of Richmond, that Tennessee would be held to the last extremity, and that if the people would but arouse themselves to sustain the conflict, eventual if not immediate foreign intervention would assure a southern victory and peace on southern terms. His listeners, delighted by a recent exploit beyond the northern lines by Colonel John H. Morgan, did not seem to doubt for a moment the validity of his contentions or predictions. Whatever dejection he might encounter in other portions of the threatened region, he found here an optimism to match his own. The thirty-seven-year-old Morgan, with four small regiments of cavalry and two of infantry — just over 2000 men in all, most of them Kentuckians like himself — had crossed the icy Cumberland by starlight, in order to strike at dawn on Sunday, December 7, a Union force of equal strength in camp at Hartsville, forty miles upstream from Nashville. Another enemy force, three times his strength, was camped nine miles away at Castalian Springs, within easy hearing distance of his guns, but had no chance to interfere. After less than an hour of fighting, in which he inflicted more than 300 casualties at a cost of 125, Morgan accepted the surrender of Colonel Absalom B. Moore of Illinois. By noon he was back across the Cumberland with 1762 prisoners and a wagon train heavily loaded with captured equipment and supplies, riding hard for Murfreesboro and the cheers that awaited him there. "A brilliant feat," Joe Johnston called it, and recommended that Morgan "be appointed brigadier general immediately. He is indispensable."

Davis gladly conferred the promotion in person when he arrived, receiving from Morgan's own hands in return one of the three sets of enemy infantry colors the cavalryman had brought home. A formal review of one corps of the Army of Tennessee next day, followed that evening by a conference with Bragg and his lieutenants, was equally satisfying, fulfilling as it did the other half of the President's double-barreled purpose. "Found the troops there in good condition and fine spirits," he wired the Secretary of War on December 14, after his return to Chattanooga the night before. "Enemy is kept close in to Nashville, and indicates only defensive purposes."

The Murfreesboro courthouse dominated the town where Jefferson Davis, along with Joseph E. Johnston, visited Bragg's headquarters in December 1862.

This last had led to a strategic decision, made on the spot and before consultation with Johnston. As Davis saw it, comparing Pemberton's plight with Bragg's, the Mississippi commander was not only more gravely threatened by a combination of army and naval forces, above and below the Vicksburg bluff; he was also far more heavily outnumbered, and with less room for maneuver. Practically speaking, despite the assurance lately given the serenaders, the loss of Middle Tennessee would mean no more than the loss of supplies to be gathered in the region; whereas the loss of Vicksburg would mean the loss of the Mississippi River throughout its length, which in turn would mean the loss of Texas, West Louisiana, Arkansas, and the last tenuous hope for the recovery of Missouri. Consequently, in an attempt to even the odds — east and west, that is; North and South the odds could never be evened, here or elsewhere — Davis decided to reinforce Pemberton with a division from Bragg. When the latter protested that this would encourage Rosecrans to attack him, he was informed that he would have to take his chances, depending on maneuver for deliverance. "Fight if you can," Davis told him, and if necessary "fall back beyond the Tennessee."

Bragg took the decision with such grace as he could muster; but not Johnston. When Davis returned to Chattanooga with instructions for the transfer to be ordered, the Virginian protested for all he was worth against a policy which seemed to him no better than robbing Peter to pay Paul. Both western armies, he declared, were already too weak for effective operations; to weaken either was to invite disaster, particularly in Tennessee, which he referred to as "the shield of the South." But in this matter the President was inflexible. Apparently reasoning that if the general would not do the job for which he had been sent here — a balancing and a taking of calculated risks in order to make the most of the advantage of operating on interior lines — then he would do it for him, Davis insisted that the transfer order be issued immediately. This Johnston did, though with a heavy heart and still protesting, convinced that he would be proved right in the end.

Whatever Davis's reaction was on learning thus that one of his two ranking commanders was opposed to availing himself of the one solid advantage strategically accruing to the South, he had other worries to fret him now: worries that threatened not a long-range but an immediate collapse, not of a part but of the whole. On his return from Murfreesboro he heard from the War Department that the national capital was menaced from two directions simultaneously. A force of undetermined strength was moving inland from coastal North Carolina against Goldsboro and the vital Weldon Railroad, and Burnside was across the Rappahannock. "You can imagine my anxiety," Davis wrote his wife, chafed by distance and the impossibility of being in two places at once. "If the necessity demands, I will return to Richmond, though already there are indications of a strong desire for me to visit the further West, expressed in terms which render me unwilling to disappoint the expectation." Presently, however, his anxiety was relieved. The Carolina invasion, though strongly mounted, had been halted at the Neuse, well short of the vital supply line, and Lee had inflicted another staggering defeat on the main northern army, flinging it back across the Rappahannock. Davis was elated at the news, but Johnston's reaction was curiously mixed. "What luck some people have," he said. "Nobody will ever come to attack me in such a place."

After a day of rest and conferences, political as well as military, Davis left Chattanooga late on the afternoon of December 16, accompanied by Johnston, who would be making his first inspection of the western portion of his command. However, with the Memphis & Charleston in Federal hands along the Tennessee-Mississippi line, their route at first led south to Atlanta, where they spent the night and Davis responded to another serenade. Continuing south to Montgomery next morning, he spoke at midday from the portico of the Alabama capitol, where he had delivered his first inaugural a week after being notified of his unexpected election to head the newly established Confederate States of America. That was nearly two years ago. Whatever thoughts he had as to the contrast between now and then, as evidenced by the demeanor of the crowd that gathered to hear him, he kept to himself as he and Johnston rode on that night to Mobile, where he spoke formally for the second time that day. Next morning, December 19, they reached Jackson, but having agreed to return for a joint appearance before the Mississippi legislature on the day after Christmas, they only stayed for lunch and left immediately afterwards for Vicksburg.

This too was a two-day visit, and mainly they spent it inspecting the town's land and water defenses, which had been extended northward a dozen miles along a range of hills and ridges overlooking the Yazoo and its swampy bayous — Chickasaw Bluffs, the range was called, or sometimes Walnut Hills — and southward about half that far to Warrenton, a hamlet near the lower end of the tall red bluff dominating the eastern shank of the hairpin bend described at this point by a whim of the Mississippi. To an untrained eye the installations might look stout indeed, bristling with guns at intervals for nearly twenty miles, but Johnston was not pleased by what he saw. To his professional eye, they not only left much to be desired in the way of execution; their very conception, it seemed to him, was badly flawed. Nor was he any slower to say so now than he had been eight months ago at Yorktown, in a similar situation down the York-James peninsula from Richmond. "Instead of a fort requiring a small garrison," which would leave the bulk of available troops free to maneuver, he protested, the overzealous engineers had made the place into "an immense intrenched camp, requiring an army to hold it." Besides, scattered as they were along the high ground north and south "to prevent the bombardment of the town, instead of to close the navigation of the river to the enemy," the batteries would not be able to concentrate their fire against naval attack. In these and other matters Johnston expressed his discontent. Davis, a professional too, could see the justice in much of this, and though he did not order the line contracted, he moved to strengthen it by wiring the War Department of the "immediate and urgent necessity for heavy guns and long-range fieldpieces at Vicksburg."

Two bits of news, one welcome, one disturbing, reached them here in the course of their brief visit. The first was that a Federal ironclad, the *Cairo,* had been sunk up the Yazoo the week before, the result of an experiment with torpedoes by Commander Isaac N. Brown, builder and skipper of the *Arkansas,* which single-handedly had raised the midsummer naval siege by an all-out attack on the two enemy fleets before she steamed downriver to her destruction in early August. The other news was that Major General Nathaniel P. Banks, whose troops were escorted upriver from New Orleans by the deep-draft fleet under Rear Admiral David G. Farragut, had reoccupied Baton Rouge, abandoned three months before by his predecessor, Major General Benjamin F. Butler. Whatever comfort the bluff's defenders found in the mishap encountered by the Yankees in their probe of the Yazoo was more than offset by the news that they were approaching in strength from the opposite direction. Johnston, for one, was convinced that, in addition to the 9000-man division already on the way from Bragg, another 20,000 troops would be required if Vicksburg and Port Hudson, another strong point on another bluff three hundred miles downriver, were to be held against the combined forces of Grant and Banks. What was more, he thought he knew just where to get them: from the adjoining Transmississippi Department, commanded by Lieutenant General Theophilus H. Holmes.

"Our great object is to hold the Mississippi," Johnston told Davis. In this connection, he firmly believed "that our true system of warfare would be to concentrate the forces of the two departments" — his and Holmes's — "on this side of the Mississippi, beat the enemy here, then reconquer the country beyond it, which [the Federals] might have gained in the meantime."

Davis had already shown his appreciation of this "true system" by recommending, a month before he left Richmond and two weeks before Johnston himself had been assigned to the western command, that Holmes send reinforcements eastward to assist in the accomplishment of the "great objective." Since then, unfortunately, and by coincidence on the December 7 of Morgan's victory at Hartsville, the Arkansas army under Major General Thomas C. Hindman, the one mobile force of any size in the department beyond the river, had fought and lost the Battle of Prairie Grove, up in the northwest corner of the state. This altered considerably Holmes's ability to comply with the request. However, instead of pointing out this and other drawbacks to Johnston's argument — 1) that to lose the Transmississippi temporarily might be to lose it permanently, as a result of losing the confidence of the people of the region; 2) that the Confederacy, already suffering from the strictures of the Federal blockade, could not afford even a brief stoppage of the flow of supplies from Texas and the valleys of the

★

Arkansas and the Red; and 3) that the transfer east of men in gray would result in a proportional transfer of men in blue, which would lengthen rather than shorten the odds on both sides of the river unless the blow was delivered with unaccustomed lightning speed — Davis was willing to repeat the recommendation in stronger terms. Accordingly, on this same December 21, he wrote to Holmes in Little Rock, apprising him of the growing danger and urging full coöperation with Johnston's plan as set forth in that general's correspondence, which was included. It was a long letter, and in it the President said in part: "From the best information at command, a large force is now ready to descend the Mississippi and coöperate with the army advancing from Memphis to make an attack upon Vicksburg. Large forces are also reported to have been sent to the lower Mississippi for the purpose of ascending the river to attempt the reduction of Port Hudson. . . . It seems to me then unquestionably best that you should reinforce Genl Johnston." After reminding Holmes that "we cannot hope at all points to meet the enemy with a force equal to his own, and must find our security in the concentration and rapid movement of troops," Davis closed with a compliment and an admonition: "I have thus presented to you my views, and trusting alike in your patriotism and discretion, leave you to make the application of them when circumstances will permit. Whatever may be done should be done with all possible dispatch."

Joseph E. Johnston disagreed with Davis about how best to use the forces at their disposal in the west.

Johnston's enthusiasm on reading the opening paragraphs of the letter, which was shown to him before it was given to a courier bound for Little Rock, was considerably dampened by the close. Judging perhaps by his own reaction the week before, when he protested against the detachment of a division from Bragg for this same purpose, he did not share the President's trust in the "patriotism and discretion" Holmes was expected to bring to bear, and he noted regretfully that, despite the final suggestion as to the need for haste, "circumstances" had been left to govern the application of what Davis called his "views."

Two days later, moreover, the general's gloom was deepened when they returned to Jackson and proceeded north a hundred miles by rail to Grenada, where Pemberton had ended his southward retreat in the face of

Grant's advance and had his badly outnumbered field force hard at work in an attempt to fortify the banks of the Yalobusha River while his cavalry, under Major General Earl Van Dorn, probed for Grant's rear in an attempt to make him call a halt, or anyhow slow him down, by giving him trouble along his lengthening supply line. Here as at Vicksburg, Johnston found the intrenchments "very extensive, but slight — the usual defect of Confederate engineering." Nor was he pleased to discover, as he said later, that "General Pemberton and I advocated opposite modes of warfare." He would have continued the retreat to a better position farther south, hoping for a stronger concentration; but as usual Davis discounted the advantage of withdrawal and sided with the commander who was opposed to delaying a showdown.

Christmas Day they returned to Jackson, which gave the President time for an overnight preparation of the speech he would deliver tomorrow before his home-state legislature. This was not so large a task as might be thought, despite the fact that he would speak for the better part of an hour. In general, what he would say here was what he had been saying for more than two weeks now, en route from Virginia, through Tennessee, Georgia, and Alabama, and elsewhere already in Mississippi. His overnight task was mainly one of consolidating his various impromptu responses to serenades and calls for "remarks" from station platforms along the way, albeit with added emphasis on his home ties and the government's concern for the welfare of the people in what he called "the further West."

★ ★ ★ *T*hat was why he began by addressing his listeners as "those who, from the days of my childhood, have ever been the trusted objects of my affection," and adding: "Whatever fortunes I may have achieved in life have been gained as a representative of Mississippi, and before all I have labored for the advancement of her glory and honor. I now, for the first time in my career, find myself the representative of a wider circle of interest, but a circle of which the interests of Mississippi are still embraced. . . . For, although in the discharge of my duties as President of the Confederate States I had determined to make no distinction between the various parts of the country — to know no separate state — yet my heart has always beat more warmly for Mississippi, and I have looked on Mississippi soldiers with a pride and emotion such as no others inspired."

Flanked on the rostrum by Governor Pettus and Senator Phelan, he waited for the polite applause to subside, then launched at once into an excoriation of the northern government: not only its leaders but also its followers, in and out of the armies of invasion.

"I was among those who, from the beginning, predicted war . . . not because our right to secede and form a government of our own was not indisputable and clearly defined in the spirit of that declaration which rests the right to govern on the consent of the governed, but because I saw that the wickedness of the North would precipitate a war upon us. Those who supposed that the exercise of this right of separation could not produce war have had cause to be convinced that they had credited their recent associates of the North with a moderation, a sagacity, a morality they did not possess. You have been involved in a war waged for the gratification of the lust of power and aggrandizement, for your conquest and your subjugation, with a malignant ferocity and with a disregard and a contempt of the usages of civilization entirely unequaled in history. Such, I have ever warned you, were the characteristics of the northern people. . . . After what has happened during the last two years, my only wonder is that we consented to live for so long a time in association with such miscreants and have loved so much a government rotten to the core. Were it ever to be proposed again to enter into a Union with such a people, I could no more consent to do it than to trust myself in a den of thieves. . . . There is indeed a difference between the two peoples. Let no man hug the delusion that there can be renewed association between them. Our enemies are a traditionless and homeless race. From the time of Cromwell to the present moment they have been disturbers of the peace of the world. Gathered together by Cromwell from the bogs and fens of the north of Ireland and England, they commenced by disturbing the peace of their own country; they disturbed Holland, to which they fled; and they disturbed England on their return. They persecuted Catholics in England, and they hung Quakers and witches in America."

He spoke next of the conscription act, defending it against its critics; reviewed the recent successes of Confederate arms, sometimes against odds that had amounted to four to one; recommended local provision for the families of soldiers in the field; urged upon the legislators "the necessity of harmony" between the national government and the governments of the states; then returned to a bitter expression of his views as to the contrast between the two embattled peoples.

"The issue before us is one of no ordinary character. We are not engaged in a conflict for conquest, or for aggrandizement, or for the settlement of a point of international law. The question for you to decide is, Will you be slaves or will you be independent? Will you transmit to your children the freedom and equality which your fathers transmitted to you, or will you bow down in adoration before an idol baser than ever was worshipped by Eastern idolators? Nothing more is necessary than the mere statement of this issue. Whatever may be the personal sacrifices involved, I am confident that you will not shrink from them whenever the question comes before you. Those men who now assail us, who have been associated with us in a common Union, who have inherited a government which they claim to be the best the world ever saw — these men, when left to themselves, have shown that they are incapable of preserving their own personal liberty. They have destroyed the freedom of the press; they have seized upon and imprisoned members of state legislatures and of municipal councils, who were suspected of sympathy with the South; men have been carried off into captivity in distant states without indictment, without a knowledge of the accusations brought against them, in utter defiance of all rights guaranteed by the institutions under which they live. These people, when separated from the South and left entirely to themselves, have in six months demonstrated their utter incapacity for self-government. And yet these are the people who claim to be your masters. These are the people who have determined to divide out the South among their Federal troops. Mississippi they have devoted to the direst vengeance of all. 'But vengeance is the Lord's,' and beneath His banner you will meet and hurl back these worse than vandal hordes."

Having attempted thus to breathe heat into what Senator Phelan had called "a cold pile of damp ashes," Davis spoke of final success as certain. "Our people have only to be true to themselves to behold the Confederate flag among the recognized nations of the earth. The question is only one of time. It may be remote, but it may be nearer than many people suppose. It is not possible that a war of the dimensions that this one has assumed, of proportions so gigantic, can be very long protracted. The combatants must soon be exhausted. But it is impossible, with a cause like ours, that we can be the first to cry, 'Hold, enough.' " He spoke of valor and determination, of his pride in the southern fighting man, and assured his listeners that the Confederacy could accomplish its own salvation. This last led him into a statement unlike any he had made before:

"In the course of this war our eyes have often been turned abroad. We have expected sometimes recognition, and sometimes intervention, at the hands of foreign nations; and we had a right to expect it. Never before in the history of the world have a people so long a time maintained their ground, and shown themselves capable of maintaining their national existence, without securing the recognition of commercial nations. I know not why this has been so, but this I say: 'Put not your trust in princes,' and rest not your hopes on foreign nations. This war is ours; we must fight it out ourselves. And I feel some pride in knowing that, so far, we have done it without the good will of anybody."

When the applause that echoed this had died away he defined what he believed to be the "two prominent objects in the program of the enemy. One is to get possession of the Mississippi River, and to open it to navigation, in order to appease the clamors of the [Northwest] and to utilize the capture of New Orleans, which has thus far rendered them no service. The other is to seize upon the capital of the Confederacy, and hold this but as proof that the Confederacy has no existence." The fourth full-scale attempt to accomplish the latter object had just been frustrated by Lee at Fredericksburg, he informed the legislature, "and I believe that, under God and by the valor of our troops, the capital of the Confederacy will stand safe behind its wall of living breasts." As for the likelihood that the Unionists might accomplish the first-mentioned object, Davis admitted that this had caused him grave concern, and was in fact the reason for his present visit.

"This was the land of my affections," he declared. "Here were situated the little of worldly goods I possessed." He had, he repeated, "every confidence in the skill and energy of the officers in command. But when I received dispatches and heard rumors of alarm and trepidation and despondency among the people of Mississippi; when I heard, even, that people were fleeing to Texas in order to save themselves from the enemy; when I saw it stated by the enemy that they had handled other states with gloves, but Mississippi was to be handled without gloves — every impulse of my heart dragged me hither, in spite of duties which might have claimed my attention elsewhere. When I heard of the sufferings of my own people, of the danger of their subjugation by a ruthless foe, I felt that if Mississippi were destined for such a fate, I would wish to sleep in her soil." However, now that he had seen for himself the condition of the army and the people of his homeland, "I shall go away from you with a lighter heart . . . anxious, but hopeful."

In closing he spoke as a man who had kept a vigil through darkness into dawn, so that now he stood in sunlight. "I can, then, say with confidence that our condition is in every respect greatly improved over what it was last year. Our armies have been augmented; our troops have been instructed and disciplined. The articles necessary for the support of our troops and our people, and from which the enemy's blockade has cut us off, are being produced by the Confederacy. . . . Our people have learned to economize and are satisfied to wear homespun. I never see a woman dressed in homespun that I do not feel like taking off my hat to her, and although our women never lose their good looks, I cannot help thinking that they are improved by this garb. I never meet a man dressed in homespun but I feel like saluting him. I cannot avoid remarking with how much pleasure I have noticed the superior morality of our troops and the contrast which in this respect they present to the invader. On their valor and the assistance of God I confidently rely."

★ ★ ★   **T**he applause that followed had begun to fade, when suddenly it swelled again, provoked and augmented by loud calls for "Johnston! Johnston!" At last the general rose and came forward, modestly acknowledging the cheers, which were redoubled. When they subsided he spoke with characteristic brevity and the self-effacement becoming to a soldier. "Fellow citizens," he said. "My only regret is that I have done so little to merit such a greeting. I promise you, however, that hereafter I shall be watchful, energetic, and indefatigable in your defense." That was all; but it was enough. According to one reporter, the applause that burst forth as he turned to resume his seat was "tremendous, uproarious, and prolonged." Apparently the general was more popular than the Chief Executive, even in the latter's own home state.

Despite this evidence of enthusiastic support from the civilians of

★

the region, now that he had completed his military inspection Johnston was more dissatisfied than ever with the task which had been thrust into his hands. His command, he told Davis as soon as they were alone, was "a nominal one merely, and useless. . . . The great distance between the Armies of Mississippi and Tennessee, and the fact that they had different objects and adversaries, made it impossible to combine their action." The only use he saw for his talents, he continued in a subsequent account of the interview, was as a substitute commander of one of the armies, "which, as each had its own general, was not intended or desirable." In short, he told the President, he asked to be excused from serving in a capacity "so little to my taste."

Davis replied that distance was precisely the factor which had caused Johnston to be sent here. However far apart the two armies were, both were certainly too far from Richmond for effective control to be exercised from there; someone with higher authority than the two commanders should be at hand to coördinate their efforts and "transfer troops from one army to another in an emergency." Unpersuaded, still perturbed, the general continued to protest that, each being already "too weak for its object," neither army "could be drawn upon to strengthen the other," and with so much distance between the two, even "temporary transfers" were "impracticable." In point of fact, he could see nothing but ultimate disaster resulting from so unorthodox an arrangement. Once more Davis disagreed. Johnston was not only here; he was *needed* here. He must do the best he could. Or, as the general put it, his "objections were disregarded."

On this discordant note the two men parted, Johnston to establish a new headquarters in the Mississippi capital and Davis to visit his eldest brother Joseph at his new plantation near Bolton, on the railroad west of Jackson. Their previous holdings on Davis Bend, just below Vicksburg — Joseph's, called The Hurricane, and his own, called Brierfield — had been overrun and sacked by Butler's men during their abortive upriver thrust, made in conjunction with Farragut's fleet the previous summer: which, incidentally, was why Davis had used the past tense in reference to "the little of worldly goods I possessed," and which, in part, was also why he referred to the Federals as "worse than vandal hordes."

In the course of his two-day visit with his septuagenarian brother, good news reached him on December 27 which seemed to indicate that Johnston's unwelcome burden already had been made a good deal lighter than he had protested it to be. Grant's army in North Mississippi was in full retreat; Van Dorn had broken loose in its immediate rear and burned its forward supply base at Holly Springs, capturing the garrison in the process, while Brigadier General Nathan Bedford Forrest, even farther in the northern commander's rear, was wrecking vital supply lines and creating general havoc all over West Tennessee. The following day, however, on the heels of these glad tidings, came word that Vicksburg itself was under assault by Major General William Tecumseh Sherman, who had

During his visit to Tennessee, Davis personally praised John Hunt Morgan for a series of cavalry raids that played havoc with Union supply and communications lines.

come downriver from Memphis with the other half of Grant's command, escorted by Rear Admiral David Porter's ironclad fleet, and was storming the Chickasaw Bluffs. With the main body off opposing Grant, this was the worst of all possible news, short of the actual capture of the place; but on the 29th the President's anxiety was relieved and his spirits lifted by word that Sherman's repulse had been accomplished as effectively and as decisively, against even longer odds, as Burnside's had been at Fredericksburg two weeks before. What was more, the means by which it had been done went far toward sustaining Davis's military judgment, since the victory had been won in a large part by two brigades from the division he had recently detached, under protest, from the Army of Tennessee.

Vicksburg, then, had been delivered from the two-pronged pressure being applied from the north. If Bragg could do even partly as well in keeping Rosecrans out of Chattanooga, and if the garrison at Port Hudson could stop Banks and Farragut in their ascent of the Mississippi, the multiple threats to the western theater would have been smashed all round, or anyhow blunted for a season, despite the dire predictions made only that week by its over-all commander. One thing at any rate was certain. The President's long train ride back to Richmond would be made in a far more genial atmosphere, militarily speaking, than he had encountered at successive stops in the course of the outward journey.

He left Jackson on the last day of the year, and after speaking again that evening from a balcony of the Battle House in Mobile, received while

retracing in reverse his route through Alabama and Georgia a double —
indeed, a triple — further measure of good tidings. "God has granted us a
happy New Year," Bragg wired from Murfreesboro. Rosecrans had ventured
out of his intrenchments to attack the Army of Tennessee, which had then
turned the tables with a dawn assault, jackknifing the Union right against
the Union left. Not only was Chattanooga secure, but from the sound of the
victorious commander's dispatch, Nashville itself might soon be recovered.
"The enemy has yielded his strong position and is falling back," Bragg exulted.
"We occupy whole field and shall follow him."

The pleasure Davis felt at this — augmented as it was by information
that John Morgan had outdone himself in Kentucky on a Christmas raid, wrecking
culverts, burning trestles, and capturing more than two thousand men, while Forrest and Van Dorn were returning safely from their separate and equally spectacular
raids, the former after escaping a convergence designed for his destruction at Parker's Crossroads, deep inside the enemy lines — was raised another notch by word
that a Federal reconnaissance force, sent upriver by Banks from Baton Rouge, had
turned tail at the unexpected sight of the guns emplaced on Port Hudson's bluff
and steamed back down without offering a challenge. And when this in turn was
followed by still a third major item in the budget of good news, the presidential
cup ran over. Major General John B. Magruder, recently arrived to take command
of all the Confederates in Texas, had improvised a two-boat fleet of "cotton-clads"
and had retaken Galveston in a New Year's predawn surprise attack, destroying
one Yankee deep-water gunboat and forcing another to strike its colors. With the
surrender of the army garrison in occupation of the island town, Texas was decon-
taminated. The only bluecoats still on her soil were Magruder's prisoners.

Leaving Mobile, Davis again visited Montgomery and Atlanta, but
passing through the latter place he proceeded, not north to Chattanooga, but eastward to Augusta, where he spent the night of January 2. Next morning he entered
South Carolina for the first time since the removal of the government to Richmond, back in May, and after a halt for a speech in Columbia, the capital, went on
that night across the state line to Charlotte. At noon the following day he spoke in
Raleigh, the North Carolina capital, then detoured south to Wilmington, the principal east coast port for blockade-runners, where he received the first really disturbing military news that had reached him since he left Virginia, nearly a month
before. Instead of "following" the defeated Rosecrans, as he had said he would do,
Bragg had waited a day before resuming the offensive, and then had been
repulsed; whereupon, having been informed that the enemy had been reinforced
— and bearing in mind, moreover, the Commander in Chief's recent advice:
"Fight if you can, and fall back [if you must]" — he fell back thirty miles to a better defensive position on Duck River, just in front of Tullahoma and still protecting
Chattanooga, another fifty-odd miles in his rear. As at Perryville, three months

★

ago, he had won a battle and then retreated. Not that Murfreesboro was not still considered a victory; it was, at least in southern eyes. Only some of the luster had been lost. Davis, however, placing emphasis on the odds and the fact that Chattanooga was secure, counted it scarcely less a triumph than before. In response to a Wilmington serenade, tendered just after he received word that Bragg had fallen back, he spoke for a full hour from his hotel balcony. Employing what one hearer called "purity of diction" and a "fervid eloquence" to match the enthusiasm of the torchlight serenaders, he characterized recent events as a vindication of the valor of southern arms, and even went so far as to repeat the words he had spoken to a similar crowd from a Richmond balcony on the jubilant morrow of First Manassas: "Never be humble to the haughty. Never be haughty to the humble."

That was a Sunday. Next day, January 5, he covered the final leg of his long journey, returning to Richmond before dark. He was weary and he looked it, and with cause, for in twenty-five days he had traveled better than twenty-five hundred miles and had made no less than twenty-five public addresses, including some that had lasted more than an hour. However, his elation overmatched his weariness, and this too was with cause. He knew that he had done much to restore civilian morale by appearing before the disaffected people, and militarily the gains had been even greater. Though mostly they had been fought against odds that should have been oppressive, if not completely paralyzing, of the several major actions which had occurred during his absence from the capital or on the eve of his departure — Prairie Grove and Hartsville, Fredericksburg and Goldsboro, Holly Springs and Chickasaw Bluffs, Galveston and Murfreesboro — all were resounding victories except the first and possibly the last. Taken in conjunction with the spectacular Christmas forays of Morgan and Forrest, the torpedoing of the *Cairo* up the Yazoo River, and Grant's enforced retreat in North Mississippi, these latest additions to the record not only sustained the reputation Confederate arms had gained on many a field during the year just passed into history; they also augured well for a future which only lately had seemed dark. Defensively speaking, indeed, the record could scarcely have been improved. Of the three objectives the Federals had set for themselves, announcing them plainly to all the world by moving simultaneously against them as the year drew to a close, Vicksburg had been disenthralled and Chattanooga remained as secure as Richmond.

Davis himself had done as much as any man, and a good deal more than most, to bring about the result that not a single armed enemy soldier now stood within fifty air-line miles of any one of these three vital cities. It was therefore a grateful, if weary, President who was met by his wife and their four children on the steps of the White House, late that Monday afternoon of the first week of the third calendar year of this second American war for independence.

★ ★ ★

*On December 13 Federal
troops on the outskirts of
Fredericksburg move to attack
Confederate positions
on Marye's Heights.*

Fredericksburg

1862 ★ ★ ★ ★ ★

Of all these various battles and engagements, fought in all these various places, Fredericksburg, the nearest to the national capital, was the largest — in numbers engaged, if not in bloodshed — as well as the grandest as a spectacle, in which respect it equaled, if indeed it did not outdo, any other major conflict of the war. Staged as it was, with a curtain of fog that lifted, under the influence of a genial sun, upon a sort of natural amphitheater referred to by one of the 200,000 participants, a native of the site, as "a champaign tract inclosed by hills," it quite fulfilled the volunteers' early-abandoned notion of combat as a picture-book affair. What was more, the setting had been historical long before the armies met there to add a bloody chapter to a past that had been peaceful up to now. John Paul Jones had lived as a boy in the old colonial town that gave its name and sacrificed the contents of its houses to the battle. Hugh Mercer's apothecary shop and James Monroe's law office were two among the many points of interest normally apt to be pointed out to strangers by the four thousand inhabitants, most of whom had lately been evacuated, however, by order of the commander of the army whose looters would presently take the place apart and whose corpses would find shallow graves on its unwarlike lawns and in its gardens. Here the widowed Mary Washington had lived, and it was here or near here that her son was reported to have

★

thrown a Spanish silver dollar across the Rappahannock. During the battle itself, from one of the dominant hills where he established his forward command post, R. E. Lee would peer through rifts in the swirling gunsmoke in an attempt to spot in the yard of Chatham, a mansion on the heights beyond the river, the old tree beneath whose branches he had courted Mary Custis, granddaughter of the woman who later married the dollar-flinging George and thus became the nation's first first lady.

Yet it was Burnside, not Lee, who had chosen the setting for the impending carnage. Appointed to succeed his friend McClellan because of that general's apparent lack of aggressiveness after the Battle of Antietam, he had shifted the Army of the Potomac eastward to this point where the Rappahannock, attaining its head of navigation, swerved suddenly south to lave the doorsteps of the town on its right bank. Washington lay fifty miles behind him; Richmond, his goal, lay fifty miles ahead. Mindful of the President's admonition that his plan for eluding Lee in order to descend on the southern capital would succeed "if you move very rapidly, otherwise not," he had indeed moved rapidly; but, as it turned out, he had moved to no avail. Though he had successfully given Lee the slip, the pontoons he had requisitioned in advance from Harpers Ferry, altogether necessary if he was to cross the river, did not reach the Fredericksburg area until his army had been massed in jump-off positions for more than a week; by which time, to his confoundment, Lee had the opposite ridges bristling with guns that were trained on the prospective bridge sites. Burnside was so profoundly distressed by this turn of events that he spent two more weeks looking down on the town from the left-bank heights, with something of the intentness and singularity of purpose which he had displayed, back in September at Antietam, looking down at the little triple-arched bridge that ever afterwards bore his name as indelibly as if the intensity of his gaze had etched it deep into the stone. Meanwhile, by way of increasing his chagrin as Lee's butternut veterans clustered thick and thicker on the hills across the way, it was becoming increasingly apparent, not only to the northern commander but also to his men, that what had begun as a sprint for Richmond had landed him and them in coffin corner.

He had troubles enough, in all conscience, but at least they were not of the kind that proceeded from any shortage of troops. Here opposite Fredericksburg, ready to execute his orders as soon as he could decide what those orders were going to be, Burnside had 121,402 effectives in his six corps of three divisions each. Organized into three Grand Divisions of two corps each, these eighteen divisions were supported by 312 pieces of artillery. Nor was that all. Marching on Dumfries, twenty miles to the north, were two more corps with an effective strength of 27,724 soldiers and 97 guns. In addition to this field force of nearly 150,000 men, supported by more than 400 guns, another 52,000 in the Washington defenses and along the upper Potomac were also included in his nominal command; so that his total "present for duty" during this second week of December — at any rate the first part of it, before the butchering began — was something over 200,000 of all arms. He did not know the exact strength of the rebels waiting for him beyond the town and at other undetermined positions downriver, but he estimated their strength at just over 80,000 men.

In this — unlike McClellan, who habitually doubled and sometimes even tripled an enemy force by estimation — he was not far off. Lee had nine divisions organized into two corps of about 35,000 each, which, together with some 8000 cavalry and artillery, gave him a total of 78,511 effectives, supported by 275 guns. He had, then, not quite two thirds as many troops in the immediate vicinity as his opponent had. By ordinary, as he had lately told the Secretary of War, he thought it preferable, considering the disparity of force, "to attempt to baffle [the enemy's] designs by maneuvering rather than to resist his advance by main force." However, he found his present position so advantageous — naturally strong, though not so formidable in appearance as to rule out the possibility of an attempted assault — that he was determined to hold his ground, despite the odds, in the belief that the present situation contained the seeds of another full-scale Federal disaster.

Except for two detached brigades of cavalry, his whole army was at hand. So far, though, he had effected the concentration of only one corps, leaving the other spread out downstream to guard the crossings all the way to Port Royal, twenty miles below. The first corps, five divisions under Lieutenant General James Longstreet — "Old Peter," his men called him, adopting his West Point nickname; Lee had lately dubbed him "my old warhorse" — was in position on the slopes and crest of a seven-mile-long range of hills overlooking the mile-wide "champaign tract" that gave down upon the town and the river, its flanks protected right and left by Massaponax Creek and the southward bend of the Rappahannock. Forbidding in appearance, the position was even more formidable in fact; for the range of hills — in effect, a broken ridge — was mostly wooded, affording concealment for the infantry, and the batteries had been sited with such care that when Longstreet suggested the need for another gun at a critical point, the artillery commander replied: "General, we cover that ground now so well that we comb it as with a fine-tooth comb. A chicken could not live on that field when we open on it."

The other corps commander, Lieutenant General Thomas Jonathan Jackson — "Old Jack" to his men, redoubtable "Stonewall" to the world at large — had three of his four divisions posted at eight-mile intervals downstream, one on the south bank of Massaponax Creek, one at Skinker's Neck, and one near Port Royal, while the fourth was held at Guiney Station, on the Richmond, Fredericksburg & Potomac Railroad, eight miles in rear of Longstreet's right at Hamilton's Crossing. Despite the possibility that Burn-

Alfred Waud sketched this view of Fredericksburg from across the Rappahannock near Falmouth before the battle. Beyond the town, on the horizon at far right, rises the soon-to-be infamous Marye's Heights.

side might swamp Longstreet with a sudden assault, outnumbering him no less than three-to-one, Lee accepted the risk of keeping the second corps widely scattered in order to be able to challenge the Union advance at the very outset, whenever and wherever it began. Jackson, on the other hand, would have preferred to fight on the line of the North Anna, a less formidable stream thirty miles nearer Richmond, rather than here on the Rappahannock, which he believed would be an effective barrier to pursuit of the beaten Yankees when they retreated, as he was sure they would do, under cover of their superior artillery posted on the dominant left-bank heights. "We will whip the enemy, but gain no fruits of victory," he predicted.

In point of fact, whatever validity Jackson might have as a prophet, Lee not only accepted the risk of a sudden, all-out attack on Longstreet; he actually preferred it. Though he expected the crossing to be attempted at some point downriver, in which case he intended to challenge it at the water's edge, it was his fervent hope that Burnside could be persuaded — or, best of all, would persuade himself — to make one here. In that case, Lee did not intend to contest the crossing itself with any considerable force. The serious challenge would

★

come later, when the enemy came at him across that open, gently undulating plain. He had confidence that Old Peter, securely intrenched along the ridge, his guns already laid and carefully ranged on check points, could absorb the shock until the two closest of Stonewall's divisions could be summoned. Their arrival would give the Confederate infantry the unaccustomed numerical wealth of six men to every yard of their seven-mile line: which Lee believed would be enough, not only to repulse the Federals, but also to enable the graybacks to launch a savage counterstroke, in the style of Second Manassas, that would drive the bluecoats in a panicky mass and pen them for slaughter against the unfordable river, too thickly clustered for escape across their pontoon bridges and too closely intermingled with his own charging troops for the Union artillery to attempt a bombardment from the opposite heights. It was unlikely that Burnside would thus expose his army to the Cannae so many Southerners believed was overdue. It was, indeed, almost too much to hope for. But Lee did hope for it. He hoped for it intensely.

Burnside, too, was weighing these possibilities, and it seemed to him also that the situation was heavy with the potentials of disaster: much more so, in fact, than it had been before he shifted his army eastward in November from the scene of Pope's late-August rout. Though so far he had escaped direct connection with a military fiasco, he had not been unacquainted with sudden blows of adversity in the years before the war. Once as a newly commissioned lieutenant on his way to the Mexican War he had lost his stake to a gambler on a Mississippi steamboat, and again in the mid-50's he had failed to get a government contract for the manufacture of a breech-loading rifle he had invented and put his cash in after leaving the army to devote full time to its promotion, which left him so broke that he had to sell his sword and uniforms for money to live on until his friend McClellan gave him a job with the land office of a railroad, where he prospered. Between these two financial upsets, he had received his worst personal shock when a Kentucky girl, whom he had wooed and finally persuaded to accompany him to the altar, responded to the minister's final ceremonial question with an abrupt, emphatic "No!" Hard as they had been to take, these three among several lesser setbacks had really hurt no one but himself, nor had they seriously affected the thirty-eight-year-old general's basically sunny disposition. But now that he had the lives of two hundred thousand men dependent on his abilities, not to mention the possible outcome of a war in which his country claimed to be fighting for survival, he did not face the likelihood of failure with such equanimity as he had shown in those previous trying situations. Formerly a hearty man, whose distinctive ruff of dark brown whiskers described a flamboyant double parabola below a generous, wide-nostriled nose, a pair of alert, dark-socketed eyes, and a pale expanse of skin that extended all the way back to the crown of his head, he had become increasingly morose and fretful here on the high left bank of the Rappahannock. "I deem it my duty," he had advised his superiors during the interim which followed the nonarrival of the pontoons at the climax of his rapid cross-country march, "to say that I cannot make the promise of probable success with the faith that I did when I supposed that all the parts of the plan would be carried out."

This was putting it rather mildly. Yet, notwithstanding his qualms, he had evolved a design which he believed would work by virtue of its daring. His balloons were up, despite the blustery weather, and the observers reported heavy concentrations of rebels far downstream. He had intended to throw his bridges across the river at Skinker's Neck, ten miles beyond Lee's immediate right, then march directly on the railroad in the southern army's rear, thus forcing its retreat to protect its supply line. However, the balloon reports convinced him that Lee had divined his purpose, and this — plus the difficulty of concealing his preparations in that quarter, which led him to suspect that he would be doing nothing more than side-stepping into another stalemate — caused him to shift the intended attack back to the vicinity of Fredericksburg itself, where he could use the town to mask the crossing. It was a bold decision, made in the be-

★

lief that, of all possible moves, this was the one his opponent would be least likely to suspect until it was already in execution: which, as he saw it from the Confederate point of view, would be too late. The troops below were Jackson's, the renowned "foot cavalry" of the Army of Northern Virginia, but a good part of them were as much as twenty miles away. By the time they arrived, if all went as Burnside intended, there would be no other half of their army for them to support; he would have crushed it, and they would find that what they had been hastening toward was slaughter or surrender.

Accordingly, early on December 9, a warning order went out for Grand Division commanders to report to army headquarters at noon, by which time they were to have alerted their troops, supplied each man with sixty rounds of ammunition, and begun the issue of three days' cooked rations. They would have the rest of today to get ready, he told them, and all of tomorrow. Then, in the predawn darkness of Thursday, December 11, the engineers would throw the six bridges by which the infantry and cavalry would cross for the attack, followed at once by such artillery as had been assigned to furnish close-up support. The crossing would be made in two general areas, one directly behind the town

Major General Edwin V. Sumner (center) poses with some of his staff for one of Mathew Brady's photographers a few weeks before marching his Grand Division toward Fredericksburg.

and the other just below it, with three bridges at each affording passage for the left and right Grand Divisions, commanded respectively by Major Generals William B. Franklin and Edwin V. Sumner. The center Grand Division, under Major General Joseph Hooker, would lend weight to the assault by detaching two of its divisions to Franklin and the other four to Sumner, giving them each a total of approximately 60,000 men, including cavalry and support artillery. Burnside's intention — not unlike McClellan's at Antietam, except that the flanks were reversed — was for Franklin's column to attack and carry the lower end of the ridge on which the Confederates were intrenched, then wheel and sweep northward along it while the enemy was being held in place by attacks delivered simultaneously by Sumner on the right. It was simple enough, as all such designs for destruction were meant to be. In fact, Burnside apparently considered it so readily comprehensible as to require little or no incidental explanation when the three generals reported to him at noon.

One additional subterfuge he would employ, but that was all. The engineers at Skinker's Neck, assisted by a regiment of Maine axmen, would be kept at work felling trees and laying a corduroy approach down to the riverbank at that point, as if for the passage of infantry with artillery support. The sound of chopping, along with the glow of fires at night, would help to delude the rebels in their expectation of a crossing there. However, even this was but a strengthening of the original subterfuge, the shifting of the main effort back upstream, on which the ruff-whiskered general based his belief, or at any rate his hope, that he would find Lee unprepared and paralyze him with his daring.

That was a good deal more than any of the northern commander's predecessors had been able to do, but Burnside's gloom had been dispelled; his confidence had risen now to zenith. As he phrased it in a dispatch telegraphed to Washington near midnight, outlining his attack plan and divulging his expectations, "I think now that the enemy will be more surprised by a crossing immediately in our front than in any other part of the river. The commanders of Grand Divisions coincide with me in this opinion, and I have accordingly ordered the movement. . . . We hope to succeed."

★ ★ ★   *L*ee was indeed surprised, though not unpleasantly. Already a firm believer in the efficacy of prayer, he might have seen in this development a further confirmation of his faith. Nor was the surprise as complete as Burnside had intended. On Wednesday night, December 10, a woman crept down to the east bank of the Rappahannock and called across to the gray pickets that the Yankees had drawn a large issue of cooked rations — always a sign that action was at hand. Then at 4.45 next morning, two hours before dawn, two guns boom-boomed the prearranged signal that the enemy was attempting a crossing here in front of

Fredericksburg. At once the Confederate bivouacs were astir with men turning out of their blankets to take the posts already assigned them along the ridge overlooking the plain that sloped eastward to the old colonial town, still invisible in the frosty darkness.

In it there was one brigade of Mississippi infantry, bled down to 1600 veterans under Brigadier General William Barksdale, a former congressman with long white hair and what one of his soldiers called "a thirst for battle glory." He had had his share of this in every major engagement since Manassas, but today was his best chance to slake that thirst; for Lee, being unwilling to subject the town to shelling, had left to these few Deep South troops the task of contesting the crossing — not with any intention of preventing it, even if that had been possible in the face of all those guns on the dominant heights, but merely to make it as costly to the Federals as he could. Barksdale received the assignment gladly, posting most of his men in stout brick houses whose rear walls, looking out upon the river, they loopholed so as to draw their beads with a minimum of distraction in the form of return fire from the men they would be dropping when the time came. Shortly after midnight, hearing sounds of preparation across the way — the muffled tread of soldiers on the march, the occasional whinny of a horse or bray of a mule, the clank of trace-chains, and at last the ponderous rumble of what he took to be pontoons being brought down from the heights — he knew the time was very much at hand. After sending word of this to his superiors, he saw to it that the few remaining civilians, mostly women and children, with a sprinkling of old men, either hastened away to the safety of the hills or else took refuge in their cellars.

He was in no hurry to open fire, preferring not to waste ammunition in the darkness. Long before daylight, however, his men could hear the Federal engineers at work: low-voiced commands, the clatter of lumber, and at intervals the loud crack of half-inch skim ice as another pontoon was launched. This last drew closer with every repetition as the bridge was extended, unit by six-foot unit, across the intervening four hundred feet of water. At last, judging by the sound that the pontoniers had reached midstream, the waiting riflemen opened fire. They aimed necessarily by ear, but the result was satisfactory. After the first yelp of pain there was the miniature thunder of boots on planks, diminishing as the runners cleared the bridge; then silence, broken presently by the boom-boom of the two guns passing the word along the ridge that the Yanks were coming.

Soon they returned to the bridge-end, working as quietly as possible since every sound, including even the squeak of a bolt, was echoed by the crack of rifles from the western bank. It was perilous work, but it was nothing compared to the trouble brought by a misty dawn and a rising sun that began to burn the fog away, exposing the workers to aimed shots from marksmen whose skill was practically superfluous at a range of two hundred feet. A pattern was

Unarmed field-engineer troops trying to bridge the Rappahannock River opposite Fredericksburg take heavy fire from Confederate marksmen early on December 11.

quickly established. The pontoniers would rush out onto the bridge, take up their tools, and work feverishly until the fire grew too hot; whereupon they would drop their tools and run the gauntlet back to bank. Then, as they got up their nerve again, their officers would lead or chevy them back onto the bridge, where the performance would be repeated. This went on for hours, to the high delight of the Mississippians, who jeered and hooted as they shot and waited, then shot and waited to shoot some more.

By 10 o'clock the northern commander's patience had run out. The movement was already hours off schedule; Longstreet's signal guns had announced Lee's alertness, and Jackson's lean marchers might well be on the way by now. Rifle fire having proved ineffective against the snipers behind the brick walls of the houses along the riverbank, Burnside ordered his chief of artillery, Brigadier General Henry Hunt, to open fire with the 147 heavy-caliber guns posted on

★

Stafford Heights, frowning down on the old town a hundred feet below. The response was immediate and uproarious, and it lasted for more than an hour, Hunt having instructed his gun crews to maintain a rate of fire of one shot every two minutes. Seventy-odd solid shot and shells a minute were thrown until 5000 had been fired. During all that time, a correspondent wrote, "the earth shook beneath the terrific explosions of the shells, which went howling over the river, crashing into houses, battering down walls, splintering doors, ripping up floors."

As a spectacle of modern war it was a great success, and it was also quite successful against the town. It wrecked houses, setting several afire; it tore up cobblestones; it shook the very hills the armies stood on. But it did not seem to dampen the spirits or influence the marksmanship of the Mississippians, who rose from the rubble and dropped more of the pontoniers, driving them again from the work they had returned to during the lull that followed the bombardment. When Barksdale sent a message asking whether he should have his men put out the fires, Longstreet replied: "You have enough to do to watch the Yankees." Back at Lee's observation post, the sight of what the Union guns had done to the Old Dominion town so riled the southern commander that he broke out wrathfully against the cannoneers and the officers who had given them orders to open fire. "Those people delight to destroy the weak and those who can make no defense," he said hotly. "It just suits them!" However, when he sent to inquire after the welfare of Barksdale's men and to see if there was anything they wanted, that general sent back word that he had everything he needed. But he added, "Tell General Lee that if he wants a bridge of dead Yankees, I can furnish him with one."

It was well past noon by now. Hunt, admitting that his guns could never dislodge the rebels, suggested that infantry use the pontoons as assault boats in order to get across the river and pry the snipers out of the rubble with bayonets. A Michigan regiment drew the duty, supported by two others from Massachusetts, and did it smartly, establishing a bridgehead in short order. During the street fighting, which used up what was left of daylight, the bridges were laid and other regiments came to their support. Barksdale's thirst was still unslaked, however. When he received permission to withdraw, he declined and kept on fighting, house to house, until past sundown. Not till dusk had fallen was he willing to call it a day, and even then he had trouble persuading some of his men to agree. This was particularly difficult in the case of the rear-guard company, whose commander somehow discovered in the course of the engagement that the Federal advance was being led by a Massachusetts company whose commander had been his classmate at Harvard. The Mississippi lieutenant called a halt and faced his men about, determined to whip his blue-clad friend then and there, until his colonel had him placed in arrest in order to continue the withdrawal. It was 7 o'clock by the time the last of Barksdale's veterans crossed

★

the plain to join their admiring comrades on the ridge, leaving Fredericksburg to the bluecoats they had been fighting for fifteen hours.

Not until well after dark did Lee order Jackson to bring his two nearest divisions to Longstreet's support, and not even then did he summon the other two from Port Royal and Skinker's Neck, where the Maine axmen on the opposite bank had kindled campfires around which they were resting from their daylong chopping. Pleased though he was with the day's work — his eyes had lighted up at each report that a new attempt to extend the bridge had been defeated — Lee simply could not believe that his hopes had been so completely fulfilled that the enemy was concentrating everything for an attack against the ridge where his guns had been laid for weeks now and his infantry was disposed at ease in overlapping lines of battle.

Across the way, on Stafford Heights, Burnside too was pleased. Despite delays that had been maddening, he had his six bridges down at last (the three lower ones, below the town, had been down since noon, but he had hesitated to use them so long as the Fredericksburg force of unknown strength was in position on their flank) and his army was assembled for the crossing. Besides, he had received balloon reports at sundown informing him that the other half of the rebel army was still in its former positions down the river, with no signs of preparation for a move in this direction. The delay, it seemed, had cost him nothing more than some nervous twinges and a few expendable combat engineers; Lee might be caught napping yet. So confidently did the ruff-whiskered general feel next morning, when observers reported Jackson's troops still in position at Skinker's Neck and Port Royal, twenty miles away, that he decided he could afford to spend another day assembling his army on the west bank of the Rappahannock for the assault across the empty plain and against the rebel ridge.

Fog shrouded the entire valley while the long blue lines of men came steeply down to the riverbank and broke step as they crossed the swaying bridges. On the heights above, the Union guns fired blindly over their heads, in case the Confederates attempted to challenge the crossing. They did not. At noon, however, the fog lifted; Lee, with a close-up view of the bluecoats massed in their thousands beyond the plain, saw at once that this was no feint, but a major effort. He sent for Jackson's other two divisions, instructing them to begin their long marches immediately in order to arrive in time for the battle, which he now saw would be fought tomorrow. Beyond that he could do no more. Though he was outnumbered worse than three-to-two, and knew it, he was in good spirits as he rode on a sundown inspection of his lines. Returning to headquarters, he seemed pleased that the Federals on the flat were about to charge him. "I shall try to do them all the damage in our power when they move forward," he said.

Down in the town, meanwhile, the Union soldiers had been having themselves a field day. Cavalrymen ripped the strings from grand pianos to make feed troughs for their horses, while others cavorted amid the rubble in women's lace-trimmed underwear and crinoline gowns snatched from closets and bureau drawers. Scarcely a house escaped pillage. Family portraits were slashed with bayonets; pier glass mirrors were shattered with musket butts; barrels of flour and molasses were dumped together on deep-piled rugs. It was all a lot of fun, especially for the more fortunate ones who found bottles of rare old madeira in the cellars. Gradually, though, the excitement paled and the looters began to speculate as to why the rebs had made no attempt to challenge the crossing today, not even with their artillery. Some guessed it was because they had no ammunition to spare, others that they were afraid of retaliation by "our siege guns." One man had a psychological theory: "General Lee thinks he will have a

Loath to besmirch the Union cause, Leslie's Illustrated Newspaper refused to run this sketch of Federal troops looting Fredericksburg on December 12.

big thing on us about the bombardment of this town. He proposes to rouse the indignation of the civilized world, as they call it. You'll see he won't throw a shell into it. He is playing for the sympathies of Europe." Still another, a veteran private, had a different idea. "Shit," he said. "They *want* us to get in. Getting out won't be quite so smart and easy. You'll see."

★ ★ ★ *T*hey would see; but not just yet. Day broke on a fog so thick that the sun, which rose at 7.17 beyond the Union left, could not pierce it, but rather gave an eerie, luminous quality to the mist that swathed the ridge where Lee's reunited army awaited the challenge foretold by sounds of preparation on the invisible plain below; "an indistinct murmur," one listener called it, "like the distant hum of myriads of bees."

Longstreet held the Confederate left. Four of his five divisions were on line, commanded north to south by Major Generals Richard Anderson, Lafayette McLaws, George Pickett, and John Bell Hood; the fifth and smallest, a demi-division under Brigadier General Robert Ransom, was in reserve. Jackson, on the right, had posted Major General A. P. Hill's large division along his entire front, backed by a second line of two close-packed divisions under Brigadier Generals William Taliaferro and Jubal Early, which in turn was supported by Major General D. H. Hill's division, just arrived from Port Royal after an all-night march. Major General J. E. B. Stuart's cavalry guarded the flank, extending it southward from Hamilton's Crossing to Massaponax Creek. Since this end of the ridge was considerably lower than the other, and consequently much less easy to defend, Lee had assigned five miles of the line to Longstreet and only two to Jackson, who thus had no less than ten men to every yard of front and could distribute them in depth. It was no wonder, then, that he replied this morning to a staff officer's expression of qualms about the enemy strength and the lowness of the ridge in this direction: "Major, my men have sometimes failed to take a position, but to defend one, never! I am glad the Yankees are coming."

Lee and Longstreet stood on an eminence known thereafter as Lee's Hill because that general had set up his forward command post here, about midway of Longstreet's line, with an excellent view — or at any rate what would be an excellent view, once the curtain of fog had lifted — of the lines in both directions, including most of Jackson's line to the south, as well as of Fredericksburg and the snow-pocked plain where the blue host was massing under cover of their guns on Stafford Heights, preparing even now to give the lower ridge across the way a long-range pounding. Today as yesterday, however, the southern commander was in good spirits. Tall and comely — nothing less, indeed, than "the handsomest man in Christendom," according to one who saw him there this morning — neatly dressed, as always, with only the three unwreathed stars on the collar of his thigh-length gray sack coat to show his rank, he gave no sign of nervousness or apprehension. Above the short-clipped iron-gray beard and beneath the medium brim of a sand-colored planter's hat, his quick brown eyes had a youthfulness which, together with the litheness of his figure and the deftness of his movements, disguised the fact that he would be fifty-six years old next month.

His companion seemed to share his confidence, if not his handsomeness of person, though he too was prepossessing of appearance. A burly, shaggy man, six feet tall, of Dutch extraction and just past forty-one, Longstreet gave above all an impression of solidity and dependability. His men's great fondness for him was based in part on their knowledge of his concern for their well-being, in and out of combat. Yesterday, for example, when some engineers protested to him that the gun crews were ruining their emplacements by digging them too deep, Old Peter would not agree to order them to stop. "If we only save the finger of a man, that's good enough," he told the engineers, and the cannoneers kept digging. Often phlegmatic, this morning he was in an expansive mood: especially after he and Lee were joined by the third-ranking member of the army triumvirate, who came riding up from the south. It was Jackson, but a Jackson quite unlike the Stonewall they had known of old. Gone were the mangy cadet cap and the homespun uniform worn threadbare since its purchase on the eve of the Valley Campaign, through the miasmic nightmare of the Seven Days, the suppression of the "miscreant Pope" at Cedar Mountain and Second Manassas, the invasion of Maryland and the hard fight at Sharpsburg. Instead he wore a new cap bound with gold braid, and more braid — "chicken guts," Confederate soldiers irreverently styled the stuff — looped on the cuffs and sleeves of a brand-new uniform, a recent gift from Jeb Stuart. Even his outsized boots were brightly polished. For all his finery, he looked as always older than his thirty-eight years. His pale blue eyes were stern, his thin-lipped mouth clamped forbiddingly behind the scraggly dark-brown beard; but this had not protected him from the jibes of his men, who greeted him with their accustomed rough affection as he rode among them. "Come here, boys!" they yelled. "Stonewall has drawed his bounty and bought hisself some new clothes." Others shook their heads in mock dismay at seeing him tricked out like some newly commissioned quartermaster lieutenant. "Old Jack will be afraid for his clothes," they said, doleful amid the catcalls, "and will not get down to work."

He had ridden all this way, exposing himself to all that raillery, for a purpose which he was quick to divulge. Turning aside Longstreet's banter, he muttered that the finery was "some doing of my friend Stuart, I believe," and passed at once to the matter that had brought him here. He wanted permission to attack. If his men surged down the ridge and onto the plain before the fog

*By early December 13 both armies were poised for battle,
but the rebels enjoyed exceptionally strong intrenched positions
on the ridges paralleling the Rappahannock.*

had lifted, he explained, they would be hidden from the guns on Stafford
Heights and could fling the startled bluecoats into the river. Lee shook his head.
He preferred to have the superior enemy force worn down by repeated charges
and repulses, in the style of Second Manassas, before he passed to the offensive.
Stonewall had his answer. As he turned to leave, Longstreet began to bait him

again. "General, do not all those multitudes of Federals frighten you?" Old Peter's humor was heavy-handed, but Jackson had no humor at all. "We shall see very soon whether I shall not frighten *them*," he said as he put one foot in the stirrup. But Longstreet kept at him. "Jackson, what are you going to do with all those people over there?" Stonewall mounted. "Sir, we will give them the bayonet," he said, and he turned his horse and rode away.

By 10 o'clock the fog had begun to thin. It drained downward, burned away by the sun, layer by upper layer, so that the valley seemed to empty after the manner of a tub when the plug is pulled. Gradually the town revealed itself: first the steeples of two churches and the courthouse, then the chimneys and rooftops, and finally the houses and gardens, set upon the checkerboard of streets. Dark lines of troops flowed steadily toward two clusters, one within the town, masked by the nearer buildings, the other two miles down the Richmond Stage Road, which ran parallel to the river and roughly bisected the mile-wide plain. Already the more adventurous Federal batteries had opened, arching their shells through sunlit rifts in the thinning mist, but the Confederates made no reply until 10.30 when Lee passed the word: "Test the ranges on the left." Longstreet's guns began to roar from Marye's Heights, the tall north end of the long ridge, directly opposite the center of the town, where the first of the two clusters of blue-clad men was thickening. All the fog was gone by now, replaced by brilliant sunlight. The drifting smoke made shifting patterns on the plain. High over Stafford Heights, where the long-range guns were adding their deeper voices to the chorus of the Union, two of Burnside's big yellow observation balloons bobbed and floated, the men in their swaying baskets looking down on war reduced to miniature.

First blood was drawn in a brief dramatic action staged in front of the Confederate right. Here the fog had rolled away so rapidly that the scene was exposed as if by the sudden lift of a curtain, showing a three-division Federal corps advancing westward in long lines so neatly dressed that watchers on the ridge could count the brigades and regiments — ten of the former, forty-six of the latter, plus eleven batteries of artillery — each with its attendant colors rippling in the sunlight. From Lee's Hill, the southern commander was surprised to see two horse-drawn guns, toy-sized in the distance, go twinkling out to the old stage road and go into position in the open, within easy range of the left flank of the 18,000 Federals, which was thrown into some disorder and came to a milling halt as the two guns began to slam their shots endwise into the blue ranks, toppling men like tenpins.

They had been brought into action by Stuart's chief of artillery, twenty-four-year-old Major John Pelham of Alabama, who in his haste to join the southern army had left West Point on the eve of graduation in '61. He had often done daring things, similar to this today, but never before with so large an audience to applaud him. As the men of both armies watched from the surrounding heights, he fired so rapidly that one general involved in the blue confusion estimated his strength at a full battery. Four Union batteries gave him their undivided attention, turning their two dozen guns against his two. One, a rifled Blakely, was soon disabled and had to be sent to the rear, but Pelham kept the other barking furiously, a 12-pounder brass Napoleon, and shifted his position each time the enemy gunners got his range. The handsome young major was in his glory, wearing bound about his cap, at the request of a British army observer, a necktie woven of red and blue, the colors of the Grenadier Guards. When Stuart sent word for him to retire, Pelham declined, though he had lost so many cannoneers by then that he himself was helping to serve the gun. "Tell the general I can hold my ground," he said. Three times the order came, but he obeyed only when his caissons were nearly empty. Back at Hamilton's Crossing, he returned the smoke-grimed necktie-souvenir to the

Artillerist John Pelham displayed such bravery at Fredericksburg that Lee dubbed him "The Gallant Pelham."

English visitor, blushing with pleasure and embarrassment at the cheers. Lee on his hill took his glasses down, smiling as he exclaimed: "It is glorious to see such courage in one so young!"

While the Federals remained halted on the plain, recovering the alignment Pelham had disturbed, their artillery began to pound the lower ridge in earnest, probing the woods in an attempt to knock out Jackson's hidden batteries before the battle passed to the infantry. The Confederate gunners made no reply, being under orders not to disclose their positions until the enemy came within easy range. At last he did, and the graybacks got their revenge for the punishment they had had to accept in silence. When the advance came within 800 yards, all of Stonewall's guns cut loose at once. The blue flood stopped, flailed ragged along its forward edge, and then reversed its flow.

The Union guns resumed the argument, having spotted their targets by the smoke that boiled up through the trees, but the infantry battle now shifted northward to where the bluecoats had been massing under cover of the town. At 11.30 they emerged and began to surge across the plain toward Marye's

★

Heights, less than half a mile away. A thirty-foot spillway, six feet deep, lay athwart their path, however, and the rebel gunners caught them close-packed as they funneled onto three bridges whose planks had been removed but whose stringers had been left in place, apparently to lure them across in single file. "Hi! Hi! Hi!" the Federals yelled as they pounded over, taking their losses in order to gain the cover of a slight roll or "dip" of ground that hid them from the guns on the heights beyond.

"It appeared to us there was no end of them," a waiting cannoneer observed. But Longstreet was not worried; he had a surprise in store for them. Along the base of Marye's Heights ran a road, flanked by stone walls four feet high, which Brigadier General T.R.R. Cobb had had his Georgians deepen, throwing the spoil over the townward wall, to add to its effectiveness as a breast-work and to hide it from the enemy. This was the advance position of the whole army, and as such it might be outflanked or enfiladed. However, when Cobb was given permission to fall back up the hill in case that happened, he replied grimly in the spirit of Barksdale and Pelham: "Well, if they wait for me to fall back, they will wait a long time."

Presently he got the chance to begin to prove his staunchness; for the Federals leaped to their feet in the swale and made a sudden rush, as if they intended to scale the heights whose base was only 400 yards away. High up the slope the guns crashed, darting tongues of flame, and the Georgians along the sunken road pulled trigger. It was as if the charging bluecoats had struck a trip wire. When the smoke of that single rifle volley rolled away, all that were left in front of the wall were writhing on the ground or scampering back to safety in the swale. After a wait, they rose and came forward again, deploying as they advanced. This time the reaction was less immediate, since they knew what to expect; but it was no different in the end. The guns on the slope and the rifles down along the wall broke into a clattering frenzy of smoke and flame, and more men were left writhing as others fell back off the blasted plain and into the swale. Again they rose. Again, incredibly, they charged. They came forward, one of them afterwards recalled, "as though they were breasting a storm of rain and sleet, their faces and bodies being only half turned to the storm, with their shoulders shrugged." Another observed that "everybody, from the smallest drummer boy on up, seemed to be shouting to the full extent of his capacity." Like the first and second, except that more men fell because it lasted longer, this third charge broke in blood and pain before a single man got within fifty yards of the wall. The survivors flowed back over the roll of earth and into the "dip," where reinforcements were nerving themselves for still a fourth attempt.

"They are massing very heavily and will break your line, I am afraid," Lee told Longstreet. But Old Peter did not believe it. He was ready for the whole Yankee nation, provided it would come at him from the direction this portion of it had done three times already, and he said so: "General, if you put every man now on the other side of the Potomac in that field to approach me over that same line, and give me plenty of ammunition, I will kill them all before they reach my line. Look to your right; you are in some danger there," he said. "But not on my line."

It was true; Lee's line was in considerable danger southward. While Sumner's men were charging the sunken road, repeatedly and headlong, taking their losses, Franklin was taking stock of the situation as Pelham's brass Napoleon and Jackson's masked batteries had left it when they disrupted his first and second advances. Both had been tentative, at best, but now he believed he knew what he had to deal with. However, as in Pleasant Valley preceding the battle on Antietam Creek, he was inclined to be circumspect: an inclination which had not been lessened here on the Rappahannock by Burnside's instructions that, once he was over the river "with a view to taking the heights," he was to be "governed by circumstances as to the extent of your movements." Further instructions had arrived this morning, warning him to keep his attack column "well supported and its line of retreat open." Accordingly, before going forward for the third time, he took care to protect the flank in Stuart's direction. The attack was delivered by the same corps, commanded by Major General John F. Reynolds, whose three divisions were under Major General George G. Meade and Brigadier Generals Abner Doubleday and John Gibbon. Doubleday was ordered to wheel left, guarding the bruised flank (sure enough, Pelham came out promptly and began to pound him) while the other two went forward in an attempt to storm the ridge. Gibbon, on the right, got as far as the railroad embankment, where he ran into murderous point-blank fire, was himself wounded, and had to be brought out on a stretcher. He was followed shortly by his men, who were not long in discovering that the Johnnies had drawn them into a trap.

That left Meade, whose division was the smallest of the three. Out of 60,000 soldiers available for the intended assault on the Confederate right, Franklin managed to get only these 4500 Pennsylvanians into slugging contact with the enemy, but they did what they could to make up in spirit for what they lacked in weight. Charging first to the railroad, then beyond it, they struck a boggy stretch of ground, about 500 yards in width, which A. P. Hill had left unmanned in the belief that it was impenetrable. It was not. Meade's troops slogged through it, burst upon and scattered a second-line brigade of startled rebels, and were still driving hard toward the accomplishment of Franklin's assignment — that is, to get astride the lower ridge and then sweep northward along it, dislodging men and guns as he went — when they themselves were struck in front and on both flanks by a horde of screaming graybacks.

These were Early's men, from over on the right. Told that Hill's line had been pierced, they came on the run, hooting as they passed the fugitives: "Here comes old Jubal! Let old Jubal straighten out that fence!" Then they struck. The Pennsylvanians were driven back through the boggy gap and out again across the open fields, where the pursuers stabbed vengefully at their rear and Confederate guns to the left and right tore viciously at their flanks. Unsupported, heavily outnumbered, thrown off balance by surprise, they paid dearly for their daring; more than a third of the men who had gone in did not come out again. There was no safety for the survivors until they regained the cover of their artillery, which promptly drove the pursuers back with severe losses and shifted without delay to the rebel batteries, blanketing them so accu-

This stone wall and deepened road provided an impenetrable breastwork for the Confederates. Only their heads and shoulders were exposed to Yankee fire.

rately with shellbursts that the fire drew an indirect compliment from Pelham himself, who happened to be visiting this part of the line at the time. "Well, you men stand killing better than any I ever saw," he remarked as he watched the cannoneers being knocked about.

At any rate, the break had been repaired, the line restored. Lee on his hill had seen it all, the penetration and repulse on Jackson's front, coincident with the bloody disintegration of the third attack on Longstreet. The ground in front of both was carpeted blue with the torn bodies of men who had challenged unsuccessfully the integrity of his line. Beyond the river, Stafford Heights were ablaze with guns whose commanding elevation and heavier metal enabled them to rake the western ridge almost at will. Even now, one of them put a large-caliber shell into the earth at the southern commander's feet, but it did not explode. A British observer saw "antique courage" in Lee's manner as he turned to Longstreet, lowering his glasses after a long look at the blasted plain where still more Federals were massing to continue their assault over the mangled remains of comrades who had tried before and failed. "It is well that war is so terrible," the gray-bearded general said. "We should grow too fond of it."

★ ★ ★ *I*f the assault was to be resumed after the comparative lull that settled over the field about 3.30, following the double failure at opposite ends of the line, it would have to be launched against that portion of the ridge where Longstreet's men were ranked four-deep in the sunken road, their rifles cocked and primed for firing at whatever came at them across the fields beyond their breast-high wall of stone and dirt. To the south, Franklin had shot his bolt with Meade's quick probe of the hole in Jackson's front: in reaction to which he was not unlike a man who has managed to salvage a good part of one hand after groping about in the dark and finding a bear trap. There might be other holes, for all he knew, but after that one costly venture the commander of the left Grand Division seemed less concerned about finding than he was about avoiding them. Whoever might deliver another attack, it was not going to be Franklin. That left Sumner and Hooker. Burnside sent them instructions to continue the assault with their right and center Grand Divisions, in hopes that the Confederates along the ridge could be breached or budged or somehow thrown into confusion as a prelude to their downfall.

Sumner, a crusty veteran of forty-four years' service, nearly forty of which had been spent accomplishing the slow climb from second lieutenant to colonel, was altogether willing, despite his heavy losses up to now. So was Hooker, whose nickname was "Fighting Joe." Shortly before 4 o'clock, the men crouched in the swale caught sight of what they thought was their best chance to storm the ridge. A whole battalion of rebel artillery began a displacement from the slopes of Marye's Heights. Quickly the word passed down the Union line; men braced themselves for the order to charge. It came and they surged forward, followed this time by several batteries, which ventured out to within 300 yards of the fuming wall, adding the weight of their metal to the attack but losing cannoneers so fast that the guns could only be served slowly. As it turned out, this was worse than ever. The artillery displacement they had spotted was not the beginning of a retreat, as they had supposed, but a yielding of the position to a fresh battalion, which arrived with full caissons in time to aid in contesting this fourth assault. Down in the sunken road, Tom Cobb had been hit by a sharpshooter firing from the upper story of a house on the edge of town; he had bled to death by now; but his men were still there, reinforced by several regiments of North Carolinians from Ransom's reserve divi-

A brilliant lawyer and ardent secessionist, Thomas R. Cobb was mortally wounded at Fredericksburg.

sion. Shoulder to shoulder along the wall, they loosed their volleys, then stepped back to reload while the rank behind stepped up to fire. So it went, through all four ranks, until the first had reloaded and taken its place along the wall, which flamed continuously under a mounting bank of smoke as if the defenders were armed with automatic weapons. This attack, like the three preceding it, broke in blood. The Federals fell back, leaving the stretch of open ground between the swale and a hundred yards of the wall thick-strewn with corpses and writhing men whose cries could be heard above the diminishing clatter of musketry.

While the carnage was being continued here ("Oh, great God!" a division commander groaned in anguish from his lookout post in the cupola of the courthouse. "See how our men, our poor fellows, are falling!") Jackson was burning to take the offensive against the inactive bluecoats at the other end of the line: so much so, indeed, that according to one observer "his countenance glowed, as from the glare of a great conflagration." If all those thousands of Federals on the plain could not be persuaded to approach the ridge, he ached to go down after them. "I want to move forward," he said impatiently; "to attack them — drive them into the river yonder," and as he spoke he threw out his arm, by way of lending emphasis to his words. The risk was great, he knew, for a repulse would expose his men to annihilation by the guns on the opposite heights. But at last, out of urgency, he devised a plan by which he hoped to nullify his prediction that the Confederates would "gain no fruits" from their victory. If the counterstroke were preceded by a bombardment, he believed, the enemy might be so stunned that the sudden charge across the plain might be made without undue sacrifice of life, and if it were launched just at sundown he could withdraw under cover of darkness in case it failed.

So conceived, it was so ordered. However, the almanac put sunset at 4.34; there was little time for preparation. Word was passed to the four divisions assigned to the attack, and as they got ready for the jump-off Stonewall's batteries went forward, out into the open, to begin their work of stunning or confusing the enemy. Instead, it was they who were stunned and confused, and in short order. Beyond the river, Stafford Heights seemed to buck and jump in

---

The object was to get there fast . . . then rely on the bayonet to do the work that would remain to be done when they got there.

---

flame and thunder as the guns on the crest redoubled their fire at the sight of these easy targets down below. Jackson quickly recalled his badly pounded artillerymen and canceled the attack, which he now saw would be shattered as soon as the infantry emerged from the woods. At that, the demonstration was not without its effect: especially on Franklin, who had already notified Burnside that "any movement to my front is impossible at present. . . . The truth is, my left is in danger of being turned. What hope is there of getting reinforcements across the river?" Of his eight divisions, only three had been employed offensively, and one whole corps of 24,000 men, the largest in the army, saw no action at all; yet he was asking after reinforcements. At the height of Jackson's abortive demonstration, orders came from Burnside for Franklin to take the offensive, but he declined. He was in grave danger here, he repeated. Besides, there was no time; the sun was down behind the western ridge.

Sunset did not slow the tempo of the fighting to the north, where a fifth major assault on Marye's Heights had been repulsed in much the same manner as all the others, though the officers in charge had attempted a somewhat different approach. Their instructions were for the men to veer northward when they left the swale and thus confront the sunken road from the right, which perhaps would enable them to lay down an enfilade as they gained the flank and bore down at an angle. But it did not work out that way. As the men went forward, attempting to bear off to the right, they encountered a marsh that forced them back to the left and a repetition of the direct approach to the stone wall, which seemed thus to draw them like a magnet. From behind it, all this while, the rebels — many of whom were shoeless, without overcoats or blankets to protect them from the penetrating mid-December chill — taunted the warmly clad Federals coming toward them in a tangle-footed huddle after their encounter with the bog: "Come on, blue-belly! Bring them boots and blankets! Bring 'em hyar!" And they did bring them, up to within fifty yards of the flame-stitched wall at any rate. There the forward edge of the charge was frayed and broken, the survivors crawling or running to regain the protection of the swale, which by now they were convinced they never should have left.

Sumner had done his best, or worst, but the carnage was by no means over. Hooker's men had crossed the river, under orders to continue the assault, and the commander of one of his divisions, Brigadier General Andrew Humphreys, believed he knew a way to get his troops up to and over the wall, so they could come to grips with the jeering scarecrows in the sunken road. While they were deploying in the dusk he rode among them, telling them not to fire while they were charging. It was obvious by now, he said, that firing did the rebels little damage behind their ready-made breastwork; it only served to slow the attack and expose the attackers to more of the rapid-fire volleys from beyond the wall. The object was to get there fast — much as a man might hurry across an open space in a shower of rain, intending to be as dry as possible when he reached the other side — then rely on the bayonet to do the work that would remain to be done when they got there.

They went forward in the twilight, stumbling over the human wreckage left by five previous charges. Prone men, wounded and unwounded, called out to them not to try it; some even caught at their legs as they passed, attempting to hold them back; but they ignored them and went on, beckoned by voices that mocked them from ahead, calling them blue-bellies and urging them to bring their boots and blankets within reach. Humphreys sat his horse amid the bullets, a slim veteran of aristocratic mien. He had left West Point in '31, two years behind R. E. Lee, and his record in the peacetime army had been a good one; yet his advancement since then, it was said, had been delayed because of suspicions aroused by his pre-war friendship with Jefferson Davis. Now he was out to prove those suspicions false. As he watched he saw the stone wall become "a sheet of flame that enveloped the head and flanks of the column." Its formations unraveled by sudden attrition, the charge was brought to a stumbling halt about forty yards from the wall. For a moment the Federals hung there, beginning to return the galling fire; but it was useless and they knew it.

Joseph Hooker (left) tries to persuade Burnside to call off the continuing suicidal Federal attacks on Marye's Heights (background right) at Fredericksburg.

Despite the shouts and pleas of their officers — including Humphreys, who remained mounted yet incredibly went unhit — the men turned and stumbled back through the gathering darkness. Or anyhow the survivors did, having added a thousand casualties to the wreckage that cluttered the open slope, ghastly under the pinkish yellow flicker of muzzle-flashes still rippling back and forth along the crest of the stone wall.

"The fighting is about over," a Union signal officer reported at 6 o'clock from the heights across the way; "only an occasional gun is heard."

It was over, as he said, but not as the result of instructions from Burnside. Hooker was the one who finally called a halt to the carnage. "Finding that I had lost as many men as my orders required me to lose," he later declared in his official report, "I suspended the attack."

Burnside himself took a much less gloomy view of the state of affairs when he crossed the river late that night for an inspection of the front. Unquestionably a great deal of blood had been shed — far more, in fact, than he would know until he received the final casualty returns — but he had little doubt that a continuation of today's work would break Lee's line tomorrow. At any rate he

★

was determined to try it, and he sent out orders to that effect, alerting his front-line commanders. Recrossing the Rappahannock at 4 o'clock in the morning, he got off a wire to Washington: "I have just returned from the field. Our troops are all over the river. We hold the first ridge outside the town, and 3 miles below. We hope to carry the crest today."

★ ★ ★ **Once more Lee had divined his opponent's purpose.** "I expect the battle to be renewed at daylight," he wired Richmond, three hours after the final assault had failed, and this opinion was reinforced within another three hours by the capture, shortly before midnight, of a courier bearing orders to Burnside's front-line commanders for tomorrow's continuation of the attack. But Sunday's dawn, December 14, brought only the soup-thick fog of yesterday, without the familiar hum of preparation from down on the curtained plain. Indeed, even after the rising sun had burned away the mist, the only change apparent to the eye was in the lines along the western ridge. Expecting a turning movement, Lee had instructed his men to improve their fortifications in order to free all but a comparative handful for action on the flanks. So well had they plied their tools, these soldiers who six months ago had sneered at digging as cowardly work "unfit for a white man" and in derision had dubbed their new commander "the King of Spades," that Lee remarked with pleasure at the sight: "My army is as much stronger for these new intrenchments as if I had received reinforcements of 20,000 men."

No longer in need of prodding, or even suggestion, they kept digging. As the sun rose higher, so did the parapets. But the observers on Lee's Hill discerned no corresponding activity among the Federals on the plain, portions of whose forward edge were carpeted solid blue with the thick-fallen dead and wounded. The only sign of preparation was that the near ends of the east-west streets of Fredericksburg had been barricaded, as if in expectation of receiving, not delivering, an attack. The morning wore on. Noon came and went: then afternoon: and still no sign that the bluecoats were about to launch the assault that had been ordered in the dispatch captured the night before. As the shadows lengthened, Lee turned at last to Longstreet, who had been acquainted with the northern commander in the peacetime army. "General," he said, "I am losing faith in your friend General Burnside."

He was by no means alone in this, although the principal loss of faith in Old Peter's friend had occurred within the luckless commander's own ranks. Refreshed by a short sleep, and still convinced that he would break Lee's line by continuing yesterday's headlong tactics, Burnside had risen early that morning, only to be confronted by Sumner, who had been five years in the army before his present chief was born. He was known to be no quitter; in fact, so pronounced was his fondness for personal combat, Burnside had ordered the old man to remain at his left-bank headquarters yesterday, lest he get himself killed leading charges. Today, though, he was quite unlike himself in this respect.

"General," he said, obviously unstrung by all he had seen the day before, if only from a distance, "I hope you will desist from this attack. I do not know of any general officer who approves of it, and I think it will prove disastrous to the army."

Burnside was taken aback, having expected to encounter a different spirit. However, as he later wrote, "Advice of that kind from General Sumner, who had always been in favor of an advance whenever it was possible, caused me to hesitate." To his further dismay, he found his other Grand Division commanders of the same opinion. Franklin did not surprise him greatly in this regard — ironically, that general had served him on the left at Fredericksburg in much the same fashion as he himself had served McClellan on the left at Antietam — but when Hooker, the redoubtable Fighting Joe, was even more emphatic than Sumner in advising no renewal of the attack, he knew the thing was off. His first reaction was one of frantic despair. He had a wild impulse to place himself at the head of his old corps and lead an all-out, all-or-nothing charge against the sunken road, intending to break Lee's line or else be broken by it. Dissuaded from this, he retired to his tent, bitter with the knowledge that all yesterday's blood had been shed to no advantage: except to the rebels, who would be facing that many fewer men next time the two armies came to grips. A corps commander, Major General W. F. Smith, followed him into the tent and found him pacing back and forth, distracted. "Oh, those men! Oh, those men!" he was saying. What men? Smith asked, and Burnside replied: "Those men over there," pointing across the river, where portions of the plain were carpeted blue: "I am thinking of them all the time!"

Sunset closed a day that had witnessed nothing more than a bit of long-range firing on one side and a great deal of digging on the other. Such spectacle as there was, and it was much, came after nightfall. A mysterious refulgence, shot with fanwise shafts of varicolored light, predominantly reds and blues — first a glimmer, then a spreading glow, as if all the countryside between Fredericksburg and Washington were afire — filled a wide arc of the horizon beyond the Federal right. It was the aurora borealis, seldom visible this far south and never before seen by most of the Confederates, who watched it with amazement. The Northerners might make of it what they chose by way of a portent (after all, these were the *Northern* Lights) but to one Southerner it seemed "that the heavens were hanging out banners and streamers and setting off fireworks in honor of our great victory."

As if to rival this gaudy nighttime aerial display, morning brought a terrestrial phenomenon, equally amazing in its way. The ground in front of the sunken road, formerly carpeted solid blue, had taken on a mottled hue, with patches of startling white. Binoculars disclosed the cause. Many of the Federal dead had been stripped stark naked by shivering Confederates, who had crept out in the darkness to scavenge the woolen clothes from the bodies of men who needed them no longer.

That afternoon, as a result of a request by Burnside for a truce during which he could bury his dead and relieve such of his wounded as had survived two days and nights of exposure without medicine for their hurts or water for their fever-parched throats, the men of both armies had a nearer view of the carnage. No one assigned to one of the burial details ever forgot the horror of what he saw; for here, close-up and life-size, was an effective antidote to the long-range, miniature pageantry of Saturday's battle as it had been viewed from the opposing heights. Up close, you heard the groans and smelled the blood. You saw the dead. According to one who moved among them, they were "swollen to twice their natural size, black as Negroes in most cases." They sprawled "in every conceivable position, some on their backs with gaping jaws, some with eyes as large as walnuts, protruding with glassy stare, some doubled up like a contortionist." Here, he wrote — approaching incoherency as the memory grew stronger — lay "one without a head, there one without legs, yonder a head and legs without a trunk; everywhere horrible expressions, fear, rage, agony, madness, torture;

In this on-the-spot sketch by Arthur Lumley, Union soldiers — some walking wounded — bear a stricken comrade away from the carnage of Marye's Heights.

lying in pools of blood, lying with heads half buried in mud, with fragments of shell sticking in oozing brain, with bullet holes all over the puffed limbs."

Not even amid such scenes as this, however, did the irrepressible rebel soldier's wry sense of humor — or anyhow what passed for such; mainly it was a biting sense of the ridiculous — desert him. One, about to remove a shoe from what he thought was a Federal corpse, was surprised to see the "corpse" lift its head and look at him reproachfully. "Beg pardon, sir," the would-be scavenger said, carefully lowering the leg; "I thought you had gone above." Another butternut scarecrow, reprimanded by a Union officer for violating the terms of the truce by picking up a fine Belgian rifle that had been dropped between the lines, looked his critic up and down, pausing for a long stare at the polished boots the officer was wearing. "Never mind," he said dryly. "I'll shoot you tomorrow and git them boots."

So he said. But as the thing turned out, neither he nor anyone else was going to be doing any shooting on that field tomorrow: not unless the Confederates started shooting at each other. Night brought a storm of sleet and driving rain, with a hard wind blowing eastward off the ridge and toward the river. When the fog of December 16 rolled away, the plain was empty. A hurried and red-faced investigation disclosed the fact that not a single live, unwounded Federal remained on the west bank of the Rappahannock. Covered by darkness, the sound of their movements drowned by the howling wind, the bluecoats had made a successful withdrawal in the night, taking up their pontoons after such a good job of salvaging equipment that one signal officer proudly reported that he had not left a yard of wire behind.

Burnside was distressed that a campaign which had opened so auspiciously should have so ignominious a close. What was more, reports of the battle were appearing by now in the northern papers, and the correspondents, ignoring the general's plea that they not treat "the affair at Fredericksburg" as a disaster, pulled out all the descriptive stops and figuratively threw up their hands in horror at the bungling and the bloodshed. An account in the *New York Times* so infuriated Burnside that he summoned the reporter to his tent and threatened to run him through with his sword. By ordinary a mild-natured man, he was souring under the goads of criticism, such as those made by two of his own colonels: one that he and his men had been committed piecemeal — "handed in on toasting forks," he phrased it — and the other that the defeat had been "owing to the heavy fire in front and an excess of enthusiasm in the rear." Nor was his temper soothed when he read such comments as the following, from an Ohio journal: "It can hardly be in human nature for men to show more valor, or generals to manifest less judgment, than were perceptible on our side that day."

In truth, the casualties were staggering: especially by contrast. The Federals had lost 12,653 men, the Confederates well under half as many: 5309.

★

The latter figure was subsequently adjusted to 4201, just under one third of the former, when it was found that more than a thousand of those reported missing or wounded had taken advantage of the chance at a Christmas holiday immediately after the battle.

Longstreet was not unhappy with the results, despite the bloodless withdrawal. Suffering fewer than 2000 casualties, he had inflicted about 9000, and he was looking forward to a repetition of the tactics which had made this exploit possible. But Jackson, whose losses were not much less than his opponent's on the right, was far from satisfied, even though 11,000 stands of arms had been gleaned from the field after the departure of the Yankees. "I did not think a little red earth would have frightened them," he said. "I am sorry they are gone. I am sorry that I fortified." Lee agreed, saying of Burnside and the punishment that general had absorbed: "Had I divined that was to have been his only effort, he would have had more of it."

That evening he wrote his wife, "They went as they came — in the night. They suffered heavily as far as the battle went, but it did not go far enough to satisfy me." His anger had been aroused by the evidence of rabid vandalism he saw when he rode into Fredericksburg that afternoon. So had Jackson's. "What can we do?" a staff officer asked helplessly when he saw how thoroughly the Federals had taken the town apart. "Do?" Stonewall replied promptly. "Why, shoot them."

The stern-lipped Jackson's ire would never cool (later he expanded this remark; "We must do more than defeat their armies," he said. "We must destroy them") but Lee's was influenced considerably by the advent of the season of the Nativity. On Christmas Day he wrote his wife: "My heart is filled with gratitude to Almighty God for His unspeakable mercies with which He has blessed us in this day, for those He has granted us from the beginning of life, and particularly for those He has vouchsafed us during the past year. What should have become of us without His crowning help and protection? Oh, if our people would only realize it and cease from vain self-boasting and adulation, how strong would be my belief in final success and happiness to our country! But what a cruel thing is war; to separate and destroy families and friends, and mar the purest joys and happiness God has granted us in this world; to fill our hearts with hatred instead of love for our neighbors, and to devastate the fair face of this beautiful world. I pray that, on this day when only peace and good-will are preached to mankind, better thoughts may fill the hearts of our enemies and turn them to peace." But he added a sort of postscript in a letter to his youngest daughter, remarking that he was "happy in the knowledge that General Burnside and his army will not eat their promised Christmas dinner in Richmond today."

★　★　★

★

*Confederate soldiers clamber
aboard the Federal steamer Harriet
Lane during their successful
recapture of Galveston, Texas, from
Union control in January 1863.*

Prairie Grove; Port Hudson; Galveston

1862 ★ ★ ★ ★ ★ ★ Near the far end of the thousand-mile-long firing line that swerved and crooked its way between North and South — westward across northern Virginia, East and Middle Tennessee, North Mississippi, central Arkansas, and thence on out to Texas — Theophilus Holmes, with less rank and not one half as many soldiers in a department better than twenty times as large, had troubles which, in multiplicity at any rate, made Lee's seem downright single. From his Transmississippi headquarters in Little Rock the lately appointed North Carolinian looked apprehensively north and west and south; he was threatened from all those quarters; while from the east he was being jogged by repeated pleas and suggestions from Johnston and the President, not to mention such comparatively minor figures as Pemberton and the Secretary of War, that he send his hard-pressed and outnumbered troops to the aid of his fellow department commander on the opposite bank of the big river that ran between them. A grim-featured man, deaf as a post, at fifty-seven Holmes was the oldest of the Confederate field commanders. Moreover, his rigidity of face, indicative of arteriosclerosis, was matched by a rigidity of mind which augured ill in a situation that called for nothing so much as it called for flexibility.

By way of compensation for this drawback, he had under him three major generals whose outstanding characteristic, individually and collectively, was the very flexibility he lacked. John Magruder, Richard Taylor, and Thomas Hindman, respectively in charge of Texas, West Louisiana, and Arkansas, were remarkable men, battle tested and of proved resourcefulness. In this regard the last was not the least accomplished of the three. A prewar Helena lawyer, thirty-four years old, Hindman had preceded his present chief to his home state, and within six months of his arrival in late May, stepping into the vacuum left by Van Dorn's April crossing of the Mississippi with all the men and weapons that could be salvaged from the defeat at Elkhorn Tavern, had created and equipped, by strict enforcement of the new conscription act and the establishment of factories and foundries where none had been before, an army of 20,000 recruits, armed and uniformed more or less in accordance with regulations and supported by 46 guns. This in itself was about as close to a miracle of improvised logistics as any general ever came in the whole war, but Hindman expected to accomplish a great deal more before he was through. Dapper, jaunty, dandified, addicted to patent leather boots and rose-colored kidskin gloves, frilled shirt fronts and a rattan cane, perhaps by way of compensation for his Napoleonic five-feet-two of height, he was accustomed to getting what he wanted, whether it was a fine brick house, a seat in Congress, or a wife whose father had sought to keep her from him by locking her away in a convent: all of which he had won, despite the odds, by extending his credit, demolishing opponents from the stump, and scaling the convent wall. What he had in mind just now, though, was not only the scourging of all bluecoats from the soil of Arkansas — including Helena, where the Federal commander of the force in occupation had taken over the fine brick house for his headquarters — but also the recovery of Missouri.

Arriving in mid-August to find the diminutive Arkansan already far along with his plans, Holmes had been infected by his enthusiasm and had approved his preparations for a counterinvasion. It was gotten under way at once. By October Hindman's advance, a combined command of cavalry and Indians, was across the Missouri border, but suffered a repulse at the hands of a superior Union force under Brigadier General John M. Schofield, in command of three divisions styled the Army of the Frontier. The Indians scattered like chaff before a fan, and the cavalry fell back to the security of the Boston Mountains, skirmishing as they went. Hindman, coming forward to Fort Smith with the main body, was not discouraged by this turn of events. Indeed, as he saw it, the Federals were being lured to their destruction in the wilds of northwest Arkansas. Accordingly, he crossed the Arkansas River and concentrated his infantry at Van Buren. All he wanted, he told Holmes, was a chance to hit the Yankees with something approaching equal strength, after which he would "move into Missouri, take Springfield, and winter on the Osage at least."

Presently he got that chance, and at odds considerably better than he had dared even to hope for. Schofield, believing in mid-November that hostilities

James G. Blunt, commander of the Federals around Fayetteville, Arkansas, at the time of the Confederate march on Prairie Grove, was an ardent abolitionist who had associated with John Brown before the war.

had ended for the winter, left the largest of his three divisions near Fayetteville under Brigadier General James G. Blunt, with the assignment of blocking the path of another Confederate incursion, and withdrew to Springfield with the other two, which he placed under Brigadier General Francis J. Herron while he himself took off on sick leave. Hindman, with a mobile force of 11,500 men and 22 guns, was preparing to take advantage of this chance to strike at Blunt, who had 7000 men and 20 guns, when word came from Holmes (who by now had received instructions from the Secretary of War, urging the necessity for reinforcing Vicksburg) for him to return posthaste to Little Rock with all his men, in preparation for an eastward march across the Mississippi. Hindman protested for all he was worth. To fall back would cost him heavily in desertions, he knew, since many of his conscripts were natives of the region through which they would be retreating. Besides, he told Holmes, "to withdraw without fighting at all would . . . so embolden the enemy as to insure his following me up." Without waiting for a reply he put his army in motion on December 3, intending to precede the retrograde movement with an advance and a victory that would leave the Federals in no condition to pursue. Slogging next day through the brushy Boston Mountains, the highest and most rugged section of the Ozark chain, he printed and distributed an address to his soldiers, designed to steel their arms for the strike at Blunt. "Remember that the enemy you engage has no feeling of mercy

★

or kindness toward you," he told them. "His ranks are made up of Pin Indians, free negroes, Southern tories, Kansas jayhawkers, and hired Dutch cut-throats. These bloody ruffians have invaded your country; stolen and destroyed your property; murdered your neighbors; outraged your women; driven your children from their homes, and defiled the graves of your kindred. If each man of you will do what I have here urged upon you, we will utterly destroy them."

Blunt now had his troops in bivouac about twenty miles southwest of Fayetteville, near the hamlet of Cane Hill, from which he had driven the gray-back cavalry that week. When he got word that Hindman was across the Arkansas with an estimated 25,000 men he reacted according to his nature, rejecting the notion of retreat. A Maine-born Kansan who had practiced medicine en route in Ohio, he was a militant abolitionist and a graduate of the border wars. Round-faced, stocky, pugnacious in manner, he was thirty-six years old and no part of his training had prepared him for running from rebels, whatever their numbers. Determined to hold his ground, he wired for reinforcements and began to organize his position for defense.

The trouble with this was that the only reinforcements available were the two small divisions under Herron, a scant 6000 men with 22 guns, and they were back near Springfield, well over a hundred miles away, whereas Hindman's camp at Van Buren was little more than a third that distance from Cane Hill, so that the chances were strong that the rebels would arrive before the reinforcements did. However, this was leaving two factors out of account. The first was that Hindman's route of march lay through the mountains; his men would be climbing and descending about as much as they would be advancing along the rugged trails. The other factor was Frank Herron. An adopted Iowan, already in command of two divisions at the age of twenty-five, he intended to accomplish a great deal more in the way of fulfilling his military ambitions before returning to civilian life as head of the Dubuque bank established for him by his wealthy Pennsylvania parents. Just now, more than anything, he wanted a chance to command those two divisions in actual battle, and he got it much sooner than he had expected. At 8 o'clock on the morning of December 3 — by which hour, unknown to him or Blunt, Hindman had put his army on the road for its trek across the Boston Mountains — Herron received the summons from Cane Hill, one hundred and thirty miles from his present camp on the somber fields where the Battle of Wilson's Creek had been fought and lost by Nathaniel Lyon, almost a year and a half ago. Drums and bugles sounded assembly and the men fell in to receive instructions for the march. It would be made without tents or baggage, they were told, except for knapsacks which would be hauled in wagons. By noon they were headed south, and before they stopped at dawn next morning, slogging at route step down the pike, they had made twenty miles. After a short rest they were off again. Across the state line on December 5,

★

munching hardtack and raw bacon as they walked, they skirted the granite slopes of Pea Ridge and saw the nine-months-old scars on the Elkhorn Tavern, where Van Dorn had come to grief. At midnight the following day, having covered better than one hundred blistering miles of road, the head of the column entered Fayetteville, where the weary marchers slept in the streets, sprawled around fires they kindled and fed by ripping pickets from front-yard fences. Another twenty miles tomorrow and they would be at Cane Hill with Blunt, ready for whatever came at them from beyond the mountains whose foothills they could presently see by the glimmer of dawn on Sunday, December 7.

The first sign they had that they were not going to make it — at least not on schedule — came later that morning, twelve miles down the pike, when they encountered long-range cannonfire as they were approaching Illinois Creek. Soon they saw that the Confederates had drawn a line of battle around

Drums and bugles sounded assembly and the men fell in to receive instructions for the march. It would be made without tents or baggage, they were told, except for knapsacks which would be hauled in wagons.

the hilltop village of Prairie Grove, a couple of miles beyond the creek, blocking the path of the road-worn bluecoats eight miles short of their goal. Herron shook out a regiment of skirmishers and advanced them to the protection of the creekbank, where to his horror he discovered that his men were so weary that once they were off their feet they promptly dropped to sleep with rebel shells and bullets whistling and twittering over their heads. Undaunted, he built up his firing line and put his batteries in position, partly by way of returning the hostile fire, but mostly by way of letting Blunt know from the racket that he had arrived, or almost arrived, and needed help. The trouble was, with all those graybacks swarming in his front, he was not even sure that Blunt and his men were still in existence. For all he knew, Hindman might have gobbled them up while he himself was on the march from Wilson's Creek.

Hindman had not gobbled up Blunt; he had gone around him. Approaching Cane Hill late the afternoon before, after a march across the shoulder of the mountains in weather so cold that water froze in the men's canteens and icicles tinkled on the beards of the horses, he had put his troops in position for a dawn attack, only to learn that Herron was on the way, already approaching Fayetteville with a force which, once it was joined to Blunt's, would give the

★

Federals the advantage of numbers, both in men and guns. In command of a brigade at Shiloh, where he had been wounded and commended for gallantry, Hindman decided to profit from the example of that battle by preventing what had caused its loss, the arrival of Buell after Grant had been pushed to the edge of desperation. That is, he would strike at the reinforcements first, then turn on the main body. Accordingly, he built up the campfires along his outpost line, left a skeleton brigade of cavalry to keep up the bluff next morning, and set off after moonset on a circuitous march with 10,000 men to intercept and defeat the blue column hurrying southward out of Fayetteville. That was how it came about that Herron encountered long-range cannonfire at the crossing of Illinois Creek and the bristling line of battle at Prairie Grove, eight miles short of a junction with Blunt at Cane Hill.

Blunt had spent the morning in constant expectation of being swamped by the rebels maneuvering boldly to his front, apparently in over-whelming numbers. Near noon, however, hearing the sudden boom of guns from across the hills to his left rear, he realized that he had been outflanked; where-upon he fell back hastily to Rhea's Mills, six miles north, in order to protect his trains. Finding them secure he turned southeast in the direction of the booms and at 4 o'clock reached Prairie Grove, where he came upon the battle still in full swing after nearly five hours of doubtful contest. Two rounds from his lead bat-tery announced his arrival — announced it all too emphatically, in fact, for both shots landed among Herron's skirmishers, causing them to think that they were being flanked by their foes instead of being supported by their friends. Herron had been holding his own despite the weariness of his foot-sore men. Two charges against the ridge had failed, breaking in blood against the rim of the rebel horseshoe line, but Hindman had had no better luck in attempting a counterat-tack with his green conscripts, who fell apart whenever he ordered them forward. The fighting continued, left and right, muzzle flashes stabbing the early darkness. Despite their superiority of numbers, especially in guns — 42 to 22, now that the Union forces were united — Blunt's fresh troops could make no more of a pene-tration of the rebel line than Herron's weary ones had been able to achieve. Gradually the firing died to a sputter. Then it stopped. The battle was over.

Losses in killed, wounded, and missing totaled 1317 for the Confed-erates and 1251 for the Federals. Of the latter only 333 were from Blunt's com-mand, indicating how much heavier a proportion of the conflict Herron's men had borne, despite the fact that both laid claim to a lion's share in having brought the victory about. Hindman's only claim in that respect was the not inconsiderable one that he had managed to hold his ground throughout the fighting. Whether he had also accomplished his main objective — to shock the enemy into immobility, escaping pursuit while he fell back southward in compliance with the previous orders from Holmes — would soon be known; for

★

he retreated that night under cover of darkness, wrapping the iron tires of his gun and caisson wheels with blankets to muffle the sound of his withdrawal. The ruse worked, and so did another he tried next morning. Not only did Blunt not hear him go, but at dawn he also granted a request for a truce, which Hindman sent forward under a white flag, to allow for tending the wounded and burying the dead. Discovering presently that the Confederate main body had departed in the night, Blunt canceled the truce, on grounds that the rebels were gleaning abandoned arms from the field, and prepared to follow. By that time, however, Schofield was on the scene. Up from his sickbed and furious that his army had been committed to battle in his absence, he censured both commanders: Blunt for not withdrawing to meet the reinforcements hurrying toward him, and Herron for attacking with troops so badly blown that some of them were

These Arkansas volunteers fought to a standoff with the Union Army of the Frontier in the Battle of Prairie Grove on December 7, 1862.

found dead on the field, not from wounds but from exhaustion and exposure after their long march from Wilson's Creek. If Schofield's purpose in this was to prevent his subordinates' advancement by discrediting their valor, that purpose failed. By way of showing its appreciation for a victory won by northern arms as the year drew to a close — a victory which presently shone the brighter by contrast with the several full-scale disasters that developed elsewhere along the thousand-mile-long firing line before the month was out — the government promptly awarded major general's stars not only to Blunt but also to Herron, who then succeeded Lew Wallace as the youngest man to hold that rank in the U.S. Army. Moreover, as soon as these promotions came through, both men would outrank their present commander.

Hindman's discomfort was considerably increased in late December, when Schofield finally unleashed his cavalry for a forced march against the Confederates who, down to about 4000 men as a result of straggling and desertions, had taken sanctuary behind the Arkansas River. Three days after Christmas the blue riders struck Van Buren, destroying five steamboats at the wharf and all of the supplies of corn and bacon Hindman had gathered over the months in order to keep his army from starvation. Once more he was thrown into dispirited retreat, losing still more soldiers as he went. The Federals withdrew to Fayetteville, and thence on back to comfortable winter quarters in Missouri, but now there was no question of Hindman's returning to Little Rock with the prospect of marching his army to the relief of Vicksburg. Practically speaking he had no army. So much of it as did not lie in shallow graves at Prairie Grove was scattered over northern Arkansas, hiding from conscription agents in Ozark coves and valleys.

Thus it was that the battle lost in northwest Arkansas had repercussions far beyond the theater it was fought in. Holmes had opposed the eastward transfer from the start, protesting that the march led through a region barren of supplies and would require no less than thirty days. "Solemnly, under the circumstances," he had informed the Adjutant General earlier that month, "I regard the movement ordered as equivalent to abandoning Arkansas." All the same, against his better judgment, he had been preparing to go along with the plan. But now, with Hindman's army practically out of existence and only the local reserves to protect Little Rock itself against an advance from occupied Helena, he had what he considered the best of specific reasons for declining to comply with the government's wishes. On December 29, the day after Schofield's cavalry hit Van Buren, he wrote Johnston in reply to the correspondence the President had forwarded from Vicksburg during his inspection of that place the week before: "My information from Helena is to the effect that a heavy force of the enemy has passed down the Mississippi on transports. . . . Thus it seems very certain that any force I can now send from here would not be able to reach Vicksburg, and if at all not before such a reinforcement would be useless, while such a diversion would enable the enemy to penetrate those portions of the Arkansas Valley where the existence of supplies of subsistence and forage would afford them leisure to overrun the entire state and gradually reduce the people to . . . dependence."

———————— ⁂ ————————

★ ★ ★   *I*t was bad enough that the Yankees were steaming down the Mississippi, but they were also steaming up it — simultaneously. Banks had reoccupied Baton Rouge in mid-December and now was giving every sign that he intended to continue the northward penetration, shortening the stretch of river necessarily rebel-held if Holmes was to keep open the supply lines vital to the feeding and reinforcement, if not indeed to the survival, of all the armies of the South. Since the loss of the armed ram *Arkansas,* three months back, the Confederacy had had no vestige of a navy with which to oppose this two-pronged challenge designed for her riving and destruction; the threat would have to be stopped, if at all, not on the river itself, but from its banks. On the east bank the responsibility was Pemberton's, and to help him meet it he had two stout high-ground bastions one hundred air-line miles apart, commanding bends of the river at Vicksburg and Port Hudson. On the west bank it was Richard Taylor's, who had nothing: not only no lofty fortresses bristling with heavy-caliber guns emplaced to blow the Union ironclads out of the water, but also no army. In fact, on his arrival from Virginia in late August, he had found that his total force consisted of two troops of home-guard cavalry, a scattering of guerillas hidden from friends and foes in the moss-hung swamps and bayous, and a battalion of mounted infantry just arrived from Texas — in all, fewer than 2000 effectives for the defense of the whole Department of Louisiana. Nonetheless, Holmes had confidence that this second of his three major generals would be ingenious and tireless in his efforts to reduce the nearly immeasurable odds, and this confidence was not misplaced.

Commander of a division used as shock troops by Stonewall Jackson throughout the Shenandoah Valley campaign, Taylor had been one of the stars of that amazing chapter in military history, and had found in that experience ample compensation for his lack of formal training in the art of war. Gripped on the eve of the Seven Days by a strange paralysis of the legs, which seemed to portend the close of a promising career and a denial of any further share in winning his country's independence, this son of Zachary Taylor had recovered in time to receive his present assignment, together with a promotion, from his brother-in-law Jefferson Davis. Happy over what in fact would be a home-coming, for he had commanded Louisianians in the Valley and had spent his ante-bellum years on a Louisiana plantation, he came West with an enthusiasm that was only slightly dampened by the discovery of conditions in his new department, as of August 20, when he established headquarters in Alexandria. Undismayed by the shortage of soldiers, which kept him from any immediate accomplishment of big things — such as the retaking of New Orleans, which was very much a part of his plans for the future — he decided to be content at first with small ones. Within two weeks of his arrival he mounted a surprise attack that captured a four-gun battery and two companies of infantry at Bayou des Allemands, a Federal post near his plantation home, fifty miles downriver from Donaldsonville and less than half that far above New Orleans. If he could not retake the Crescent City just yet, he could at least draw near it — and profitably, too.

Slight though it was, this first success gained locally by Confederate arms in the four months since the fall of the South's first city was heartening indeed to the people of the district. Not even the recapture of the post in late October, when the resurgent Louisianians were driven away by a Federal amphibious force that included four regiments of infantry and a quartet of light-draft gunboats, detracted from the brilliance of that first strike. What was more, Taylor was planning others of still larger scope. Denied access to the Lafourche, that fertile region lying between the Mississippi and the Atchafalaya, he moved into the Teche country, which lay between the Atchafalaya basin and the Gulf of Mexico, and here, despite the fact that his government, as he said, "had no soldiers, no arms or munitions, and no money within the limits of the district," he set about the task of raising, equipping, and training the army with which he hoped, in time, not only to capture but also to hold the series of fortified posts that blocked the path between him and his goal, New Orleans. Meanwhile, intent on preventing further enemy penetrations, he had to disperse what forces he had in order to meet threats from all directions. With few trained subordinates and almost no telegraph or railway lines, the problem of central control was well-nigh insoluble. However, now that December had come on and the year drew toward a close, Taylor went far toward solving it. By using relays of fast-stepping mules and an ambulance in which he could sleep while traveling, the thirty-six-year-old general managed to employ what might have been his immobile hours for visits to the various scattered points in his large department. "Like the Irishman's bird," he subsequently wrote, "I almost succeeded in being in two places at the same time."

In this respect, as well as in several others, he was easily distinguishable from his opposite number, the newly arrived commander of all the Union forces in the region. Ten years Taylor's senior, of humbler birth but with much larger accomplishments in public life, having been a three-term governor of Massachusetts and speaker of the national House of Representatives, Nathaniel Banks was nothing like the Irishman's bird and had nothing like his opponent's

Richard Taylor, son of President Zachary Taylor and brother-in-law of Jefferson Davis, had served well with Jackson in the Valley and during the Seven Days' Battles, before being transferred west.

nighttime mobility — though the fact was, he had perhaps an even greater need for it if he was to carry out the multiple assignment given him by his superiors when he set out from Hampton Roads on his voyage down and around the coast to relieve his fellow Bay State politician, Benjamin Butler, as military ruler of New Orleans and commander of the Department of the Gulf. Vicksburg and Mobile were his primary objectives, he was told, and after the fall of the former place had opened the Mississippi to Union traffic throughout its length he was to move up the Red in order to gain control of northern Louisiana and, eventually, Texas. It was a large order, particularly for a general who not only had not a single battlefield victory to his credit, but rather had been whipped twice already in open contest — once at Winchester, in the Shenandoah Valley, and again at Cedar Mountain, both times by Stonewall Jackson, whose lean marchers had captured so many of his supplies that they had dubbed him "Commissary" Banks — but he apparently had no doubt that it could be filled and that he was the man to fill it. He docked at New Orleans, December 14, and took over formally next day from Butler, who issued an address to his army — "I greet you, my brave comrades, and say farewell!" it began, and ended: "Farewell, my comrades! Again, Farewell!" — and promptly departed for Washington to take the government to task for having made what seemed to him an improvident substitution.

Banks wasted no time on speeches. On the day he took command he issued orders for one of the divisions he had brought along to proceed at once upriver, without unloading from its transports, and to reoccupy Baton Rouge, which Butler had abandoned after repulsing an all-out attack on the place in early August. Two days later, when the Louisiana capital fell without even a show of resistance, Banks was greatly pleased at having made so prompt and effective a beginning toward fulfilling his government's outsized expectations. Including the reinforcements still arriving after their long voyage from New York and Fort Monroe, he had 36,508 effectives in his department, exclusive of navy personnel, and he felt that these were ample for the accomplishment of his task. What was more, he reported that he had found in Farragut, who was to be his partner in continuing the bold upriver thrust, a sailor who was "earnest for work." After a conference with the Tennessee-born admiral he added that he was delighted with his enthusiasm and frankness, and that he looked forward to "a most satisfactory result from our mutual labors." Banks was feeling chipper, and he said so. "All the indications of our campaign are auspicious," he notified Washington on December 18, the day after the fall of Baton Rouge, "and I hope to make good the most sanguine expectations in regard to my expedition."

There were, however, two previously unsuspected matters for concern, one military, one civil, and both grave. The first was the presence, thirty-five miles above Baton Rouge, which in turn was a hundred miles above New Orleans, of the fortifications at Port Hudson. Neither his Washington superiors nor Banks himself, until he arrived, had known of the existence of any such obstacle south of Vicksburg, another 250 winding miles upstream; yet intelligence reports informed him now that the Confederates had no less than 12,000 troops in the place, strongly intrenched on the landward side and with 21 heavy guns emplaced on the high bluff, waiting to sink or blow sky high whatever came their way across the chocolate-colored surface of the river. This in itself, placing as it did a new complexion on the problem of ascent, was enough to give Banks pause. But the other concern, the civil one, was even more disturbing in its way, since it showed that the command of the department was going to be a far more complex occupation than he had supposed, early that month, when he set out from Virginia. Less than two weeks after his arrival, for example, he received a note from one C. A. Smith, commission agent for certain northern interests, and Andrew Butler, whose brother Ben had set him up in business when he took over as military ruler of New Orleans. "Dear Sir," it read. "If you will allow our commercial program to be [carried] out as projected previous to your arrival in this department, giving the same support and facilities as your predecessor, I am authorized on [receiving] your assent to place at your disposal $100,000."

In the course of his rise from bobbin boy to the top of the heap in Massachusetts politics Banks no doubt had encountered other offers of this nature, but hardly one that was made so blatantly or with such apparent confidence in his basic corruptibility. "It was no temptation," he told his wife. "I thank God every night that I have no desire for dishonest gains." All the same, he felt obliged to report to Washington "that as much, or more, attention has been given to civil than to military matters," including the training of his army, and that, in consequence, the troops were "not in condition for immediate service." Though he declared on Christmas Eve, "We hope to move up the river at the close of the week," he was still in New Orleans after New Year's, complaining that he was cramped by a shortage of siege artillery. "The enemy's works at Port Hudson have been in progress many months and are formidable," he explained. "Our light field guns would make no impression on them." In fact, having learned by now of the reverses lately suffered by the column supposed to be working its way southward out of Memphis while he moved northward from New Orleans, he was beginning to "feel some anxiety as to the defenses of this city. . . . The enemy is concentrating all available forces on the river, and in the event of disasters North will not fail to turn their attention to this quarter."

So it was that, now in January — while Taylor kept busy raising and training an army in the bayous, lulled to sleep each night in his ambulance by the clopping of hoofs as he traveled the moon-drenched roads of the Teche and dreamed of retaking the South's first city — Banks stayed where he was, bedeviled by itchy-handed speculators, made apprehensive by rebel successes upriver, and fretted by shortages while he continued his preparations for the upstream movement which he had assured his superiors in December would be launched without delay.

★ ★ ★   **A**nother part of his assignment, albeit one that was no more than incidental, he had also placed in the way of execution, though so far on a scale that was small indeed. Its conception was provoked by the shortage of cotton for the textile mills of New England, 3,252,000 of whose 4,745,750 spindles had fallen idle by the middle of the year, with the result that production was down to less than one fourth of normal before its close. New Orleans having failed to yield more than a comparative handful of bales, the hungry manufacturers had cast their eyes on Texas. What they had in mind was conquest and colonization; they saw their chance to make of it what one observer called "another and a fairer Kansas," where Yankee know-how and industry, replacing the slovenly farming methods now employed, would produce more cotton in a single year than had previously been grown in all the history of the vast Lone Star expanse. That way, the idle spindles would be fed, the mill hands would return to work, and the owners would get rich. First, however, the army would have to clear the path for immigration, and in this connection Banks had in his entourage a Texas Unionist, Andrew Jackson Hamilton, upon whom the War Department, at the behest of the New England manufacturers, had conferred the rank of brigadier general, together with appointment as military governor of Texas. He would take office, preparing the way for the textile-sponsored "colonists," when and if Banks won control of some portion of the state for him to govern.

So far, all there was for him in this regard was Galveston harbor, seized two months ago by the navy and now being patrolled by gunboats of the West Coast Blockading Squadron, part of Farragut's command. Texas was far down on the list of Banks's assigned objectives; though his department had been enlarged to include that state, its occupation was scheduled to follow the opening of the Mississippi and the conquest of the Red River Valley in northwest Louisiana; but at Hamilton's urging he agreed to send a Massachusetts regiment to take and hold the island town at once, thus giving the newly appointed governor at least the shadow of a dry-land claim to his high title. Accordingly, an advance party of three companies left New Orleans on December 22, before they had had time for more than a hurried look at the sights of the city, and landed at Galveston on Christmas Eve. There, under the muzzles of the gunboats anchored in the harbor, they set to work barricading the wharf as a precaution against attack from the landward side while awaiting the arrival of the rest of the infantry by sea, together with attached units of cavalry and field artillery.

They had need for greater caution than they suspected, for this action brought them into immediate contact with the first in rank of Holmes's three major generals, John Magruder. Known to be unpredictable and tricky, he was also first in reputation; "Prince John" he had been called in the old army, partly because of his aristocratic manner and his fondness for staging amateur theatricals, partly too because of his flared mustache, luxuriant sideburns, gaudy clothes, and imperial six-feet-two of height. As flamboyant in the Transmississippi as he had been in his native Virginia — where, previous to becoming somewhat unstrung in the jangle of the Seven Days, he had put on such a show of strength with a handful of men that McClellan had been awed into immobility before Yorktown — his ache for distinction and love of flourish were no less pronounced in the Lone Star State. The difference here, eight months later, was that Magruder was thinking offensively. For some time now, in fact ever since his assignment to command the District of Texas, Arizona, and New Mexico on October 10, five days after the Union flotilla steamed in and put Galveston under its guns, he had had it in mind not only to liberate the island town, less than fifty miles southeast of his Houston headquarters, but also to sink or capture the warships riding insolently at anchor in the harbor. So far as Prince John was concerned, the addition of those three companies of Massachusetts infantry, now barricading the wharf against attack, only fattened the prize within his grasp and added to the glory about to be won.

Nor was his plan for making a naval assault deterred by his lack of anything resembling a navy. If he had none then he would build one, or at any rate improvise one, and he did so in short order. Workmen off the Houston docks piled bales of cotton around the paddle boxes and decks of the *Bayou City,* a two-story side-wheel Mississippi steamboat, and the stern-wheeler *Neptune,* a smaller vessel. The former was armed with a rifled 32-pounder, located forward of her stacks, and the latter's bow was faced with railroad iron to stiffen her punch as a ram. Their crews were army volunteers, including some 300 riflemen stationed about the decks as sharpshooters. These two "cotton-clads" would stage the naval assault, descending Buffalo Bayou to come booming down on the five Union gunboats, *Westfield, Harriet Lane, Owasco, Clifton,* and *Sachem,* which had a combined displacement of over 3000 tons and mounted a total of 28 guns, mostly heavy. For the land attack there were in all about 500 men; Texans under Colonel Tom Green, who had led them at Valverde, they were survivors of Brigadier General Henry Sibley's nightmare expedition up the Rio Grande, back in the spring. Magruder divided them into three assault columns, taking the center one himself. By New Year's Eve his preparations were complete. He gave the signal and the attack got under way, bringing in the new year with a bang.

Crossing from the mainland by the unguarded bridge, he struck the barricade shortly after midnight — only to find that his scaling ladders were too short. All he could do was work his men up close and keep exchanging shots with the defenders, who had turned out at the first alarm and were laying down a heavy fire. Everything depended now on the untried two-boat navy. The first the Federals knew of its existence was when lookouts on the *Westfield,* Commander W. B. Renshaw's flagship, spotted two ungainly-looking steamboats, apparently overloaded with cotton bales, driving hard toward the anchored flotilla. Attempting to take evasive action, the *Westfield* went aground on Pelican Island Bar, removed from the fight as effectively as if she had been sunk. Aboard the *Bayou City,* bearing down on the *Harriet Lane,* the gun captain of the 32-pounder shouted: "Well, here goes for a New Year's present!" and pulled the lanyard. The first shot missed, as did the second, and on the third the gun exploded at the breech, killing him and four of its crew; whereupon the *Neptune* came up, churning the water in her wake, and struck the *Lane* such a tremendous thump that she broke her own nose and had to run up on the flats to keep from sinking. Afloat as ashore, the battle seemed lost by mishap or miscalculation.

By now, however, the *Bayou City* had pulled up alongside the *Lane,* her upper-deck riflemen firing down on the rattled bluejackets while a boarding party swarmed over the bulwarks and began slashing at the survivors in the style of John Paul Jones. In the course of this melee the Union skipper was killed and his lieutenant ran up the white flag of surrender; observing which, the other three nearby captains did the same. Across the way, still hard aground, Renshaw saw that the *Westfield* was next on the rebel target list. Determined not to have

*A charge meant to prevent the capture of the stranded
Federal gunboat Westfield explodes prematurely as much
of her crew looks on from rescuing rowboats.*

her fall into enemy hands, he ordered the crew to abandon ship while he low-
ered into an open magazine a barrel of turpentine equipped with a slow fuze
which he set and started before he turned to go. That was his last act on earth
or water, for the fuze was defective or wrongly set. Before he made it out of
range, a flame-shot column of black smoke roared skyward and the *Westfield*
blew apart, her wreckage enveloped in fire and steam.

 Watching this abrupt disintegration of the naval support for the
defenders of the wharf, the Texans in front of the barricade took heart and
the Federals behind it were dejected; so much so, indeed, that the three Massachusetts companies, warned by a step-up in the firing that an assault was about
to be launched, surrendered in a body. But the commanders of the gunboats
Clifton, Owasco, and *Sachem,* claiming that this forcing of the issue ashore was in
violation of the naval "truce" — for so they had considered it, they later affirmed

★

by way of rebuttal to the outrage expressed by the rebels — hauled down their white flags and made a sudden run for open water. The Confederates, unable to pursue out into the Gulf, could do nothing but howl in protest at foul play. They had lost 143 killed and wounded. Including captives, the Federals had lost about 600 soldiers and sailors: plus, of course, two gunboats and the town. At a single stroke, boldly conceived and boldly delivered, Magruder had cleared Texas of armed bluecoats. Nor did he intend to grant them another foothold. Moving his headquarters triumphantly to Galveston, he notified his government next day: "We are preparing to give them a warm reception should they return."

The navy might (and in fact did, the following week, withdrawing the 2000-ton screw steamer *Brooklyn* and six gunboats from the blockade squadron off Mobile and bringing them to Galveston, where they were careful however to maintain station well outside the harbor and thus beyond reach of another eruption of Magruder's cotton-clads) but Banks had no intention of returning, not even with a token force. He counted himself lucky that the whole Bay State regiment, together with its artillery and cavalry supports, had not landed in time to be gobbled up, and he brought the still-loaded transports back to New Orleans, turning a deaf ear to Would-Be-Governor Hamilton's disgruntled protestations. That gentleman and his party — a sizable group, characterized by one critic as "friends, patrons, and creditors," who had meant to be front runners in the intended Lone Star colonization — returned instead to Washington, complaining bitterly that they had been "deliberately and purposely humbugged."

Though Holmes of course was quick to congratulate Magruder, whose amphibious coup made the one bright spot in the entire Transmississippi as the new year came in, Hamilton's dejection and disgust were not matched by any corresponding elation on the part of the over-all commander of the Confederate Far West. Though he had managed, on the face of it, to achieve a sort of balance within the limits of his deparartment — defeat in northwestern Arkansas, stalemate in West Louisiana, victory in coastal Texas — he knew that it was precarious in nature, tenuous at best and, in consideration of the odds, most likely temporary. Nor was the maintenance of that shaky balance only dependent on what occurred within the borders of the monster region. Cut off, Holmes and all those under him would be left as it were to wither on the vine; so that what happened beyond or along those borders was equally important, and this was true in particular as to what happened along the eastern border, the Mississippi itself, down which he had reported the "heavy force" of Union ironclads and transports steaming the week before past Helena. It was headed, according to his conjecture, for Vicksburg, the linchpin whose loss might well result in the collapse of the whole Confederate wagon.

★　★　★

★

*This fanciful engraving shows
Sherman's Federal troops reaching
the crest of Chickasaw Bluffs,
when in fact his assault was stopped
at the foot of the hill.*

Parker's Crossroads; Holly Springs; Walnut Hills

1862 ★ ★ ★ ★ ★ **H**aste made waste and Grant **knew it,** but in this case the haste was unavoidable — unavoidable, that is, unless he was willing to take the risk of having another general win the prize he was after — because he was fighting two wars simultaneously: one against the Confederacy, or at any rate so much of its army as stood between him and the river town that was his goal, and the other against a man who, like himself, wore blue. That was where the need for haste came in, for the rival general's name was John McClernand. A former Springfield lawyer and Illinois congressman, McClernand was known to have political aspirations designed to carry him not one inch below the top position occupied at present by his friend, another former Springfield lawyer and Illinois congressman, Abraham Lincoln. Moreover, having decided that the road to the White House led through Vicksburg, he had taken pains to see that he traveled it well equipped, and this he had done by engaging the preliminary support, the active military backing, not only of his friend the President, but also of the Secretary of War, the crusty and often difficult Edwin M. Stanton. With the odds thus lengthened against him, Grant — when he belatedly found out what his rival had been up to — could see that this private war against McClernand might well turn out to be as tough, in several ways, as the public one he had been fighting for eighteen months against the rebels.

★

In the first place, he had not even known that he had this private war on his hands until it was so well under way that his rival had already won the opening skirmish. McClernand had gone to Washington on leave in late September, complaining privately that he was "tired of furnishing brains" for Grant's army. Arriving in the capital he appealed to Lincoln to "let one volunteer officer try his abilities." His plan was to return to his old political stamping ground and there, by reaching also into Indiana and Iowa, raise an army with which he would descend the Mississippi, capture Vicksburg, "and open navigation to New Orleans." Lincoln liked the sound of that and took him to see Stanton, who liked it too. McClernand left Washington in late October, armed with a confidential order signed by Stanton and indorsed by Lincoln, giving official sanction to his plan. By early November Grant was hearing rumors from upriver in Illinois: rumors which were presently reinforced by a dispatch from General-in-Chief Henry W. Halleck, whom the three former lawyers had not taken into their confidence. Memphis, which was in Grant's department, was to "be made the depot of a joint military and naval expedition on Vicksburg." Alarmed at hearing the rumors confirmed, Grant wired back: "Am I to understand that I lie still here while an expedition is fitted out from Memphis, or do you want me to push south as far as possible?" Halleck was something of a lawyer, too, though he now found himself at cross-purposes with the men who had not let him in on the secret. "You have command of all troops sent to your department," he replied, "and have permission to fight the enemy where you please."

Grant considered himself unleashed. Organizing his mobile force of about 40,000 effectives into right and left wings, respectively under Major General W. T. Sherman and Brigadier General C. S. Hamilton, with the center under Major General J. B. McPherson, he began to move at once, southward along the Mississippi Central Railroad from Grand Junction. Ordinarily he would have preferred to wait for reinforcements, but not now. "I feared that delay might bring McClernand," he later explained. Vicksburg was 250 miles away, and as he saw it the town belonged to the man who got there first. By mid-November he was in Holly Springs, where he set up a depot of supplies and munitions, then continued on across the Tallahatchie, leapfrogging his headquarters to Oxford while the lead division was fording the Yocknapatalfa, eight miles north of Water Valley, which was occupied during the first week of December. The movement had been rapid and well coördinated; so far, it had encountered only token resistance from the rebels, who were fading back before the advance of the bluecoats. Presently Grant discovered why. Pemberton — whose strength he considerably overestimated as equal to his own — was avoiding serious contact while seeking a tactical advantage, and at last he found it. He called a halt near Grenada, another twenty-five miles beyond Water Valley, and put his gray-clad troops to work improving with intrenchments a position of great natural strength along the Yalobusha. Approaching Coffeeville on December 5, midway between Water Valley and Grenada, the Federal cavalry was struck a blow that signified the end of easy progress. Still 150-odd miles from Vicksburg, Grant could see that the going was apt to be a good deal rougher and slower from here on.

Something else he could see as well, something that disturbed him even more. While he was being delayed in the piny highlands of north-central Mississippi, facing the rebels intrenched along the high-banked Yalobusha, McClernand might come down to Memphis, where advance contingents of his expedition were awaiting him already, and ride the broad smooth highway of the Mississippi River down to Vicksburg unopposed: in which case Grant would not only have lost his private war, he would even have helped his opponent win it by holding Pemberton and the greater part of the Vicksburg garrison in position, 150 miles away, while McClernand captured the weakly defended town with little more exertion than had been required in the course of the long boat ride

"I wish you would come over this evening and stay tonight, or come in the morning. I would like to talk with you."

— Ulysses S. Grant

south from Cairo. That was what rankled worst, the thought that he would have helped to pluck the laurels that would grace his rival's brow. But as he thought distastefully of this, it began to occur to him that he saw here the possibility of a campaign of his own along these lines. "You have command of all troops sent to your department," Halleck had told him, and presumably this included the recruits awaiting McClernand's arrival at Memphis. So Grant, still at his Oxford headquarters on December 8, sent a note to Sherman, whose command was at College Hill, ten miles away: "I wish you would come over this evening and stay tonight, or come in the morning. I would like to talk with you."

Sherman did not wait for morning. Impatient as always, he rode straight over, a tall red-haired man with a fidgety manner, concave temples, glittering hazel eyes, and a scraggly, close-cropped beard. "I never saw him but I thought of Lazarus," one observer was to write. A chain smoker who, according to another witness, got through each cigar "as if it was a duty to be finished in the shortest possible time," he was forty-two, two years older than the comparatively stolid Grant and once his military senior, too, until Donelson brought the younger brigadier fame and a promotion, both of which had been delayed for Sherman until Shiloh, where he fought under — some said, saved — his former junior. He felt no resentment at that. In fact, he saw Grant as "the coming man

★

in this war." But he had never had better reason for this belief than now at Oxford, when he was closeted with him and heard his plan for the sudden capture of Vicksburg with the help of a kidnaped army.

As usual in military matters, geography played a primary part in determining what was to be done, and how. Various geographic factors made Vicksburg an extremely difficult nut to crack. First there was the bluff itself, the 200-foot red-clay escarpment dominating the hairpin bend of the river at its base, unscalable for infantry and affording the guns emplaced on its crest a deadly plunging fire — as Farragut, for one, could testify — against whatever naval forces moved against or past it. As for land forces, since they could not scale the bluff itself, even if they had been able to approach it from the front, their only alternative was to come upon it from the rear; that is, either to march overland down the Mississippi Central to Grenada, as Grant was now attempting to do, and thence along the high ground lying between the Yazoo and the Big Black rivers, or else debark from their transports somewhere short of the town and make a wide swing east, in order to approach it from that direction. However, the latter was nearly impossible, too, because of another geographic factor, the so-called Yazoo-Mississippi alluvial delta. This incredibly fertile, magnolia-leaf-shaped region, 200 miles in length and 50 miles in average width, bounded east and west by the two rivers that gave it its compound name, and north and south by the hills that rose below and above Memphis and Vicksburg, was nearly roadless throughout its flat and swampy expanse, was subject to floods in all but the driest seasons, and — except for the presence of a scattering of pioneers who risked its malarial and intestinal disorders for the sake of the richness of its forty-foot topsoil, which in time, after the felling of its big trees and the draining of its bayous, would make it the best cotton farmland in the world — was the exclusive domain of moccasins, bears, alligators, and panthers. It was, in short, impenetrable to all but the smallest of military parties, engaged in the briefest of forays. An army attempting to march across or through it would come out at the other end considerably reduced in numbers and fit for nothing more strenuous than a six-month rest, with quinine as the principal item on its diet. Anyhow, Grant did not intend to try it that way. He had his eye fixed on the mouth of the Yazoo, twelve miles above Vicksburg, and it seemed to him that an amphibious force could ascend that river for a landing on the southeast bank, which would afford the troops a straight shot at the town on the bluff. True, there were hills here, too — the Walnut Hills, they were called, the beginning of the long ridge known as the Chickasaw Bluffs, which lay along the left bank of the Yazoo, overlooking the flat morass of the delta — but they were by no means as forbidding as the heights overlooking the Mississippi, a dozen miles below. It was Grant's belief that determined men, supported by the guns of the fleet, could swarm over these comparatively low-lying hills,

★

By the time General William Tecumseh Sherman posed for this tranquil portrait just weeks before his attack on Walnut Hills, he was already Grant's most trusted subordinate and confidant.

brushing aside whatever portion of the weakened garrison tried to stop them, and be inside the town before nightfall of the day they came ashore.

That was why he had sent for Sherman, who seemed to him the right man for the job. Sherman happily agreed to undertake it, and Grant gave him his written orders that same evening. He was to return at once to Memphis with one of his three divisions, which he would combine with McClernand's volunteers, already waiting there. This would give him 21,000 troops, and to these would be added another 12,000 to be picked up at Helena on the way downriver, bringing his total strength to four divisions of 33,000 men, supported by Porter's fleet. Grant explained that he himself would continue to bristle aggressively along the line of the Yalobusha "so as to keep up the impression of a continuous move," and if Pemberton fell back prematurely he would "follow him even to the gates of Vicksburg," in which event he and Sherman would meet on the Yazoo and combine for the final dash into the town. Delighted with the prospect, Sherman was off next day for Memphis, altogether mindful of the need for haste if he was to forestall both McClernand and Pemberton. "Time now is the great object," he wired Porter. "We must not give time for new combinations."

He did not make it precisely clear whether these feared "combinations" were being designed in Richmond or in Washington — whether, that is, they threatened the successful prosecution of Grant's public or his private war. By mid-December, however, Grant's worries in regard to the latter were

★

mostly over. Sherman was in Memphis, poised for the jump-off, and McClernand's men had become organic parts of the army the redhead was about to take downriver. There was still one danger. McClernand outranked him; which meant that if he arrived before Sherman left, he would assume command by virtue of seniority. But Grant considered this unlikely. Sherman was thoroughly aware of the risk and would be sure to avoid the consequences. Besides, with Halleck's telegram in his files as license for the kidnap operation, Grant felt secure from possible thunder from on high. "I doubted McClernand's fitness," he later wrote, "and I had good reason to believe that in forestalling him I was by no means giving offense to those whose authority to command was above both him and me."

The arrival of a telegram from Washington on the 18th, instructing him to divide his command (now and henceforward to be called the Army of the Tennessee) into four corps, with McClernand in charge of one of those assigned to operations down the Mississippi — which meant of course that, once he joined it, he would be in charge of the whole column by virtue of his rank, unless Grant himself came over and took command along the river route — did not disturb the plans Grant had described in a letter home, three days ago, as "all complete for weeks to come," adding: "I hope to have them all work out just as planned." Sherman was ready to leave, he knew, and in fact would be gone tomorrow, before McClernand could possibly arrive from Illinois. Blandly he wired his new subordinate word of the Washington order, which dispelled McClernand's illusion that his command was to be an independent one. Instructing him to come on down to Memphis, Grant even managed to keep a straight face while remarking: "I hope you will find all the preliminary preparations completed on your arrival and the expedition ready to move."

★ ★ ★ *M*cClernand found no such thing, of course. All he found when at last he reached Memphis on December 29 were the empty docks his men had departed from, ten days ago under Sherman, and Grant's telegram, delayed eleven days in transmission. Nor did Grant's own plans, "all complete for weeks to come," work out as he had intended and predicted. In both cases — entirely in the former and largely in the latter — the cause could be summed up in three two-syllable nouns: Nathan Bedford Forrest.

"He was the only Confederate cavalryman of whom Grant stood in much dread," a friend of the Union general's once remarked. Then he told why. "Who's commanding?" Grant would ask on hearing that gray raiders were on the prowl. If it was some other rebel chieftain he would shrug off the threat with a light remark; "but if Forrest was in command he at once became apprehensive, because the latter was amenable to no known rules of procedure, was a law unto himself for all military acts, and was constantly doing the unexpected at all times and places."

Grant's apprehensions were well founded as he looked back over his shoulder in the direction of his main supply base at Columbus, Kentucky; or, more specifically, since the far-off river town was adequately garrisoned against raiders, as he traced on the map the nearly two hundred highly vulnerable, not to say frangible, miles of railroad which were his sole all-weather connection with the munitions and food his army in North Mississippi required if it was to continue to shoot and eat. Without that base and those railroads, once he had used up the reserve supplies already brought forward and stored at Holly Springs, his choice would lie between retreat on the one hand and starvation or surrender on the other. Just now, moreover, the reason his apprehensions were so well founded was that Forrest was looking — and not only looking, but moving — in that direction too: as Grant learned from a dispatch received December 15 from Jackson, Tennessee, a vital junction about midway of his vulnerable supply line. "Forrest is crossing [the] Tennessee at Clifton," the local commander wired. Four days later, Jackson itself was under attack by a mounted force which the Federal defenders estimated at 10,000 men, with Forrest himself definitely in charge.

Pemberton had begun it by appealing to Bragg in late November for a diversion in West Tennessee, which he thought might ease the pressure on his front, and Bragg had responded by sending Forrest instructions to "throw his command rapidly over the Tennessee River and precipitate it upon the enemy's lines, break up railroads, burn bridges, destroy depots, capture hospitals and guards, and harass him generally." Receiving these orders December 10 at Columbia, forty miles south of Nashville, Forrest was off next day with four regiments of cavalry and a four-gun battery, 2100 men in all, mostly recruits newly brigaded under his command and mainly armed with shotguns and flintlock muskets. Four days later and sixty miles away, he began to cross the Tennessee at Clifton on two flatboats which he had built for the emergency and which he afterwards sank in a nearby creek in case he needed them coming back. Deep in enemy country, with the bluecoats warned of his crossing while it was still in progress, he encountered on the 18th, near Lexington, two regiments of infantry, a battalion of cavalry, and a section of artillery, all under Colonel Robert G. Ingersoll, who had been sent out to intercept him. The meeting engagement was brief and decisive. Falling back on the town, Ingersoll took up what he thought was a good defensive position and was firing rapidly with his two guns at the rebels to his front, when suddenly he "found that the enemy were pouring in on all directions." The fight ended quite as abruptly as it had begun. "If he really believed that there is no hell," one grayback later said of the postwar orator-agnostic, "we convinced him that there was something mightily like it." Captured along with his two guns and 150 of his men, while the rest made off "on the full run" for Jackson, twenty-five miles to the west, Ingersoll greeted his captors with aplomb: "Is this the army of your Southern Confederacy for which I have so diligently sought? Then I am your guest until the wheels of the great Cartel are put in motion."

Following hard on the heels of the fugitives, who he knew would stumble into Jackson with exaggerated stories of his strength, Forrest advanced to within four miles of the place and began to dispose his "army" as if for assault, maneuvering boldly along the ridge-lines and beating kettledrums at widely scattered points to keep up the illusion, or, as he called it, "the skeer." It worked quite well. Convinced that he was heavily outnumbered, though in fact he had about four times as many troops inside the town as the Confederates had outside it, Brigadier General Jeremiah Sullivan prepared to make a desperate house-to-house defense. All next day the rebel host continued to gather, waxing bolder hour by hour. When dawn of the 20th showed the graybacks gone, Sullivan took heart and set out after them, pushing eastward — into emptiness, as it turned out, for Forrest had swung north. Today in fact, having thrown the Federal main body off his trail, he began in earnest to carry out his primary assignment, the destruction of the sixty miles of the Mobile & Ohio connecting Jackson and Union City, up near the Kentucky line. The common complaint of army commanders, that cavalry could seldom be persuaded to get down off their horses for the hard work that was necessary if the damage to enemy installations was to be more than temporary, was never leveled against Forrest's men. Besides forcing the surrender of the several blue garrisons in towns along the line, they tore up track, burned crossties and trestles, and wrecked culverts so effectively that this stretch of the M&O was out of commission for the balance of the war. In Union City on Christmas Eve, resting his troopers after their four-day rampage with axes and sledges, Forrest reported by courier to Bragg that, at a cost so far of 22 men, he had killed or captured more than 1300 of the enemy, "including 4 colonels, 4 majors, 10 captains, and 23 lieutenants." That he considered this no more than a respectable beginning was shown by his closing remark: "My men have all behaved well in action, and as soon as rested a little you will hear from me in another quarter."

His problem now, after paroling his captives and sending them north to Columbus to spread bizarre reports of his strength — reports that were based on bogus dispatches, which he had been careful to let them overhear while their papers were being made out at his headquarters — was, first, what further damage to inflict and, second, how to get back over the river intact before the various Federal columns, still chasing phantoms all over West Tennessee,

★

Although lacking a formal education, Confederate cavalryman Nathan Bedford Forrest was a natural military leader who became known as the "Wizard of the Saddle."

converged on him with overwhelming numbers. The first was solved on Christmas Day, when he marched southeast out of Union City and spent the next two days administering to the Nashville & Northwestern the treatment already given the M&O. Reaching McKenzie on the 28th in an icy, pelting rain, he headed south across the swampy bottoms of the swollen Obion River, and now began his solution of the second part of his problem. Instead of trying to make a run for the Tennessee, with the chance of being caught half-over and hamstrung, he decided to brazen out the game by thrusting in among the Federals attempting a convergence, and by vigorous blows, struck right or left at whatever came within his reach, stun them into inaction or retreat, while he continued his movement toward the security of Middle Tennessee.

The fact was, he had little to fear from the direction of Columbus. Brigadier General Thomas A. Davies, commander of the 5000 bluecoats gathered there, had been so alarmed by demonstrations within ten miles of the town on Christmas Eve, as well as by the parolees coming in next day with reports of 40,000 infantry on the march from Bragg, that he had spiked the guns at New Madrid and Island Ten, throwing the powder into the Mississippi to keep it out of rebel hands, and now was concentrating everything in order to protect the $13,000,000 worth of supplies and equipment being loaded onto steamboats

---

"I have Forrest in a tight place. My troops are moving on him from three directions, and I hope with success."

— Jeremiah Sullivan

---

at the Columbus wharf for a getaway in case Forrest broke his lines. Conditions were scarcely better, from the Union point of view, 250 miles downriver at Memphis, where the citizens had become so elated over rumors that their former alderman was coming home, along with thousands of his troopers, that Major General S. A. Hurlbut, perturbed by their reaction and the fact that his garrison was down to a handful since the departure of Sherman, telegraphed Washington: "I hold city by terror of heavy guns bearing upon it and the belief that an attack would cause its destruction." Grant, however, was of a different breed. He was thinking not of his safety, but of the possible destruction of Forrest and his men. "I have directed such a concentration of troops that I think not many of them will get back to the east bank of the Tennessee," he informed a subordinate. Nor was this opinion ill-founded. One superior blue force was coming south from Fort Henry, another north from Corinth, and both were now much closer to the Clifton crossing than Forrest was. So, for that matter, were Jere Sullivan and his three brigades, two of which were back by now from their goose chase east of Jackson and headed north. Undiscouraged by his lack of luck so far, he believed he knew just where the raiders were, and he intended to bag them. "I have Forrest in a tight place," he wired Grant on December 29. "My troops are moving on him from three directions, and I hope with success."

★

Forrest was indeed in a tight place, and that place was about to get tighter. Emerging from the flooded Obion bottoms, which he had crossed by an abandoned causeway, he paused on December 30 to let Sullivan's unsuspecting lead brigade go by him, then resumed his march past Huntingdon and toward Clarksburg, nearing which place on the morning of the last day of the year he encountered the other brigade, forewarned and drawn up to meet him at Parker's Crossroads. By way of precaution he had sent four companies to guard the road from Huntingdon and warn him in case the lead brigade turned back, and now, secure in the belief that his rear was well protected against surprise, he settled down to a casualty-saving artillery duel with the blue force to his front. It lasted from about 9 o'clock until an hour past noon, by which time he had captured three of the enemy guns and 18 wagonloads of ammunition and had driven the skirmishers back on their supports. He had in fact ceased firing, in response to several white flags displayed along the Union line, and was sending in his usual demand for "unconditional surrender to prevent the further effusion of blood," when an attack exploded directly in his rear. For the first last only time in his career, Forrest was completely surprised in battle. His reaction was immediate. Quickly resuming the fight to his front, he simultaneously charged rearward, stalling the surprise attackers with blows to the head and flanks, and withdrew sideways before his opponents recovered from the shock. It was smartly done — later giving rise to the legend that his response to a staff officer's flustered question, "What shall we do? What shall we do?" was: "Charge both ways!" — but not without sacrifice. The captured guns were abandoned, along with three of his own, for lack of horses to draw them, as well as the 18 wagonloads of ammunition. Three hundred men who had been fighting afoot were taken, too, while trying to catch their mounts, which had bolted at the sudden burst of gunfire from the rear. Sullivan, coming up from behind Jackson with his third brigade next day, was elated. "Forrest's army completely broken up," he wired Grant. "They are scattered over the country without ammunition. We need a good cavalry regiment to go through the country and pick them up."

So he said. But while he and his three brigades were waiting for that "good regiment," Forrest and his troopers were riding hard for the Tennessee and eluding the columns approaching cautiously from Corinth and Fort Henry. All in high spirits on New Year's Day — except possibly the captain who by now had been verbally blistered for taking yesterday's rear-guard companies up the wrong road and thus permitting the Federals to march past him unobserved — they reached Clifton about midday, raised the sunken flatboats, and were across the icy river before dawn. The basis for their high spirits was a sense of accomplishment. They had gone out as green recruits, miserably armed, and had returned within less than three weeks as veterans, equipped with the best accouterments and weapons the U.S. government could provide. In the course of a brief midwinter campaign, which opened and closed with a pontoonless crossing of one of the nation's great rivers, and in the course of which they more than made up in recruits for what they lost in battle or on the march, they had killed or paroled as many men as they had in their whole command and had kept at least ten times their number of bluecoats frantically busy for a fortnight. Besides the estimated $3,000,000 they had cost the Federals in wrecked installations and equipment, they had taken or destroyed 10 guns and captured 10,000 rifles and a million badly needed cartridges. Above all, they had accomplished their primary assignment by cutting Grant's lifeline, from Jackson north to the Kentucky border. They saw all this as Forrest's doing, and it was their pride, now and for all the rest of their lives — whether those lives were to end next week in combat or were to stretch on down the years to the ones they spent sunning their old bones on the galleries of crossroads stores throughout the Deep and Central South — that they had belonged to what in time would be known as his Old Brigade.

★ ★ ★   **P**emberton was highly pleased, not only with the results of this cavalry action outside the limits of his department, but also with another which had been carried out within those limits and which he himself had designed as a sort of companion piece or counterpart to the raid-in-progress beyond the Tennessee line. Both had a profound effect on the situation he had been facing ever since he called a halt and began intrenching along the Yalobusha, preparatory to coming to grips with Grant's superior army: so profound an effect, indeed, that it presently became obvious that if he and Grant were to come to grips, it would be neither here nor now. Like that of the first, the success of this second horseback exploit — which in point of fact was simultaneous rather than sequential, beginning later and ending sooner — could also be summed up in three nouns, though in this case the summary was even briefer, since all three were single-syllabled: Earl Van Dorn.

"Buck" Van Dorn, as he had been called at West Point and by his fellow officers in the old army, had leaped at the chance for distinction, not only because it was part of his nature to delight in desperate ventures, but also because he was badly in need just now of personal redemption. After a brilliant pre-Manassas career in Texas, he had been called to Virginia, then reassigned to Arkansas, where his attempt at a double envelopment had been foiled disastrously at Elkhorn Tavern. Crossing the Mississippi after Shiloh, he had suffered an even bloodier repulse at Corinth in October, which gave him so evil a reputation in his home state that a court had been called to hear evidence of his bungling. Although he was cleared by the court, the government soon afterwards promoted Pemberton over the head upon which the public was still heaping condemnations. The accusation that he was "the source of all our woes," Senator Phelan wrote President Davis, was "so fastened in the public belief that an acquittal by a court-martial of angels would not relieve him of the charge." Van Dorn was depressed, but he was not without hope. A court-martial of angels was one thing; a brilliant military exploit, characterized by boldness and attended by great risk, was quite another. So when Pemberton summoned him to army headquarters and gave him his assignment — an all-out raid on Grant's communications and supply lines, including the great depot lately established at Holly Springs — the diminutive Mississippian saw in it the opportunity to retrieve his reputation and bask once more in the warmth of his countrymen's affection. Always one to grasp the nettle danger, he embraced the offered chance without delay.

He left Grenada on December 18 with 3500 cavalry, heading east at first to skirt Grant's flank, then north as if for a return to Corinth. Next day, however, he turned west beyond New Albany and came thundering into Holly Springs at dawn, December 20. The Federal commander there, Colonel R. C. Murphy, had been placed in a similar uncomfortable position in September at Iuka, which he had abandoned without a fight or even destruction of the stores to keep them from falling into enemy hands. Grant had forgiven him then because of his youth and inexperience, and now he was given another chance to prove his mettle. He did no better. In fact, despite advance warning that a heavy column of graybacks was moving in his direction, he did far worse. This time, he lost not only the stores in his charge but also the soldiers, 1500 of whom were captured and paroled on the spot by the jubilant rebels, caracoling their horses at the sight of the mountains of food and equipment piled here for Grant's army. "My fate is most mortifying," he reported that night amid the embers which were all that remained of the million-dollar depot of supplies. "I have done all in my power — in truth, my force was inadequate."

Grant reacted "with pain and mortification" at the news of his loss and ordered Murphy dismissed from the service, as of "the date of his cowardly and disgraceful conduct." With Forrest loose on the railroad north of Jackson that same day, and his own wife spared embarrassment at Holly Springs only because she had left to join him in Oxford the day before, Grant began to design combinations of forces in North Mississippi, not unlike those already sent out after Forrest in West Tennessee, to accomplish Van Dorn's destruction before he could return to safety behind the Yalobusha. "I want those fellows caught, if possible," he said.

The trouble with this was that by the time the various columns could be put in motion Van Dorn was no longer in North Mississippi. Instead of racing for home, and perhaps into the arms of superior forces already gathering in his rear, he pushed on northward into Tennessee. Before he left his native state, however, the commander of a small outpost at Davis Mill, twenty miles north of Holly Springs and just south of the Tennessee line, gave him — and, incidentally, Murphy — a lesson in how well an "inadequate" force could hold its own against "overwhelming" numbers. His name was Colonel W. H. Morgan and he had less than 300 men for the defense of a point made critical by the presence of a trestle by which the Mississippi Central crossed Wolf River. Hearing that the raiders were coming his way, he converted an old sawmill into a blockhouse, reinforcing its walls with cotton bales and crossties, and a nearby Indian mound into a moated earthwork, both of which covered the railroad approach with converging fire. About noon of the 21st, the Confederates came up and launched a quick assault, which was repulsed. After a two-hour long-range skirmish, finding the fire too hot for a storming party to reach and ignite the trestle, let alone cross the river, the attackers sent forward, under a flag of truce, a note asking whether the defenders were ready to surrender. Morgan replied with what he later termed "a respectful but decided negative," and the Confederates withdrew, leaving 22 dead and 30 wounded on the field, along with another 20 prisoners who had ventured up too close to be able to pull back without exposing themselves to slaughter. Morgan's loss was 3 men slightly wounded.

Earl Van Dorn's raid on the Federal supply depot at Holly Springs and the surrounding area refurbished his tarnished reputation resulting from earlier defeats at Elkhorn Tavern and Corinth.

Except for the further damage it did to his former opinion that one Southerner was worth ten Yankee hirelings in a scrap, Van Dorn was not greatly disturbed by this tactical upset. In the course of his approach to the fight, and even while it was in progress, he had done the railroad enough damage to be able to afford to let the trestle go. By-passing Morgan's improvised blockhouse, he crossed upstream and pushed on northward between Grand Junction and LaGrange, where he tore up sections of the Memphis & Charleston for good measure. Near Bolivar on the 23rd, he circled Middleburg, still ripping up track and wrecking culverts, and headed back south on Christmas Eve, riding through Van Buren and Saulsbury to reënter Mississippi. South of Ripley on Christmas Day, he had a brush with one of the converging Union columns, but pressed on without delay, through Pontotoc and thence on back to Grenada, which he reached by midafternoon of December 28. He had carried out his mission in fine style, destroying Grant's reserve supplies of food, forage, and munitions. What was more, at least from a particular point of view, he had refurbished his tarnished reputation. Households which formerly had mentioned his name only with frowns of disapproval or downright scowls of condemnation now drank his health with shouts of joy and praised him to the skies.

Pemberton, then, was delighted at the manner in which Van Dorn had achieved redemption; but not Grant, who paid the bill which thus was added to all that Forrest was costing him simultaneously. With Columbus in a panic, Memphis cowed by heavy guns, his communications disrupted, and his supply line almost a continuous wreck from Holly Springs north to the Kentucky border, he was stymied and he knew it. Van Dorn having destroyed his supplies on hand and Forrest having made it impossible for him to bring up more, he could neither move forward nor stand still. There was no way he could go but back, and this he proceeded to do, meanwhile solving the problem of immediate subsistence by sending out "all the wagons we had, under proper escort, to collect and bring in all supplies of forage and food from a region of fifteen miles east and west of the road from our front back to Grand Junction." At the news of this, the broad smiles caused by Van Dorn's coup faded from the faces of the people around Oxford. Their former mocking question, "What will you do now?" was changed to: "What are *we* to do?" Grant replied that he had done his best to feed his soldiers from their own northern resources, but now that these had been cut off "it could not be expected that men, with arms in their hands, would starve in the midst of plenty." In short, as he said later, "I advised them to emigrate east, or west, fifteen miles and assist in eating up what we left."

To his amazement — for he had thought the pickings would be slim and had lately advised his government that an army could not "subsist itself on the country except in forage"; "Disaster would result in the end," he had predicted — the wagons returned heavy-laden with hams, corn on the cob, field peas and beans, sweet and Irish potatoes, and fowls of every description, accompanied by herds of beef on the hoof. "It showed that we could have subsisted off the country for two months instead of two weeks without going beyond the limits designated," he subsequently wrote, adding: "This taught me a lesson."

The knowledge thus gained might prove to be of great use in the future, but for the present one thing still bothered him beyond all others. This was the thought that, putting it baldly, he was leaving his friend Sherman in the lurch. He had promised to hold Pemberton in position, 150 miles from Vicksburg, while Sherman was storming its thinly held defenses; yet Pemberton was already hurrying troops in that direction, as Grant knew, and might well arrive in time to smother the attackers in the Yazoo bottoms. However, there was little Grant could do about it now, except depend on Sherman to work out his own salvation. Out of touch as he was, because of his ruptured communications, Grant did not even know whether Sherman had left Memphis yet — or, if so, whether he was still in command of the river expedition; McClernand, in event of delay, might have arrived in time to take over. All Grant could do was send a courier to Memphis with a message addressed to "Commanding Officer Expedition down Mississippi," advising him, whoever he was, "that farther advance by this route is perfectly impracticable" and that he and his men were falling back, while Pemberton did likewise. Whether this would arrive in time to forestall disaster, he did not know.

★ ★ ★   *S*herman was already downriver, and so far his only thought of disaster had been the intention to inflict it. "You may calculate on our being at Vicksburg by Christmas," he wrote Grant's adjutant on December 19, the day he left Memphis. "River has risen some feet, and all is now good navigation. Gunboats are at mouth of Yazoo now, and there will be no difficulty in effecting a landing up Yazoo within twelve miles of Vicksburg." Two days later at Helena, where he picked up his fourth division, he received from upriver his first intimation that Grant might be having trouble in the form of rebel cavalry, which was reported to have captured Holly Springs. If this was so, then Sherman's first letter most likely had not got through to Oxford; nor would a second. Nevertheless, he refused to be disconcerted, and wrote again. "I hardly know what faith to put in such a report," he said, "but suppose whatever may be the case you will attend to it."

All was indeed "good navigation" for the fifty-odd army transports and the 32,500 soldiers close-packed on their decks, steaming rapidly toward their destiny below, as well as for the naval escort of three ironclads, two wooden gunboats, and two rams. But for the rest of Porter's fleet — three ironclads and two "tinclads," so called because their armor was no more than musket-proof — the going had been less easy. Sent downriver two weeks before, they had succeeded in clearing the Yazoo from its mouth upstream to Haines Bluff, where a stout Confederate battery defined the limit of penetration, 23 winding miles from the point of entrance. This had not been accomplished without cost, however, for the defenses were in charge of Isaac Brown, and Brown was known to be hungry for vengeance because of the recent loss above Baton Rouge of the steam ram *Arkansas,* which he had built up this same river the summer before and with which he had charged and sundered the two flotillas then besieging Vicksburg. He had no warship now, but he had notions about torpedoes, five-gallon whiskey demijohns packed with powder, fuzed with artillery friction tubes, and each suspended a few feet below a float on the muddy surface. On December 12 the five-boat Union reconnaissance squadron appeared up the Yazoo, shelling the banks and fishing up Brown's torpedoes as it advanced. Approaching Haines Bluff, the ironclad *Cairo* made contact with one of the glass demijohns at five minutes before noon, and at 12.03 she was out of sight, all but the tips of her stacks, in thirty feet of water.

Celerity and good discipline made it possible for the crew to abandon ship within the allowed eight minutes. No lives were lost, but the *Cairo*'s skipper, Lieutenant Commander T. O. Selfridge, Jr., a young man with a lofty forehead and luxuriant sideburns, was greatly disturbed by the loss of his boat and the possible end of his career as well, depending on the admiral's reaction to the news. Steaming back down the Yazoo aboard one of the tinclads, he found Porter himself at the mouth of the river, just arrived from Memphis, and stiffly requested a court of inquiry. "Court!" the admiral snorted. "I have no time to order courts. I can't blame an officer who puts his ship close to the enemy. Is there any other vessel you would like to have?" Without waiting for an answer he turned abruptly to the flag captain standing beside him on the bridge. "Breese, make out Selfridge's orders to the *Conestoga.*"

Porter was like that, when he chose to be. Just short of fifty and rather hard-faced, with a hearty manner and a full dark beard, he had been given his present assignment, together with the rank of acting rear admiral, over the heads of eighty seniors. For the present, though, despite this cause for self-congratulation, the heartiness and bluster were cover for worry. Most of his old sailors had broken down, with the result that his heavy boats were half-manned, while ten light-draft vessels were laid up for lack of crews, and he was complaining to Washington that a draft of new men, lately arrived from New York, were "all boys and very ordinary landsmen." Characteristically, however, in a letter written this week to Sherman, after protesting of these and other matters, including a shortage of provisions, fuel, medicines, and clothing — not to mention the loss of the *Cairo* — he closed by observing: "I expected that the government would send men from the East, but not a man will they send or notice my complaints, so we will have to go on with what we have."

Reaching Milliken's Bend, on the west bank of the Mississippi ten miles above the mouth of the Yazoo, Sherman landed a brigade on Christmas Day and sent it out to wreck a section of the railroad connecting Vicksburg and Monroe, Louisiana. Next morning, while the brigade was returning, its mission accomplished, the rest of the armada proceeded downstream, entered the Yazoo, and steamed up its intricate channel. A light gunboat and an ironclad led the way, followed by twenty transports, each with two companies of riflemen charged with returning the fire of snipers. Then came another ironclad and twenty more transports, similarly protected. So it went, to the tail of the 64-boat column, until a landing was made at Johnson's Farm, on the Vicksburg shore of the Yazoo ten miles above its mouth. Alertness had paid off, or else it had been unnecessary. "Some few guerilla parties infested the banks," Sherman explained, "but did not dare to molest so strong a force as I commanded." It occurred to some of his soldiers, though, that the rebels were going to let geography do their fighting for them. Wide-eyed as the Illinois and Indiana farmboys were in this strange land, that seemed altogether possible. First there had been the big river itself — or himself; the Old Man, natives called the stream, taking their cue from the Indians, who had named it the Father of Waters — the tawny, mile-wide Mississippi, so thick with silt that recruits could almost believe the steamboat hands who solemnly assured them that if you drank its water for as much as a week "you will have a sandbar in you a mile long." Then had come the smaller stream, with its currentless bayous and mazy sloughs, whose very name was the Indian word for death. And now there was this, the land itself, spongelike under their feet as they came ashore, desolate as the back side of the moon and brooded over by cypresses and water oaks with long gray beards of Spanish moss. North was only a direction indicated by a compass — if a man had one, that is, for otherwise there was no north or south or east or west; there was only the brooding desolation. If this was the country the rebs wanted to take out of the Union, the blue-coated farmboys were ready to say good riddance.

The molestation Sherman had said the Confederates did not dare to attempt began the following day, December 27, against the navy. Commander William Gwin, a veteran of all the river fights since Fort Henry, took his ironclad *Benton* upstream to shell out some graybacks lurking in the woods on the left flank, but got caught in a narrow stretch of the river and was pounded by a battery on the bluffs. Three of the more than thirty hits came through the *Benton*'s ports, cutting her crew up badly, and Gwin, who refused to take cover in the shot-proof pilot house — "A captain's place is on the quarterdeck," he protested when urged to step inside — was mortally wounded by an 8-inch solid

*Converted from a snag boat, as these drawings show, the
U.S.S. Benton became an ironclad with 16 cannons —
one of the most powerful vessels of the Federal river fleet.*

that took off most of his right arm and breast, exposing the ribs and lung in a sudden flash of white and scarlet. Meanwhile the army was having its share of opposition, too, as it floundered about in the Yazoo bottoms and tried to get itself aligned for the assault on the Walnut Hills. The four division commanders, Brigadier Generals A. J. Smith, M. L. Smith, G. W. Morgan, and Frederick Steele, were in the thick of things next morning, dodging bullets like all the rest, when suddenly their number was reduced to three by a sniper who hit the second Smith in the hip joint and retired him from the campaign.

These two high-placed casualties only added to a confusion that was rife enough already. Johnson's Farm, which was little more than a patch of cleared ground in the midst of swampy woods, was separated from the hills ahead by a broad, shallow bayou, a former bed of the Yazoo, and hemmed in on the flanks by two others, Old River Bayou on the right and Chickasaw Bayou on the left. All three looked much alike to an unpracticed eye, so that there was much consequent loss of direction, misidentification of objectives, and countermarching of columns. A bridge ordered constructed over the shallow bayou to the front was built by mistake over one of the others, too late to be relaid. Whole companies got separated from their regiments and spent hours ricocheting from one alien outfit to another. As a result of all this, and more, it was Monday morning, December 29, before the objectives could be assigned and pointed out on the ground instead of on the inadequate maps. Sherman's plan for overrunning the hilltop defenses was for all four divisions to make "a show of attack along the whole front," but to concentrate his main effort at two points, half a mile apart, which seemed to him to afford his soldiers the best chance for a penetration. One of these was in front of Morgan's division, and when Sherman pointed it out to him and told him what he wanted, Morgan nodded positively. "General, in ten minutes after you give the signal I'll be on those hills," he said.

His timing was a good deal off. Except for one brigade, which "took cover behind the [opposite] bank, and could not be moved forward," as Sherman later reported in disgust, Morgan not only did not reach "those hills," he did not even get across the bayou, in ten or any other number of minutes after the signal for attack was given by the batteries all along the Federal line. Presently, however, it was demonstrated that, all in all, this was perhaps the best thing to have done in the situation in which their red-headed commander had placed them. A brigade of Steele's division, led by Brigadier General Frank Blair, Jr., a former Missouri congressman and brother of the Postmaster General, got across in good order and excellent spirits, only to encounter a savage artillery crossfire that sent it staggering back, leaving 500 killed, wounded, and captured at the point where it had been struck. One regiment kept going but was stopped by the steepness of the bluff and a battery firing directly down the throats of the attackers. With their hands they began to scoop out burrows in the face of the nearly perpendicular hillside, seeking overhead cover from enemy riflemen who held their muskets out over the parapet and fired them vertically into the huddled, frantically digging mass below. Indeed, so critical was their position, as Sherman later said, "that we could not recall the men till after dark, and then one at a time." He added, in summation of the day's activities: "Our loss had been pretty heavy, and we had accomplished nothing, and had inflicted little loss on our enemy."

"Pretty heavy" was putting it mildly, as he would discover when he found time for counting noses, but the rest of this estimation was accurate enough. Federal losses reached the commemorative figure 1776, of whom 208 were killed, 1005 were wounded, and 563 were captured or otherwise missing. The Confederates lost 207 in all: 63 killed, 134 wounded, and 10 missing.

Unwilling to let it go at that — "We will lose 5000 men before we take Vicksburg," he had said, "and may as well lose them here as anywhere else" — Sherman decided to reload Steele's division aboard transports and move it upstream for a diversionary strike in the vicinity of Haines Bluff, which might induce the defenders to weaken their present line. Porter was no less willing than before. Moreover, by way of disposing of Brown's remaining torpedoes, he conceived the idea of using one of the rams to clear the path. "I propose to send her ahead and explode them," he explained. "If we lose her, it does not matter much." Colonel Charles R. Ellet, youthful successor to his dead father as commander of the former army vessels, did not take to this notion of a sacrificial ram. With Porter's consent, he added a 45-foot boom extending beyond the prow and equipped it with pulleys and cords and hooks for fishing up the floats and demijohns. Ram and transports set out by the dark of the moon on the last night of the year, while Sherman alerted his other three divisions for a second all-out assault on the Walnut Hills as soon as they heard the boom of guns

---

"Our loss had been pretty heavy, and we had accomplished nothing, and had inflicted little loss on our enemy."

— William T. Sherman

---

upstream. What came instead, at 4 a.m. on New Year's Day, was a note from Steele, explaining that the boats were fog-bound and could not proceed. So Sherman called a halt and took stock. He had been waiting all this time for some word from Grant, either on the line of the Yalobusha or here on the Yazoo, but there had been nothing since the rumor of the fall of Holly Springs. From Vicksburg itself, ten air-line miles away, its steeples visible from several points along his boggy front, he had been hearing for the past three days the sound of trains arriving and departing. It might be a ruse, as at Corinth back in May. On the other hand, it might signify what it sounded like: the arrival from Grenada or Mobile or Chattanooga, or possibly all three, of reinforcements for the rebel garrison. Also, rain had begun to fall by now in earnest, and looking up he saw watermarks on the trunks of trees "ten feet above our heads." In short, as he later reported, seeing "no good reason for remaining in so unenviable a position any longer," he "became convinced that the part of wisdom was to withdraw."

Withdraw he did, reëmbarking his soldiers the following day and proceeding downriver without delay. There was more room on the decks of the transports now, and Sherman was low in spirits: not because he was dissatisfied with his direction of the attempt — "There was no bungling on my part," he

Stephen D. Lee deployed his outnumbered troops in strong defensive positions atop Walnut Hills and stopped Sherman's attack, forcing the Federals to withdraw.

wrote, "for I never worked harder or with more intensity of purpose in my life" — but because he knew that the journalists, whom he had snubbed at every opportunity since their spreading of last year's rumors that he was insane, would have a field day writing their descriptions of his repulse and retreat. Presently he was hailed by Porter, who signaled him to come aboard the flagship. Sherman did so, rain-drenched and disconsolate.

"I've lost 1700 men," he said, "and those infernal reporters will publish all over the country their ridiculous stories about Sherman being whipped."

"Pshaw," the admiral replied. "That's nothing; simply an episode of the war. You'll lose 17,000 before the war is over and think nothing of it. We'll have Vicksburg yet, before we die. Steward! Bring some punch."

When he got the red-head settled down he gave him the unwelcome news that McClernand was at hand, anchored just inside the mouth of the Yazoo and waiting to see him. Sherman, who could keep as straight a face as his friend Grant when so inclined, afterwards remarked of his rival's sudden but long-expected appearance on the scene: "It was rumored he had come down to supersede me."

★

McClernand, too, had news for him when they met later that day. Grant was not coming down through Mississippi; he had in fact been in retreat for more than a week, leaving Pemberton free to concentrate for the defense of Vicksburg. Sherman suggested that this meant that any further attempt against the town with their present force was hopeless. Indeed, in the light of this disclosure, he began to consider himself most fortunate in failure, even though it had cost him a total of 1848 casualties for the whole campaign. "Had we succeeded," he reasoned, "we might have found ourselves in a worse trap, when General Pemberton was at full liberty to turn his whole force against us."

Dark-bearded McClernand agreed that the grapes were sour, at least for now. Next day, January 3, he and Sherman withdrew their troops from the Yazoo and rendezvoused again at Milliken's Bend where McClernand took command.

"Well, we have been to Vicksburg and it was too much for us and we have backed out," Sherman wrote his wife from the camp on the west bank of the Mississippi. Reporting by dispatch to Grant, however, he went a bit more into detail as to causes. "I attribute our failure to the strength of the enemy's position, both natural and artificial, and not to his superior fighting," he declared; "but as we must all in the future have ample opportunities to test this quality, it is foolish to discuss it."

Pemberton would have agreed that it was foolish to discuss it, not for the reason his adversary gave, but because he considered the question already settled. The proof of the answer, so far as he was concerned, had been demonstrated in the course of the past two weeks, during which time he had stood off and repulsed two separate Union armies, each superior in numbers to his own. What was more, he had gained new confidence in his top commanders: in Van Dorn, whose lightning raid, staged in conjunction with Forrest's in West Tennessee, had abolished the northward menace: in the on-the-spot Vicksburg defenders, Major General Martin L. Smith and Brigadier General Stephen D. Lee, who with fewer than 15,000 soldiers, most of whom had arrived at the last minute from Grenada, had driven better than twice as many bluecoats out of their side yard, inflicting in the process about nine times as many casualties as they suffered: and in himself, who had engineered the whole and had been present for both repulses. Not that he did not expect to have to fight a return engagement. He did. But he considered that this would be no more than an occasion for redemonstrating what had been proved already.

"Vicksburg is daily growing stronger," he wired Richmond soon after New Year's. "We intend to hold it."

★ ★ ★

★

*M*en of the Washington Light
Artillery's 5th Company, seen
here relaxing in camp, held a
contested ridge at Murfreesboro
until their ammunition gave out.

Murfreesboro: Bragg Retreats

1862 ★ ★ ★ ★ ★

Rosecrans too was aware that **haste made waste,** but unlike Grant he was having no part of it. In reply to Halleck's frequent urgings that he move against Bragg and Chattanooga without delay — it was for this, after all, that he had been appointed to succeed his fellow Ohioan, Don Carlos Buell, whose characteristic attitude had seemed to his superiors to be one of hesitation — he made it clear that he intended to take his time. He would move when he got ready, not before, and thus, as he put it, avoid having to "stop and tinker" along the way. His policy, he explained in a series of answers to the telegraphic nudges, was "to lull [the rebels] into security," then "press them up solidly" and "endeavor to make an end of them." When Halleck at last lost patience altogether, informing the general in early December that he had twice been asked to designate a successor for him — "If you remain one more week in Nashville," he warned, "I cannot prevent your removal" — Rosecrans set his heels in hard and bristled back at the general-in-chief: "I need no other stimulus to make me do my duty than the knowledge of what it is. To threats of removal or the like I must be permitted to say that I am insensible."

"Old Rosy" the men called him, not only because of his colorful name, but also because of his large red nose, which one observer classified as "intensified Roman." He was a tall, hale man, a heavy drinker but withal an ar-

★

dent Catholic; he carried a crucifix on his watch chain and a rosary in his pocket, and he so delighted in small-hours religious discussions that he sometimes kept his staff up half the night debating such fine points as the distinction between profanity, which he freely employed, and blasphemy, which he eschewed. One such discussion achieved marathon proportions, going on for ten nights running, and though this was hard on the staff men, who missed their sleep, Rosecrans considered the problem solved beforehand by the fact that, like himself, they were all blond; "sandy fellows," he remarked upon occasion, were "quick and sharp," and, being more industrious by nature than brunets, required less rest — although he, for his own part, often slept till noon on the day following one of the all-night sessions devoted to eschatology or the question of how many angels could stand tiptoe on a pinpoint. Like Bardolph, whom he so much resembled in physiognomy, he could swing rapidly from gloom to equanimity or from abusiveness to affability. The bristly reply to Halleck was characteristic, for he would often flare up on short notice; but he was likely to calm down just as fast. All of a sudden, on the heels of an outburst of temper, he would be all smiles and congeniality, stroking and cajoling the very man he had been reviling a moment past, and if this was sometimes confusing to those around him, it was also a rather welcome relief from the dour and noncommittal Buell. Rosecrans was forty-three, two years younger than his present opponent Bragg, who had graduated five years ahead of him at West Point, where each had stood fifth in his class. Sometimes he seemed older than his years, sometimes not, depending on his mood, but in general he was liked and even admired, especially by the volunteers, who found him approachable and amusing. For instance, he would stroll through the camps after lights-out, and if he saw a lamp still burning in one of the tents he would whack on the canvas with the flat of his sword. The response, if not blasphemous, would at any rate be profane and abusive. Prompt to apologize when they saw the red-nosed face of their general appear through the tent flap, the soldiers would explain that they had thought he was some rowdy prowling around in the dark. He took it well, including the muffled laughter that followed the extinguishing of the lamp on his departure, and the result was a steady growth of affection between him and the men of the army which Halleck was protesting he was slow to commit to battle.

That army's present over-all strength was 81,729 effectives, divided like Grant's into Left Wing, Center, and Right Wing, commanded respectively by Major Generals T. L. Crittenden, George Thomas, and Alexander McCook, all veterans of the bloody October fight at Perryville, Kentucky, under Buell. By mid-December — Halleck having more or less apologized for the previous nudgings by explaining that they had not been intended as "threats of removal or the like," but merely as expressions of the President's "great anxiety" over the fact that, Middle Tennessee being the Confederacy's only late-summer gain which had not been erased, pro-Southern members of the British parliament, scheduled to convene in January, might find in this apparent stalemate persuasive arguments for the intervention France was already urging — Rosecrans became more optimistic, despite the drouth which kept the Cumberland River too shallow for it to serve as a dependable supply line. "Things will be ripe soon," he assured his nervous superiors on the 15th, and followed this dispatch with another, put on the wire within an hour: "Rebel troops say they will fight us. . . . Cumberland still very low; rain threatens; will be ready in a few days."

The few days stretched on to Christmas, and still he had not moved. By then, however, he had received encouraging reports from scouts and spies beyond the rebel lines. In the first place, Morgan and Forrest were on the prowl, and though normally this would have been considered alarming information, in this case it was not so, for the former was now so far in his rear as not to be able

William S. Rosecrans was, wrote one of his staff, "a man from whom the people are each day expecting some extraordinary action, some tremendous battle."

to interfere with any immediate action south or east of Nashville, while the latter was clean outside his department. Whatever harm they might do in Kentucky and West Tennessee (which, as it turned out, was considerable) Rosecrans could wish them Godspeed, so long as they kept their backs in his direction. Moreover, he had learned of the visit to Murfreesboro by Jefferson Davis and the subsequent detachment of one of Bragg's six divisions to Pemberton. Now if ever was the time to strike, and the Union commander was ready. Orders went out Christmas Day for the advance to begin next morning in three columns: Crittenden on the left, marching down the Murfreesboro turnpike through La Vergne and paralleling the Nashville & Chattanooga Railroad; McCook in the middle, cross-country through Nolensville; Thomas on the right, due south through Brentwood, then eastward across McCook's rear to take his rightful position in the center. Each of the three "wings" was well below its normal three-divisional strength because of guard detachments. Thomas, for example, had left a whole division on garrison duty at Nashville, in case Morgan or Forrest turned back or some other pack of raiders struck in that direction while the main body was attending to Bragg, and Crittenden and McCook were almost equally reduced by piecemeal detachments on similar duty elsewhere along the lines of supply and communication. The result was that Rosecrans had barely 44,000 troops in his three columns — Crittenden 14,500, Thomas 13,500, McCook 16,000 — or only a little more than half of his total effective strength. But he was not ruffled by this reduction of the numerical odds in his favor; he knew that he was still a good deal stronger than his opponent. What was more, his deliberate preparations had paid off. Not only would he be free of the necessity to "stop and tinker" for lack of engineering equipment; he had within reach "the essentials of ammunition and twenty days' rations." Thus he had notified Washington on Christmas Eve, while planning the movement of his eight attack divisions, and he added in regard to the enemy, thirty miles southeastward down the pike: "If they meet us, we shall fight tomorrow; if they wait for us, next day."

It was neither "tomorrow" nor the "next day" — which was in fact the day he actually got started. Nor was it the day after that, or the day after that, or even the day after that. Still, Rosecrans was not unduly perturbed. Delay had already gained him much, including the loss by the Confederates of one infantry division and two brigades of cavalry; further delay might gain him more. Such was not the case, as it turned out, but what fretted him most just now was the slashing efficiency of the cavalry retained by Bragg, which cost the advancing Federals portions of their wagon train, as well as isolated detachments of their own horsemen assigned to protect the flanks and rear of the main body, slogging forward in three columns. As these drew near Murfreesboro on the 29th and 30th, consolidating at last to form a continuous line of battle along the west bank of the south fork of Stones River, two miles short of the town, they

★

began to encounter infantry resistance, spasmodic at first and then determined, which seemed to promise fulfillment of the vow Rosecrans had passed along to Halleck two weeks before: "Rebel troops say they will fight us." However, he had followed this with a vow of his own, which he also believed was moving toward fulfillment: "If we beat them, I shall try to drive them to the wall."

★ ★ ★   **Bragg had 37,713 effectives, well under half as many as his opponent, but he had them all at hand,** with the result that the attackers were only about fifteen percent stronger than the defenders. Not that he considered himself committed to the tactical defensive. If the opportunity arose he intended to hit Rosecrans first, and hard. By way of preparation, however, he wanted him within reach, and therefore he gave his outpost commanders instructions to offer the advancing blue columns no more than a token resistance. "General Bragg sent us word not to fight them too much, but to let them come on," one gray cavalryman afterwards recalled.

In the course of the four-day Federal approach march — which was impeded, but not "too much," by the nearly 4000 troopers under Brigadier General Joseph Wheeler — Bragg assembled his 34,000 infantry at Murfreesboro, the center of the wide arc along which his five divisions had been disposed so as to cover the roads out of Nashville. Lieutenant General Leonidas Polk's two-division corps was there already, and Lieutenant General William J. Hardee's came in on December 28 from Triune, fifteen miles west. With the arrival next day of Major General John McCown's division from Readyville, a dozen miles east, the concentration was complete, and the army formed for combat astride Stones River, which was fordable at practically all points because of the drouth. Hardee was on the right, northwest of the town and with a bend of the river to his front; Polk was on the left, due west of the town and with another bend of the river to his rear; McCown was in reserve behind the center, which was pierced by the Nashville turnpike and the Nashville & Chattanooga Railroad, pointing arrow-straight in the direction from which Rosecrans was expected. Except for Wheeler's horsemen, who, now that the consolidation of the infantry had been effected with time to spare, were turned loose with a vengeance on the flanks and rear of the still approaching Federals, the Confederates settled down to wait for the opening of the battle everyone knew was about to be fought.

Many of them — particularly the officers, whose opportunities were larger in this respect — were still suffering from the aftereffects of a Christmas which they had celebrated with the fervor of men who knew only too well that the chances were strong that it would be their last. "I felt feeble," a Georgia lieutenant wrote in his diary the morning after, "but, being anxious to be with my men, reported for duty." Things had been that way for weeks now. Murfreesboro, a former state capital named for a colonel in the Revolution, was a lively place whose citizens, decidedly pro-rebel no matter which army happened to be in occupation, afforded their gray-clad defenders entertainments and amusements of all kinds, including horse races, balls, whist parties, and midnight gatherings in their parlors. President Davis's visit, two weeks before, had been the occasion for much rejoicing and pride, but all agreed that the social high point of the season had been the marriage on December 14, the day after the President's departure, of John Morgan and a local belle. Spirited in her defense of all things southern, when she heard some northern officers disparaging the raider during the Union occupation the previous summer, she told them off so roundly that one of the bluecoats asked her name. "It's Mattie Ready now," she said. "But by the grace of God one day I hope to call myself the wife of John Morgan." Hearing the story, the widower cavalryman came to call on her as soon as the town was again in southern hands, and in due time — for the young lady was apparently as skilled in her brand of tactics as the colonel was in his — they became engaged. Because of the size of the guest list, which included Bragg and his ranking commanders, Morgan's fellow officers and kinsmen from Kentucky, and a host of civilians invited from round about by the bride's family, the wedding was held in the courtroom of the Murfreesboro courthouse, Leonidas Polk officiating and wearing over the uniform of a Confederate lieutenant general the vestments of an Episcopal bishop. Thus it was that Mattie Ready, by the grace of God, became Mrs John Hunt Morgan.

Within a week, apparently not content with his exploit at Hartsville earlier that month, the bridegroom was off on what would be known as his Christmas Raid, a twofold celebration of his marriage and the brigadier's commission recently handed him by the President himself. His goal, assigned by Bragg, was Rosecrans' supply line, specifically the Louisville & Nashville Railroad north of Bowling Green, with particular attention to be paid to the great trestles at Muldraugh's Hill. He left Alexandria, thirty miles northeast of Murfreesboro, on December 21 with 2500 horsemen, crossed the Cumberland the following day, and reëntered his home state the day after that. Passing through Glasgow on the 24th, he forded the Green on Christmas Day, skirmishing as he went and taking prisoners by the hundreds, and struck suddenly north of Munfordville to lay siege to the Federal garrison at Elizabethtown, which surrendered on the 27th, opening the way to Muldraugh's Hill, where the garrison also surrendered. After burning the trestles, enormous structures five hundred feet long and eighty feet tall, he continued east through Bardstown to Springfield, then turned south, skirting heavily garrisoned Lebanon and fighting off pursuers for a getaway through Campbellsville, Columbia, and Burkesville, to reach Smithville, Tennessee, on January 5, fifteen miles southeast of his starting point at Alexandria. In two weeks, having covered better than 400 miles, he had fought four engagements and numerous skirmishes. At a total cost of 2 men

★

Shortly after marrying Confederate cavalry raider John Hunt Morgan in December 1863, 17-year-old Mattie Ready Morgan wrote, "They say we are a love-struck couple."

killed and 24 wounded, plus about 300 stragglers — victims not of enemy guns but of the weather, which was bitter, and of confiscated bourbon — he had destroyed the vital railroad trestles and four important bridges, along with an estimated $2,000,000 in Union stores, and had torn up more than twenty miles of L&N track, while capturing and paroling 1887 enemy soldiers.

Joe Wheeler, West Point '59, was not to be outdone by Morgan or Forrest, who were his subordinates as a result of Bragg's appointment of the twenty-six-year-old Georgian as commander of all the cavalry in the Army of Tennessee. Unleashed on the night of December 29, after screening the concentration of the gray infantry in his rear and delaying the advance of the blue columns to his front, he rode north on the Lebanon pike with 2000 troopers, then swung west to Jefferson, where he attacked a brigade of infantry on the march and gobbled up a 20-wagon segment of Crittenden's supply train. At La Vergne by noon, halfway to Nashville and well in the Union rear, he captured and burned McCook's whole train of 300 wagons, packed with stores valued by Wheeler at "many hundred thousands of dollars," and paroled 700 prisoners, including the teamsters and their escort. "The turnpike, as far as the eye could reach, was filled with burning wagons," a Federal officer reported when he rode through the town next morning and surveyed the ruin the graybacks left behind. "The country was overspread with disarmed men [and] broken-down horses and mules. The streets were covered with empty valises and trunks, knapsacks, broken guns, and all the indescribable débris of a captured and rifled army train." Wheeler and his horsemen were over the southwest horizon by then, having taken two more trains, one at Rock Spring and another at Nolensville. Beyond there, more prisoners were paroled while the weary raiders snatched a few hours' sleep before swinging back into their saddles and heading east for Murfreesboro to rejoin the infantry drawn up along Stones River. Completing his two-day circuit of Rosecrans — in the course of which he had captured more than a thousand men, destroyed all or parts of four wagon trains, brought off enough rifles and carbines to arm a brigade, remounted all of his troopers who needed fresh horses, and left a train of devastation along both flanks and around the rear of the entire Union army — Wheeler made contact with Bragg's left at 2 a.m. on the last day of the year, in time for a share in the battle which was now about to open.

★ ★ ★ A certain amount of reshuffling had occurred during his absence. Rosecrans, coming forward with his main body on the 30th while Wheeler was clawing at his flanks and rear, put his three corps in line, left to right, Crittenden and Thomas and McCook, the first opposite Hardee, the second opposite Polk, and the third — the largest of the three — opposite nothing more than a thin line of skirmishers extending the rebel left. Because of skillful screening by the gray cavalry during the approach march, the Federal commander was not aware of the opportunity he had created for a lunge straight into Murfreesboro around the Confederate flank; but Bragg was, and he moved at once to correct his dispositions, shifting McCown's reserve division from its post behind the center to a position on Polk's left, extending his line of battle southward to meet the threat. Rosecrans meanwhile was planning and issuing orders for an attack. His intention was to execute a right wheel, sending Crittenden forward on the north, with instructions to pivot on the left of Thomas, who would also move forward in sequence to assist in the capture of the town, cutting the rebels off from their supplies and setting them up for annihilation. McCook was thus to serve as anchor man. "If the enemy attacks you," Rosecrans told him, "fall back slowly, refusing your right, contesting the ground inch by inch. If the enemy does not attack you, you will attack him, not vigorously but warmly." As an added piece of deception, McCook was ordered about 6 p.m. to build a

*On the morning of December 31, Hardee's Confederates
smashed northward into the Federal right flank
to open the Battle of Murfreesboro.*

line of fires beyond his right, simulating a prolongation of his line so as to
draw Bragg's attention away from the main effort at the far end of the field.

The southern commander was indeed deceived, and quite as thoroughly as Rosecrans had intended, but his reaction was something different
from what the northern commander had hoped for. Or, rather, it was what he
had hoped for, only more so. When Bragg observed the fires and heard sounds
of movement on the Federal right, not only did he take the bait, but he
proceeded, so to speak, to run away with it. Devising an offensive of his own to
meet what he conceived to be a new threat to his left, he instructed Hardee,
whose two divisions were under Major Generals John C. Breckinridge and
Patrick R. Cleburne, to leave the former posted where it was, guarding the river

crossings on the right, and move the latter southward to a position in support of McCown, who had been shifted earlier that day. Hardee himself was to come along, moreover, and take command of these two divisions on the left for a slashing assault on the Federals seemingly massed in that direction. Bragg's plans called for a right wheel by both corps on the west bank of Stones River, with the pivot on Polk's right division near the Nashville pike, the brigades attacking in rapid sequence from left to right, obliquing northward as they advanced, in order to throw the bluecoats back against the stretch of river whose crossings were covered by Breckinridge's guns and infantry.

Just before tattoo, while this additional shift was being completed under cover of darkness and orders were going out for the assault next morning, the military bands of both armies began to play their respective favorite tunes. Carrying sweet and clear on the windless wintry air, the music of any one band was about as audible on one side of the line as on the other, and the concert thus became something of a contest, a musical bombardment. "Dixie" answered the taunting "Yankee Doodle"; "Hail Columbia" followed "The Bonnie Blue Flag." Finally, though, one group of musicians began to play the familiar "Home Sweet Home," and one by one the others took it up, until at last all the bands of both armies were playing the song. Soldiers on both sides of the battle line began to sing the words, swelling the chorus east and west, North and South. As it died away on the final line — "There's no-o place like home" — the words caught in the throats of men, who, blue-coat and butternut alike, would be killing each other tomorrow in what already gave promise of being one of the bloodiest battles in that fratricidal war.

★ ★ ★   **A**s at First Manassas, a year and a half ago, both com-manders had identical plans of battle: in this case, an advance on the left to strike the enemy right. Here as there, if they had moved simultaneously, the two armies might have grappled and swung round and round, like a pair of dancers clutching each other and twirling to the accompaniment of cannon. So it might have been, but it was not. For one thing, the lines were closer together on the south than on the north, and there was no natural obstacle such as the river to delay the Confederate attack in its initial stages. For another, with his usual attention to preparatory matters, Rosecrans had told his generals to advance as soon as possible after breakfast; whereas Bragg, with less concern for the creature comforts, had called for a dawn assault, and that was what he got.

McCown went forward in the steely twilight before sunrise, Cleburne following 400 yards behind. Between them they had 10,000 men and Mc-Cook had 16,000, but the latter were still preparing breakfast when the rebel skirmishers, preceding a long gray double line of infantry extending left and right, shoulder to shoulder as far as the eye could reach, broke through the cedar thickets and bore down on them, yelling. Coming as it did, with all the advantage of surprise, the charge was well-nigh irresistible. A Tennessee private later recalled that his brigade, in the front rank of the attackers, "swooped down on those Yankees like a whirl-a-gust of woodpeckers in a hail storm." The fact was, in this opening phase, everything went so smoothly for the aggressors that even their mistakes seemed to work to their advantage. When McCown, who had had little combat experience, having been left behind in command of Knoxville during the invasion of Kentucky, drifted wide because he neglected to oblique to the right as instructed, Pat Cleburne, whose soldierly qualities had grown steadily since Shiloh despite the wounds he had taken at Richmond and Perryville, moved neatly forward into the gap without even the need to pause for alignment. Advancing on this extended front the two divisions swept everything before them, their captures including several front-line batteries taken before the cannoneers could leap to their posts and get a round off. Such knots of bluecoats as managed to form for individual resistance in clumps of cedar or behind outcroppings of rock, finding themselves suddenly outflanked on the left or right, cried as they had cried under Buell twelve weeks before: "We are sold! Sold again!" and broke for the rear, discarding their weapons as they ran.

McCook's three divisions, on line from right to left under Brigadier Generals R. W. Johnson, Jefferson Davis, and Philip Sheridan, caught the full force of the initial assault. Johnson and Davis were under personal clouds, the former because he had been captured by Morgan early that month and exchanged on the eve of battle, the latter because of his assassination of Major General William Nelson in a Louisville hotel lobby back in September; but they had little chance to earn redemption here. Johnson's division, on the far right of the army, practically disintegrated on contact, losing within the opening half-hour more than half its members by sudden death, injury, or capture. Davis, next in line, fared scarcely better, though most of his men at least had time to put up a show of resistance before falling back, dribbling skulkers as they went. That left Sheridan. As pugnacious here as he had been at Perryville, where he first attracted general attention, the bandy-legged, bullet-headed Ohioan was determined to yield no ground except under direct pressure, and only then when that pressure buckled his knees. "Square-shouldered, muscular, wiry to the last degree, and as nearly insensible to hardship and fatigue as is consistent with humanity" — thus a staff man saw him here, on the eve of his thirty-second birthday — he rode his lines, calling on his men to stand firm while the storm of battle drew nearer, then broke in fury against his front.

Polk's corps, with its two divisions under Major Generals J. M. Withers and Benjamin Cheatham, had taken up the assault by now, and it was Withers who struck Sheridan first — and suffered the first Confederate repulse. The Federals were in a position described by one of its defenders as "a confused mass of rock, lying in slabs, and boulders interspersed with holes, fissures, and caverns which would have made progress over it extremely difficult even if there had been no timber." But there was timber, a thick tangle of cedars whose trunks "ran straight up into the air so near together that the sunlight was obscured." Fighting here, with all that was happening on the right or left hidden from them "except as we could gather it from the portentous avalanches of sound which assailed us from every direction," Sheridan's men repulsed three separate charges by Withers. Then Cheatham came up. A veteran of Mexico and all the army's battles since Belmont, where he had saved the day, Cheatham was forty-two, a native Tennessean, and had earned the distinction of being the most profane man in the Army of Tennessee, despite the disadvantage in this respect of having as his corps commander the distinguished and watchful Bishop of Louisiana. "Give 'em hell, boys!" he shouted as he led his division forward. Polk, who was riding beside him, approved of the intention if not of the unchurchly language. "Give them what General Cheatham says, boys!" he cried. "Give them what General Cheatham says!"

General McCook, on horseback beneath the red flag, gestures with his sword toward a distant Confederate line as he tries to rally his corps at Stones River.

That was what they gave them, though they received in return a goodly measure of the same. Sheridan, down to his last three rounds and having lost the first of his three brigade commanders, his West Point classmate Brigadier General Joshua Sill — he would lose the other two before the day was over — fell back under knee-buckling pressure from Cheatham in front and Cleburne on the flank, abandoning eight guns in the thicket for lack of horses to draw them off. He then replenished his ammunition and took a position back near the Nashville turnpike, facing south and east alongside Brigadier General J. S. Negley's division, one of the two belonging to Thomas, who had been forced to give ground during the struggle. It was now about 10 o'clock; Bragg's initial objectives had been attained, along with the capture of 28 guns and no less than 3000 soldiers. The enemy right had been driven three miles and the center had also given way, until now the Union line of battle resembled a half-closed jackknife, most of it being at right angles to its original position. Bragg was about to open the second phase, intending to break the knife at the critical juncture of blade and handle; after which would come the third phase, the mop-up.

Rosecrans meanwhile had used to good advantage the interlude afforded him by Sheridan's resistance, though it was not until the battle had been raging for more than an hour that he realized he was face to face with probable disaster. For some time, indeed, having joined Crittenden on the left so as to supervise the opening attack, he assumed that what was occurring on the right — the uproar being considerably diminished by distance and acoustical peculiarities — was in accordance with his instructions to McCook, whereby Bragg had been deceived into stripping the flank about to be assaulted, in order to bolster the flank beyond which the untended campfires had been kindled the night before. One of Crittenden's divisions was already crossing Stones River, and he was preparing to follow with the other two. Not even the arrival of a courier from McCook, informing Rosecrans that he was being assailed and needed reinforcements, changed the Federal commander's belief in this regard.

"Tell General McCook to contest every inch of ground," he told the courier, repeating his previous instructions. "If he holds them we will swing into Murfreesboro with our left and cut them off." To his staff he added, with apparent satisfaction: "It's working right."

Discovering presently, however, that it was "working" not for him but for Bragg, who was using his own battle plan against him and had got the jump in the process — with the result that McCook, far from being able to conduct an inch-by-inch defense, had lost control of two of his three divisions before he was able to conduct a defense that was even mile-by-mile — Rosecrans reacted fast. To one observer he seemed "profoundly moved," but that was putting it rather mildly. Even his florid nose "had paled and lost its ruddy luster," the officer added, the glow apparently having been transferred to his eyes, which "blazed with sullen

No death at Stones River was mourned more than that of Colonel Julius P. Garesché, who was decapitated by a Confederate cannonball (near right) while riding next to Rosecrans.

An actual sketch, made on the spot by one of the Special Artists of Frank Leslie's Illustrated Newspaper.

Mr. Leslie holds the copyright and reserves the exclusive right of publication.

fire." Canceling the advance on the left, he told Crittenden to send the two uncrossed divisions of Brigadier Generals John Palmer and Thomas Wood to reinforce the frazzled right. Brigadier General Horatio Van Cleve's division was to be recalled from the opposite bank of the river and sent without delay after the others, except for one brigade which would be left to guard against a crossing, in case the rebels tried to follow up the withdrawal in this quarter. Crittenden passed the word at once, and: "Goodbye, General," Wood replied as he set out in the direction of the uproar, which now was swelling louder as it drew nearer. "We'll all meet at the hatter's, as one coon said to another when the dogs were after them."

Rosecrans had no time for jokes. His exclusive concern just now was the salvation of his army, and it seemed to him that there was only one way for this to be accomplished. "This battle must be won," he said. He intended to see personally to all the dispositions, especially on the crumbling right, but first he needed a feeling of security on the left — if for no other purpose than to be able to forget it. Accordingly, accompanied by his chief of staff, he rode to the riverbank position of the one brigade Van Cleve had left behind to prevent a rebel crossing, and inquired who commanded.

"I do, sir," a colonel said, stepping forward. He was Samuel W. Price, a Union-loyal Kentuckian.

"Will you hold this ford?" Rosecrans asked him.

"I will try, sir," Price replied.

Unsatisfied, Rosecrans repeated: "Will you hold this ford?"

"I will die right here," the colonel answered stoutly.

Still unsatisfied, for he was less interested in the Kentuckian's willingness to lay down his life than he was in his ability to prevent a rebel crossing, the general pressed the question a third time: "Will you hold this ford?"

"Yes, sir," Price said.

"That will do," Rosecrans snapped, and having at last got the answer he wanted, turned his horse and galloped off.

As he drew near the tumult of battle, which by now was approaching the turnpike on the right, he received another shock in the form of a cannonball which, narrowly missing him, tore off the head of his chief of staff, riding beside him, and so bespattered Rosecrans that whoever saw him afterwards that morning assumed at first sight that he was badly wounded. "Oh, no," he would say, in response to expressions of concern. "That is the blood of poor Garesché." However, this did nothing to restrict or slow his movements; he would not even pause to change his coat. "At no one time, and I rode with him during most of the day," a signal officer afterwards reported, "do I remember of his having been one half-hour at the same place." To Crittenden, whose troops he was using as a reserve in order to shore up the line along the turnpike, he "seemed ubiquitous," and to another observer he appeared "as firm as iron and fixed as fate" as he moved about the field, rallying panicked men and hoicking them into line. "This battle must be won," he kept repeating.

Arriving in time to meet Sheridan, who had just been driven back, he directed him to refill his cartridge boxes from the ammunition train and to fall in alongside Negley and Major General Lovell Rousseau, commanding Thomas's other division. As a result of such stopgap improvisations, adopted amid the confusion of retreat, there was much intermingling of units and a resultant loss of control by division and corps commanders. Some of Crittenden's brigades were on the right with McCook, who had set up a straggler line along which he was doing what he could to rally the remnants of Johnson and Davis, and some of McCook's brigades were on the left with Crittenden, who was nervously making his dispositions on unfamiliar ground. Between them, with his two divisions consolidated and supported by Van Cleve, George Thomas was calm as always, whatever the panic all around him. Where his left joined Crittenden's right there was a salient, marking the point where the half-closed knife blade joined the handle, and within this angle, just east of the pike and on both sides of the railroad, there was a slight elevation inclosed by a circular four-acre clump of cedars, not unlike the one Sheridan had successfully defended against three separate all-out rebel assaults that morning. Known locally as the Round Forest, this tree-choked patch of rocky earth was presently dubbed "Hell's Half-Acre" by the soldiers; for it was here that Bragg seemed most determined to score a breakthrough, despite the heavy concentration of artillery of all calibers which Rosecrans had massed on the high ground directly in its rear.

He struck first, and hard, with a brigade of Mississippians from Withers. They surged forward across fields of unpicked cotton, yelling as they had yelled at Shiloh, where they had been the farthest to advance, and were staggered by rapid-fire volleys from fifty guns ranked hub to hub on the high ground just beyond the clump of dark-green trees. At that point-blank range, one cannoneer remarked, the Federal batteries "could not fire amiss." Deafened by the uproar, the Confederates plucked cotton from the fallen bolls and stuffed it in their ears. Still they came on — to be met, halfway across, by sheets of musketry from the blue infantry close-packed under cover of the cedars; whereupon, some regiments having lost as many as half a dozen color-bearers, the Mississippians wavered and fell back, leaving a third of their number dead or wounded in the furrows or lying crosswise to the blasted rows. Next to try it, about noon, was a Tennessee brigade from Cheatham, which lately had helped throw Sheridan out of a similar position. They charged through the rattling dry brown stalks, yelling with all the frenzy of those who had come this way before, but with no better luck. They too were repulsed, and with even crueler losses. More

★

than half of the men of the 16th Tennessee were casualties, while the 8th Tennessee lost 306 out of the 424 who had started across the fields in an attempt to drive the bluecoats out of the Round Forest.

Bragg was by no means resigned, as yet, to the fact that this could not be done. Though he had no reserves at hand — McCown and Cleburne were still winded from their long advance, around and over the original Federal right, and Withers and Cheatham had just been fought to a frazzle by the newly established left — the five-brigade division of Breckinridge, the largest in the army, was still posted beyond the river, having contributed nothing to the victory up to this point except the shells its batteries had been throwing from an east-bank hill which the former Vice President had been instructed to hold at all costs, as "the key to the position." So far, he had had no trouble doing this, despite an early-morning cavalry warning that a large body of enemy troops had crossed the river well upstream and was headed in his direction. This was of

---

They charged through the rattling dry brown stalks, yelling with all the frenzy of those who had come this way before, but with no better luck.

---

course Van Cleve's division, whose advance had been spotted promptly, but whose subsequent withdrawal had gone unnoticed or at any rate unreported; so that when Bragg's order came, about 1 o'clock, for him to leave one brigade to guard the right while he marched to the support of Polk and Hardee with the other four, Breckinridge was alarmed and sent back word that it was he who needed reinforcements; the enemy, in heavy force, was moving upon him even now, intending to challenge his hold on "the key to the position." Bragg's reply was a peremptory repetition of the order, which left the Kentuckian no choice except to obey. He sent two brigades at 2 o'clock, and followed with the other two himself, about an hour later.

That way, they came up piecemeal, and piecemeal they were fed into the hopper. The Federals, allowed an hour or more in which to improve their dispositions in the Round Forest and replenish the ammunition for the guns posted just behind it, caught the third wave of attackers much as they had caught the first and second, naked in the open fields, with devastating effect. Here again there was no lack of valor. One defender said of the charge that it was "without doubt the most daring, courageous, and best-executed attack which the Confederates made on our line between pike and river." But it broke in blood, as the others had done, and the survivors fell back across the fields, leaving their dead and wounded behind with the dead and wounded Tennesseans and Mississippians. Again there was a lull, until about 4 o'clock, when the last two brigades arrived from Breckinridge and the fourth gray wave rolled out across the fields of cotton.

"The battle had hushed," a Union brigadier reported, "and the dreadful splendor of this advance can only be conceived, as all descriptions must fall vastly short." While the attackers moved forward, "steadily, and, as it seemed, to certain victory," he added, "I sent back all my remaining staff successively to ask for support, and braced up my own lines as perfectly as possible." The bracing served its purpose; for though the defenders suffered heavily, too — it was here that Sheridan lost the third of his three brigade commanders — the charge was repulsed quite as decisively as the others. The sun went down at 4.30 and the racket died away. After eleven hours of uproar, a mutual hush fell over the glades and copses, and the brief winter twilight faded into the darkness before moonrise.

★ ★ ★   *B*ragg's losses had been heavy — about 9000 — but he had reason to believe that the enemy's, which included several thousand prisoners, had been much heavier. Moreover, in thus reversing the usual casualty ratio between attacker and defender, he had not only foiled the attempt to throw him out of his position covering Murfreesboro and Chattanooga; he had overrun the original Union position at every point where he had applied pressure, driving major portions of the blue line as far as three miles backward and taking guns and colors in abundance as he went. By all the logic of war, despite their stubborn stand that afternoon in the Round Forest, the Federals were whipped, and now they would have to accept the consequences. As Bragg saw it, they had little choice in this respect. They could stay and suffer further reverses, amounting in the end to annihilation; or they could retreat, hoping to find sanctuary in the Nashville intrenchments. Perhaps because it was the one he himself would have chosen, he believed the latter course to be the one Rosecrans was most likely to adopt. At any rate, this opinion seemed presently to have been confirmed by the arrival of outpost reports informing him that long lines of wagons had been heard rumbling through the darkness behind the Union lines and along the Nashville pike. Elated by this apparent chance to catch the northern army strung out on the roads and ripe for slaughter, Bragg prepared to follow in the morning. Proudly reviewing today's accomplishments while anticipating tomorrow's, he got off a wire to Richmond before he went to bed: "The enemy has yielded his strong position and is falling back. We occupy whole field and shall follow him. . . . God has granted us a happy New Year."

★

He was mistaken, at least in part. The rumble of wagons, northwestward along the turnpike, had not signified an attempt on the part of the Federal commander to save his trains before the commencement of a general retreat, but rather was the sound made by a long cavalcade of wounded — part of today's total of about 12,000 Union casualties — being taken back to the Tennessee capital for treatment in the military hospitals established there as another example of foresight and careful preparation. Not that Rosecrans had given no thought to a withdrawal. He had indeed. In fact, in an attempt to make up his mind as to the wisdom of retreating, he was holding a council of war to debate the matter and share the responsibility of the decision, even as Bragg was composing his victory message. It was a stormy night, rain beating hard on the roof of the cabin which Rosecrans had selected the day before as his headquarters beside the Nashville pike, never suspecting that the battle line would be drawn today practically on its doorstep. All three of his corps commanders were present, along with a number of their subordinates, and all presented a rather bedraggled aspect, "battered as to hats, tousled as to hair, torn as to clothes, and depressed as to spirits." An adjutant in attendance described them thus, and added: "If there was a cheerful-expressioned face present I did not see it."

After a long silence, broken only by the drumming of rain on shingles, Rosecrans began the questioning, addressing the several generals in turn, clockwise as they sat about the room. "General McCook, have you any suggestions for tomorrow?" Smooth-shaven and round-faced, the thirty-one-year-old McCook was somewhat more subdued tonight than he had been on the night after Perryville — where, as here, his had been the corps that was surprised and routed — but he showed by his reply that at least a part of his rollicking nature still remained. "No," he said. "Only I would like for Bragg to pay me for my two horses lost today." Others were gloomier and more forthright, advising retreat as the army's best way out of its predicament. Characteristically, George Thomas had fallen asleep in his chair before the discussion got well under way. When the word "retreat" came through to him, he opened his eyes. "This army doesn't retreat," he muttered, and fell back into the sleep he had emerged from. The discussion thus interrupted was resumed, but it led to no clear-cut decision before the council broke up and the commanders returned to their units. Except for incidental tactical adjustments, specifically authorized from above, they would hold their present positions through tomorrow, unless they received alternate instructions before dawn.

Still undecided, Rosecrans rode out for a midnight inspection of his lines, in the course of which he looked out across the fields and saw an alarming sight. On the far side of Overall's Creek, which crossed the turnpike at right angles and covered his right flank and rear, firebrands were moving in the night. The explanation was actually simple: Federal cavalrymen, suffering from the

General Rosecrans, on a dappled gray (center), was, said one observer, "in his saddle almost constantly, and ate as often on horseback as at the table."

cold, had disobeyed orders against kindling fires and were carrying brands from point to point along the outpost line: but Rosecrans, never suspecting that his orders would be flaunted in this fashion, assumed that they were rebels. "They have got entirely in our rear," he said, "and are forming line of battle by torch-light!" With retreat no longer even a possibility, let alone an alternative — or so at any rate he thought — he returned at once to army headquarters and, adopting the dramatic phraseology of the Kentucky colonel which he had rejected that morning beside the upper Stones River ford, sent word for his subordinates to "prepare to fight or die."

    Except for the surgeons and the men they worked on, blue and gray, whose screams broke through the singing of the bone saws, both sides were bedded down by now amid the wreckage and the corpses, preparing to sleep out as best they could the last night of the year. Simultaneously, from a balcony of the Mobile Battle House, Jefferson Davis lifted the hearts of his listeners with a review of recent Confederate successes, unaware that even as he spoke the list was about to be lengthened by John Magruder, whose two-boat navy of cotton-clads was steaming down Buffalo Bayou to recapture Galveston. Lee's Army of Northern Virginia still occupied the field of its two-weeks-old long-odds victory on the southwest bank of the Rappahannock, and the Federal invaders from coastal North Carolina were back beneath the shelter of their

★

siege guns, licking the wounds they had suffered in their repulse along the Neuse. In North Mississippi, where Van Dorn was resting his troopers after their exploits in Holly Springs and beyond the Tennessee line, Grant was in retreat on Memphis, while Sherman, three hundred winding miles downriver, was counting his casualties under Chickasaw Bluffs and preparing to give it one more try before falling back down the Yazoo to meet the general whose army he had kidnaped and depleted to no avail. Forrest and Morgan, the former moving east from Parker's Crossroads, the latter riding south through Campbellsville, both having eluded their pursuers, were returning in triumph from disruptive raids on their respective home regions in West Tennessee and Kentucky. In all these scattered theaters, where so recently the Confederacy had seemed at best to be approaching near-certain disaster, fortune had smiled on southern arms; yet nowhere did her smile seem broader than here, southeast of Nashville and northwest of vital Chattanooga, where Bragg with such alacrity had snatched up the gage flung down by Rosecrans and struck him smartly with it, first on the flank, a smashing blow, and then between the eyes. Now both rested from their injuries and exertions. Wrapped in their blankets, those who had them, the soldiers of both armies huddled close to fires they had kindled against orders. The waxing moon set early and the wind veered and blew coldly from the north; the screams of the wounded died away with the singing of the bone saws. Unlike the night before, on the eve of carnage, there were no serenades tonight, no mingled choruses of "Home Sweet Home," for even the bandsmen had fought in this savage battle, and expected to have to fight again tomorrow, bringing in the new year as they had ushered out the old.

———————— ❦ ————————

★ ★ ★ $\mathcal{S}$o they thought; but they were wrong, at least so far as the schedule was concerned. Though there were tentative skirmishes, fitful exchanges of artillery fire, and some readjustment of the tactical dispositions on both sides, New Year's Day saw nothing like the carnival of death that had been staged on New Year's Eve. In point of fact, the two armies were rather like two great jungle cats who, having fought to mutual exhaustion, were content — aside, that is, from the more or less secret hope on the part of each that the other would slink away — to eye one another balefully, limiting their actions to licking their wounds and emitting only occasional growls and rumbles, while storing up strength to resume the mortal contest.

Considerably surprised, in the light of last night's cavalry reports of a withdrawal, to find the enemy not only still there, but still there in line of battle, Bragg sent Polk forward about midmorning to discover what effect a prod would have. He soon found out. Though the troops moved unopposed into the Round Forest, which Rosecrans had ordered evacuated so as to straighten out his line, and which in turn gave validity to the bishop's subsequent claim that "the opening of the new year found us masters of the field," Polk encountered resistance just beyond it too stiff to permit his men to emerge from the woods on the far side. All he had gained for his pains were more blue corpses, along with the unwelcome task of digging their graves in order to rid his nostrils of their stench. Likewise, on the Union left, Rosecrans advanced Van Cleve's division — now under Colonel Samuel Beatty; Van Cleve had caught a bullet in the leg — beyond Stones River, retracing the route it had taken the previous morning by moving today into the vacuum created by the withdrawal of Breckinridge the afternoon before, and occupied a hill overlooking the ford. These were the only major readjustments, North or South, though the Federals were reinforced by a brigade arrived from Nashville, accompanied as one officer said by "an army of stragglers" picked up along the pike. For the most part, the soldiers on both sides roved the field, looking for fallen comrades among the wounded and the slain. The search for food was even more intensive, and for once, as a result of Wheeler's depredations in the course of his pre-battle ride around the Union forces, the Yankees were worse off in this respect than the rebels. One brigade commander later recorded that he made his supper off a piece of raw pork and a few crackers he found in his pocket. No food had ever tasted sweeter, he declared. Even so high-ranking an officer as Crittenden was not exempt from want, but as he went to bed, complaining of hunger pangs, he was delighted to hear his orderly say he could get him "a first-rate beefsteak." The Kentuckian accepted the offer gladly, and presently, when the promised meal was brought, consumed it with gusto — only to learn next morning that the "beefsteak" had been cut from a horse that had been killed in the battle. "I didn't know this at the time I ate it," he afterwards explained, somewhat ruefully.

Day ended; night came down. Although Rosecrans had no apparent notion of resuming the offensive, or indeed any definite plan at all beyond holding onto the ground he had fallen back to, he was pleased to have had this day-long opportunity to consolidate his forces and recover in some measure from the shock to his army and his nervous system. Bragg on the other hand seemed to have no more of a plan than his opponent. Convinced that he had won a victory, he apparently did not know what to do with it beyond setting various details to work collecting the arms and matériel scattered about the field and paroling the thousands of captives he had taken the day before. What he mainly wanted, still, was for the enemy to admit defeat by retreating, and thus substantiate his claim; then he would follow, as he had promised in his wire to Richmond, hoping to catch the blue mass in motion on the pike and tear its flanks and rear, which now were inaccessible to him beyond the guns parked

★

hub to hub behind the long lines of close-spaced bayonets weaving in and out of the cedar brakes and among the gray outcroppings of rock that scarred the landscape. The prospect was altogether grim. After nightfall, however, he was again encouraged by cavalry reports that well-guarded Federal trains were in motion on the roads leading back to Nashville. If this meant what Bragg hoped it did, that the Unionists were finally admitting they were whipped and were preparing to retire, bag and baggage, he would be up and after them tomorrow.

Tomorrow's dawn showed the prospect unimproved. Whatever might be moving along the rearward roads, the bayonets defining the Union front glinted quite as close-spaced as ever and the guns frowned every bit as grim. In fact, as Bragg conducted a personal inspection of his lines that morning, combining with it a long-range binocular reconnaissance of the enemy position, he began to perceive that, despite his bloodless occupation of the Round Forest, which increased his claim to the honors of the field, it was his own army

The afternoon of January 2, Breckinridge's initially successful attack on Crittenden's Federals was stopped and the Confederates were driven back by a fierce counterattack.

★

which was in the graver danger as a result of yesterday's tactical readjustments. The advance of Van Cleve's division, which put it in possession of the hill just east of the river, gave him particular concern. Artillery emplaced on that height could fire across the stream and enfilade Polk's flank if he attempted to advance. With this in mind, Bragg decided the enemy guns must be dislodged. Accordingly he sent for Breckinridge, whose troops had returned to their east-bank position north of Murfreesboro, along a ridge about a mile short of the hill overlooking the ford. When the former Vice President reached army headquarters, under a large sycamore that stood alongside the Nashville pike just west of the wrecked bridge that had spanned Stones River, Bragg told him what he wanted. He was going to resume the offensive by sending Polk forward, he explained. First, though, he wanted Van Cleve's men flung off the dominant height. This was admittedly a tough assignment, he continued, but to protect the attackers from the added strain of having to repulse a counterattack, he was directing that the movement be made less than an hour before sundown, which would give the Federals no time to reorganize or bring up reinforcements before dark. Then next morning Polk could jump off, not only with his flank secure, but also with the enemy mouse-trapped out of position to his front.

Breckinridge, who was not yet forty-two despite his distinguished prewar career in national politics — a hearty-looking man with a prominent forehead, somewhat bulging eyes, a plump but firm jaw, and the swooping dark mustache of a Sicilian brigand, he was a leading contender among the many candidates for the title of the handsomest general in the southern army — protested at once and for all he was worth. The hill was well-nigh impregnable, he said, and Van Cleve's division had now been reinforced by two brigades from Palmer; besides which, he added, guns from the main Union line across the river would tear his flank as he advanced, thus exposing his men to the very horror he would be sparing Polk's if he was successful, which was doubtful. Warming to the subject, he took up a stick and began to draw in the soft dirt a map that emphasized the difficulty of the terrain. Bragg stopped him in mid-sketch. The Kentuckian had delayed the battle two days ago with similar protests which had turned out to be ill-founded, and the army commander was having no more of that. "Sir," Bragg said curtly, "my information is different. I have given the order to attack the enemy in your front and expect it to be obeyed."

That was that, and Breckinridge returned to his troops, most of whom were Bluegrass natives like himself, exiles from their homeland since midwinter nearly a year ago; "my poor orphans," he sometimes called them, jokingly but not without an undertone of sadness and homesickness. Rejoining them he sought out his friend Brigadier General William Preston — now commanding one of his brigades, but formerly chief of staff to his brother-in-law Albert Sidney Johnston, who had died in his arms at Shiloh — to whom he now ad-

Breckinridge . . . a hearty-looking man with a prominent forehead, somewhat bulging eyes, a plump but firm jaw, and the swooping dark mustache of a Sicilian brigand . . . was a leading contender among the many candidates for the title of the handsomest general in the southern army.

dressed himself concerning the assignment he had just been given. "General Preston," he said, speaking formally and with a tone that strangely combined dejection and determination, "this attack is made against my judgment and by the special orders of General Bragg. Of course we all must try to do our duty and fight the best we can. But if it should result in disaster and I be among the slain, I want you to do justice to my memory and tell the people that I believed this attack to be very unwise and tried to prevent it." And having thus unburdened his mind he ordered his five brigades to form for the assault.

Across the way, Crittenden was inspecting his dispositions along the west bank of Stones River, accompanied by his chief of artillery Captain John Mendenhall, when he looked over the ford near the base of the occupied hill beyond and saw the graybacks forming in heavy columns along the ridge to the south, obviously preparing for a blow at Beatty, who commanded not only Van Cleve's division but also the two brigades of reinforcements which had joined him that morning. It was now about 3.30; the sun was within an hour of the landline. According to Mendenhall, "The general asked me if I could not do something to relieve Colonel Beatty with my guns." The Indiana-born West Pointer could indeed, and he moved to do so promptly. Assembling within the next half hour a total of 58 pieces of various calibers, he stationed 37 of these on the crest of a west-bank hill, cradled by a bend of the stream and overlooking the opposite bank, and placed the other 21 along its eastern base for flat-trajectory fire that would catch the rebel columns end-on as they charged across the rolling slopes beyond the river. Then he waited; but not for long.

The five Confederate brigades, with a total effective strength of 4500 men, started down off their sheltering ridge at 4 o'clock, moving steadily across the valley which lay between them and the hill from whose crest Beatty's cannoneers and riflemen soon took them under fire. As at Baton Rouge five months ago, where they had fought in isolation while the rest of Bragg's army was preparing to set out for their native Bluegrass, the Kentuckians did not falter as they swung down the long slope of the intervening valley, crossed its floor, and began to climb the other side. Halfway up the face of the hill, taking heavier losses now at closer range, they fired their first volleys and then, beginning to yell, broke into a run for the crest. The bluecoats did not wait for them, but whirled and fled from the threat of contact, and the attackers came on after them, yelling now with shrill screams of triumph as they topped the rise and pursued the defenders down the rearward slope. However, they could not close the gap created by the quick retreat, and this gave Mendenhall the chance he had been waiting for all this time, to shoot at his foes without injuring his friends. At the signal "Fire!" his 58 double-shotted guns began to roar in chorus, flinging more than a hundred rounds a minute against the flank of the butternut mass across the way. "Thinned, reeling, broken under that terrible hail" — thus one reporter described the instantaneous effect — the graybacks milled in confusion, scarcely knowing at first what had struck them. When they saw what it was, they attempted to change front to the left and move against the fuming hill beyond the ford; but to no avail. "The very forest seemed to fall before our fire," one Federal observer wrote — without exaggeration, for men in the gray ranks were actually crushed under fallen limbs that were torn from the trees by exploding shells when they tried to find shelter in a patch of woods — "and not a Confederate reached the river." Shattered, they changed front again to the left, of one accord, and ran for the ridge that had marked their line of departure. A Union colonel, watching this sudden turn of events, was the amused witness of a double, simultaneous retreat. "It was difficult to say which was running away the more rapidly," he later reported, "the division of Van Cleve to the rear, or the enemy in the opposite direction."

Breckinridge watched his men come stumbling back through the dusk that followed sunset of the brief winter day. They had been gone just seventy minutes in all, and of their number 1700 had fallen: which meant that better than one man out of every three who descended the slope did not return unhurt. As their commander, who had protested the slaughter in advance and done what he could to prevent it, watched them close ranks to fill the gaps as they formed their line behind their own ten guns on the ridge, his eyes filled with tears. "My poor orphans! My poor orphans!" he exclaimed.

★ ★ ★   **T**he lament for the fallen need not have been limited to the Confederate right, nor indeed to either side of the line of battle; for the over-all Federal losses had been even heavier. According to final reports and computations, in two days of conflict — the day-long struggle of the 31st and the sunset repulse on the 2d — only a dozen less than 25,000 casualties had been suffered by the two armies. (Which, incidentally, indicated something of the fury of western fighting. With fewer than half as many troops involved, the butcher bill at Murfreesboro, Tennessee, was more than one-third greater than the one presented at Fredericksburg, Virginia, three weeks back.) The South lost 1294 killed, 7945 wounded, and 2500 captured or missing, a total of 11,739. The North lost 1730 killed, 7802 wounded, and 3717 captured or missing, a total of 13,249. The over-all total thus was 24,988: which was to say, and more could scarcely *be* said, that the battle had been bloodier than Shiloh or Sharpsburg.

  At any rate, though neither commander yet recognized the fact, the carnage was over. Polk, who had learned of the sunset assault only just before it was launched, when Bragg came to his headquarters for a better view of the action across the river, had protested almost as vehemently as Breckinridge had done, but with no more success; Bragg's mind was quite made up. And now that the attack had met with predicted disaster, the blue defenders returned to the abandoned hill in greater strength than ever, reinforced by another whole division. Tactically, all was as it had been before the assault was launched, only more so; Polk would be less able to advance tomorrow than he had been today. Whether the enemy was under a similar disadvantage he did not know, but his two division commanders were not only doubtful that such was the case, they were also doubtful that their troops were in any fit condition to block the way: as was shown by a letter they wrote, shortly after midnight, and sent through channels to Bragg. "We deem it our duty to say to you frankly," Cheatham and Withers declared, "that, in our judgment, this army should be promptly put in retreat. . . . We do fear great disaster from the condition of things now existing, and think it should be averted if possible." Polk added his endorsement to the unusual document: "I greatly fear the consequences of another engagement at this place in the ensuing day. We could now, perhaps, get off with some safety and some credit, if the affair is well managed," and forwarded it to Bragg.

★

Waked at 2 a.m., the grim-faced commander sat up in bed and read the letter halfway through, then stopped and told the aide who had disturbed his sleep: "Say to the general we shall maintain our position at every hazard."

When he rose at daylight, however, he began to discover how great that hazard was. Rain was falling steadily and the river was rising fast, threatening to isolate the two wings of his army. Moreover, unlike the previous ones, this morning's cavalry reports gave no hint of signs in the night that the enemy was considering withdrawal, but rather informed him that another fresh brigade of reinforcements had just arrived on the Union right, accompanying a train of supplies from the Tennessee capital. By now, too, his staff had found time to study the papers captured when McCook's headquarters were overrun, which indicated an effective strength of nearly 70,000 bluecoats to his front. This gave Bragg pause, and having paused he wavered. At 10 o'clock that morning he sent for Polk and Hardee, who found him in a different frame of mind from the one he had shown eight hours ago, when he was roused out of sleep to read the letter advising retreat. With the enemy heavily reinforced, as he believed and later wrote in his report, "Common prudence and the safety of my army, upon which even the safety of our cause depended, left no doubt on my mind as to the necessity of my withdrawal from so unequal a contest." The retrograde movement got under way that night, January 3, and was conducted with such skill that not even a rear-guard action was fought with the unsuspecting Federals, who seemed no more anxious to pursue than Bragg had been to stay. He himself went to Winchester, fifty miles southeast, planning to establish a new line along Elk River. Polk was instructed to fall back on Shelbyville, Hardee on Tullahoma, respectively twenty-three and thirty-five miles from Murfreesboro, but when the former reached his goal and reported that the bluecoats had not ventured beyond Stones River, Bragg ordered Hardee to stop at Wartrace, on line with Polk. Returning at once to establish headquarters at Tullahoma, on the railroad about midway between Nashville and Chattanooga, he began to organize a new defensive position along the Duck, whose rich valley offered much in the way of subsistence and adequate

Federals enter Murfreesboro after the battle. Though unscathed by the fighting, almost every building in town was used as a hospital for the wounded of both sides.

camp sites, including level fields for the daily hours of close-order drill in which he placed great store as a disciplinarian.

His pride in his army and its conduct during the battle — which was in a way a coda to the Kentucky excursion, launched soon after he took command at Tupelo, Mississippi, back in June — was expressed in his report, where he listed with satisfaction the capture of 6273 prisoners and enemy colors in abundance, along with 31 cannon and 6000 small arms, as well as "a large amount of other valuable property, all of which was secured and appropriated to proper uses." Moreover, he declared by way of final proof of moral superiority over his antagonist, "the army retired to its present position behind Duck River without giving or receiving a shot." Within the ranks of that army, however, though the men agreed that they had won a victory, there were fewer signs of elation. The retreat was made in wretched weather, and as they plodded southward through the mud, alternately drenched with rain and pelted with sleet, bent beneath the weight of their sodden packs, it seemed to them that the Perryville technique — fight; win; fall back — had been repeated. "What does he fight battles for?" they grumbled, beginning to discern a discouraging pattern to their efforts under Bragg. Similarly at home, as one civilian diarist recorded, "It was small surcease to the sob of the widow and the moan of the orphan that 'the retreat to Tullahoma was conducted in good order.' "

Rosecrans, on the other hand — who had not made a single offensive move since the explosive attack on his right wing at dawn of the 31st, who had allowed a foe he claimed was beaten to withdraw from his immediate front without so much as a threat of molestation, and who was so cautious in pursuit that his eventual movement to the east bank of Stones River, from which he had withdrawn on the night of January 3 lest the rising waters expose his troops to destruction in detail, amounted to practically no pursuit at all — was praised not only by those below and above him in the army, but also by the public at large, including the Ohio legislature, which tendered him before the month was out a resolution of thanks "for the glorious victory resulting in the capture of Murfreesboro and the defeat of the rebel forces at that place." Cheered by his soldiers as he rode among them, he received equally gratifying responses to the dispatches by which he announced his victory to the authorities in Washington. "God bless you, and all of you," the President replied, and the Secretary of War (who had said of Rosecrans' appointment at the outset, "Well, you have made your choice of idiots. Now you can await the news of a terrible disaster") was quite expansive, wiring: "The country is filled with admiration of the gallantry and heroic achievement of yourself and the officers and troops under your command. . . . There is nothing you can ask within my power to grant to yourself or your noble command that will not be cheerfully given." Even Halleck, who had prodded and nudged him for weeks beyond endurance, eventually joined the chorus of praise, though not before he had waited a few days for verification in Confederate newspapers smuggled across the border. "Rebel accounts fully confirm your telegrams from the battlefield," he wired, and added: "You and your brave army have won the gratitude of your country and the admiration of the world. . . . All honor to the Army of the Cumberland — thanks to the living and tears for the lamented dead."

Bragg, he knew, was playing a cagey game at Tullahoma ("We shall fight him again at every hazard if he advances, and harass him daily if he does not," the terrible-tempered general was telling his superiors even now) but Rosecrans was firm in his intentions and had already reverted to the use of vigorous phrases he had been employing two weeks back, on the eve of battle. "We shall press them as rapidly as our means of traveling and subsistence will permit," he notified Stanton on January 5. Next day, though he was still at Murfreesboro, he boldly repeated words he had used at Nashville in mid-December: "I now wish to press them to the wall."

★ ★ ★ When Davis returned to Richmond that same January 5, to be met on the portico of the White House by his wife and their four children — three sons and a daughter, stair-stepped at two-year intervals so that their ages ranged from just past one to almost eight — Mrs Davis, observing that her husband was near exhaustion, insisted that he retire at once to rest from the exertions of his journey. Presently, however, they heard the thump and blare of drums and horns and the cheers of a crowd that had gathered in front of the house to welcome him back with a serenade. Weary though he was, and despite his desire to be alone with his family — "Every sound is the voice of my child and every child renews the memory of a loved one's appearance," he had written home from Tennessee, "but none can equal their charms, nor can any compare with my own long-worshipped Winnie" — he felt that he could not ignore the shouts of the crowd or fail to acknowledge the courtesy being tendered.

The cheers were redoubled as the big front door swung ajar once more and the President came out onto the steps. Captain J. B. Smith's Silver Band played "Listen to the Mocking Bird" and several other airs which the crowd enjoyed while waiting for the speech they had come to hear. Davis did not disappoint them. Carried forward perhaps by a sort of verbal secondary inertia, he spoke as he had been speaking now for more than three weeks, to similar crowds and with similar words, in the course of his nearly three-thousand-mile trip to "the further West" and back.

"I am happy to be welcomed on my return to the capital of the Confederacy — the last hope, as I believe, for the perpetuation of that system of government which our forefathers founded — the asylum of the oppressed, and the home of true representative liberty." His voice, as he thus began, showed the strain to which it had been exposed, but as usual it gathered strength as he continued, reverting to the deeds of olden days in the Old Dominion, where the earlier Revolution had been proclaimed and, finally, won. Now once more, he told these latter-day Virginians, "anticipating the overthrow of that government which you had inherited, you assumed to yourselves the right, as your fathers had done before you, to declare yourself independent, and nobly have you advocated the assertion which you have made. Here, upon your soil, some of the fiercest battles of the Revolution were fought, and upon your soil it closed by the surrender of Cornwallis. Here again are men of every state; here they have congregated, linked in the defense of a most sacred cause. They have battled, they have bled upon your soil, and it is now consecrated by blood which cries for vengeance against the insensate foe of religion as well as of humanity, of the altar as well as of the hearthstone." Thus he repeated the bitterness he had voiced in his home state, ten days ago. Nor, with first-hand accounts of the sack of Fredericksburg now added to the list of northern depredations — not the least of them being the recently issued Emancipation Proclamation, which, as he saw it, incited the slaves to the murder of their masters — had that reaction been tempered by second thought. Rather, the bitterness had increased: as he now showed. "It is true," he told his listeners, "you have a cause which binds you together more firmly than your fathers were. They fought to be free from the usurpations of the British crown, but they fought against a manly foe. You fight against the off-scourings of the earth."

Applauded, he passed on to a brief review of recent Confederate successes in the field, which he predicted would bring discord to northern councils, and then returned to his condemnation, not only of the conduct of the Federal armies of invasion, but also of the men who had sent them South. "Every crime which could characterize the course of demons has marked the course of the invader . . . from the burning of defenseless towns to the stealing of silver forks and spoons." In this last he had particular reference to Ben Butler, known as "Beast" Butler and "Spoons" Butler as a result of his alleged brutality and deftness in the exercise of his authority in command of the occupation of New Orleans, and Davis made the charge explicit, asserting that the Massachusetts general had "exerted himself to earn the excoriations of the civilized world, and now returns [to Washington] with his dishonors thick upon him to receive the plaudits of the only people on earth who do not blush to think he wears the human form. . . . They have come to disturb your social organization on the plea that it is a military necessity. For what are they waging war? They say to preserve the Union.

Can they preserve the Union by destroying the social existence of a portion of the South? Do they hope to reconstruct the Union by striking at everything which is dear to man? — by showing themselves so utterly disgraced that if the question was proposed to you whether you would combine with hyenas or Yankees, I trust every Virginian would say: 'Give me the hyenas.' "

"Good! Good!" his listeners cried, and there was laughter. They wanted more along these lines.

But Davis spoke calmly now, as if to refute the charge made by his critics that he was cold in his attitude toward the people, unconcerned for their welfare, and anxious to avoid commingling with them — as if, indeed, he had brought back East from his journey West an increased awareness of the warmth and strength proceeding from contact with those who looked to him for leadership not only as their President but also as a man. "My friends, constant labor in the duties of office, borne down by care, and with an anxiety which has left me scarcely a moment for repose, I have had but little opportunity for social intercourse among you. I thank you for this greeting, and hope the time may come soon when you and I alike, relieved of the anxieties of the hour, may have more of social intercourse than has heretofore existed." Flushed with confidence as a result of the victories won by the nation's armies in the course of his trip, he added: "If the war continues we shall only grow stronger and stronger as each year rolls on. Compare our condition today with that which existed one year ago. See the increasing power of the enemy, but mark that our own has been proportionately greater, until we see in the future nothing to disturb the prospect of the independence for which we are struggling. One year ago, many were depressed and some were despondent. Now deep resolve is seen in every eye; an unconquerable spirit nerves every arm. And gentle woman, too; who can estimate the value of her services in this struggle? . . . With such noble women at home, and such heroic soldiers in the field, we are invincible."

He waited for the applause to die away, and then concluded his remarks, once more on a personal note. "I thank you, my friends, for the kind salutation tonight; it is an indication that at some future time we shall be better acquainted. I trust we shall all live to enjoy some of the fruits of the struggle in which we are engaged. My prayers are for your individual and collective welfare. May God prosper our cause, and may we live to give to our children untarnished the rich inheritance which our fathers gave us. Good night!"

★   ★   ★

*Late in January 1863, Federals
slog knee-deep across a rain swollen
stream during the mud march,
Burnside's ill-fated second attempt
to take Fredericksburg.*

Lincoln; Mud March; Hooker

1862 ★ ★ ★ ★ ★ **N**ew Year's 1863 was for Abraham Lincoln perhaps the single busiest day of his whole presidential life, and it came moreover at dead center of what was perhaps his period of deepest gloom and perplexity of spirit. Not only was there political division within his party, and even within his own official family, but with the possible exception of Rosecrans, whose battle was in mid-career and appeared worse than doubtful, all his hand-picked commanders had failed him utterly, through enemy action or their own inaction, in his hopes for a multifaceted early-winter triumph in which he himself had assigned them the parts they were to play in putting a quick end to rebellion. One by one, sometimes two by two, they had failed him. Burnside and his fellow generals on the Rappahannock, having blundered into defeat at Fredericksburg, were engaged in a frenzy of backbiting such as not even the highly contentious Army of the Potomac had ever known before. Grant, according to the *New York Times*, remained "stuck in the mud of northern Mississippi, his army of no use to him or anybody else." Banks, caught in a toil of imported New Orleans cotton speculators, was stymied by a previously unsuspected fort on the Mississippi, two hundred and fifty miles downstream from his assigned objective. And McClernand, from whom the Commander in Chief had perhaps expected most, was apparently the worst off of all. He not only had done nothing

★

with his army; the last Lincoln had heard from him, he could not even find it.

Nor had these and other failures of omission and commission gone unnoticed by the country at large, the voters and investors on whose will and trust the prosecution of the war depended. The Democrats, still on the outside looking in, but with substantial gains in the fall elections to sharpen their appetite for more, had seen to that: especially Ohio Representative Clement L. Vallandigham, who was savagely pointing out, from the vantage point of his seat in Congress, the administration's errors. "Money you have expended without limit," he told Republicans in the House, "and blood poured out like water. Defeat, debt, taxation, and sepulchers — these are your only trophies." Others, less violent but no less earnest, including his disaffected former allies, were accusing the President in a similar vein; so that now, perhaps, with his own critics crying out against him, he could feel more sympathy for James K. Polk than he had felt when he

"Money you have expended without limit and blood poured out like water. Defeat, debt, taxation, and sepulchers — these are your only trophies."

— Clement L. Vallandigham

spoke against him in Congress, fifteen years ago this month, in the midst of another war. "I more than suspect already," the youthful Lincoln had declared from a seat in the rear of the House, "that he is deeply conscious of being in the wrong; that he feels the blood of this war, like the blood of Abel, is crying to heaven against him; that originally having some strong motive . . . to involve the two countries in a war, and trusting to escape scrutiny by fixing the public gaze upon the exceeding brightness of military glory . . . he plunged into it and has swept on and on, till, disappointed in his calculation . . . he now finds himself he knows not where. . . . His mind, tasked beyond its power, is running hither and thither, like some tortured creature on a burning surface, finding no position on which it can settle down and be at ease. . . . He is a bewildered, confounded, and miserably perplexed man. God grant he may be able to show there is not something about his conscience more painful than all his mental perplexity!"

The words rebounded from the target, boomeranged down the years, and came back in other forms to strike the sender. Orestes Brownson, the prominent Boston author and former transcendentalist, wrote of Lincoln: "His soul seems made of leather, and incapable of any grand or noble emotion. Compared with the mass of men, he is a line of flat prose in a beautiful and spirited lyric. He lowers, he never elevates you. You leave his presence with your enthusiasm dampened, your better feelings crushed, and your hopes cast to the winds. You ask not, can this man carry the nation through its terrible struggles? but can the nation carry this man through them, and not perish in the attempt?" Brownson was of no uncertain mind where Lincoln was concerned. "He is thickheaded; he is ignorant; he is tricky, somewhat astute, in a small way, and obstinate as a mule. . . . He is wrong-headed, the attorney not the lawyer, the petty politician not the statesman, and, in my belief, ill-deserving of the soubriquet of Honest. I am out of all patience with him," he added, rather anticlimactically, and inquired: "Is there no way of inducing him to resign, and allow Mr Hamlin to take his place?" Senator William Pitt Fessenden, a Maine Republican high in the party's councils, replied in somewhat the same vein when told that he should be a member of the cabinet in order to be at Lincoln's elbow and give the nation the full benefit of his advice. "No friend of mine should ever wish to see me there," he answered. "You cannot change the President's character or conduct. He remained long enough in Springfield, surrounded by toadies and office-seekers, to persuade himself that he was specially chosen by the Almighty for this crisis, and well chosen. This conceit has never yet been beaten out of him, and until it is, no human wisdom can be of much avail. I see nothing for it but to let the ship of state drift along, hoping that the current of public opinion may bring it safely into port." Similarly, a Boston philanthropist, railroad magnate J. M. Forbes, convinced that Lincoln was badly off the track, was asking: "Can nothing be done to reach the President's ear and heart? I hear he is susceptible to religious impressions; shall we send our eloquent divines to talk to him, or shall we send on a deputation of mothers and wives, or can we, the conservators of liberty, who have elected him, combine with Congress in beseeching him to save the country?"

In point of fact, one such group of "eloquent divines" as Forbes suggested did come to call on Lincoln at this time, protesting with considerable heat the lack of progress in the war; but he gave them little satisfaction beyond a brief, short-tempered lecture comparing the administration's predicament to that of a tightrope walker in mid-act. "Gentlemen," he told them, "suppose all the property you were worth was in gold, and you had put it in the hands of Blondin to carry across the Niagara River. Would you shake the cable or keep shouting out to him, 'Blondin, stand up a little straighter!' 'Blondin, stoop a little more!' 'Go a little faster'; 'Lean a little more to the north'; 'Lean a little more to the south'? No. You would hold your breath as well as your tongue, and keep your hands off until he was safe over. The government is carrying an immense weight. Untold treasures are in their hands. They are doing the very

best they can. Don't badger them. Keep silence, and we'll get you safe across."
The visit, he said afterwards, made him "a little shy of preachers" for a time.
"But the latchstring is out," he added, "and they have the right to come here
and preach to me if they will go about it with some gentleness and moderation."

Gentleness and moderation were easier to prescribe than they were
to practice. An infinitely patient man, he was beginning to lose patience: with the
result that some who formerly had complained that he lacked firmness were now
protesting that he had assumed the prerogatives of a dictator, spurning their
counsels and high-handedly overruling their objections. It was true in some
respects. His accustomed tact sometimes failed him under pressure nowadays,
and he gave short answers, though rarely without the saving grace of humor, the
velvet glove that softened the clutch of the iron hand. This was evident, for
example, in a clash with Secretary of the Treasury Salmon P. Chase about this
time. An economist came to Lincoln with a plan for issuing greenbacks. Lincoln
heard him out, liked the notion, but told him: "You must go to Chase. He
is running that end of the machine." The man left, then presently returned,
saying that the Secretary had dismissed him with the objection that the proposal was unconstitutional. Lincoln grimaced. "Go back to Chase," he said,
and tell him not to bother himself about the Constitution. Say that I have that
sacred instrument here at the White House, and am guarding it with great care."

Such brusque, not to say cavalier, treatment of his highly respected
Treasury chief was prologue to an even rougher handling of that dignitary in
mid-December, when he tripped him neatly from behind as he tried a sprint up
several rungs of the political ladder. This was a time of crisis and division, in the
cabinet as in the nation at large. One member, Secretary of the Interior Caleb
Blood Smith, who had received his appointment as the result of a convention
bargain, was leaving to accept a judgeship Lincoln had offered him in his native
Indiana; his post would go to John Palmer Usher, another Hoosier, at present
the Assistant Secretary. The other six members were split on the question of
whether to admit West Virginia as a state under an act just passed by Congress,
divorcing Virginia's northwest counties from the Old Dominion and validating
the rump government set up in Charleston during the Sumter furor. Three cabinet officers — Chase, Stanton, and Secretary of State William H. Seward —
wanted Lincoln to sign the bill, converting slave soil into free soil by the stroke
of a pen, and incidentally adding good Republican votes on whatever questions
Congress might decide needed settling in the future; while three others —
Secretary of the Navy Gideon Welles, Attorney General Edward Bates, and Postmaster General Montgomery Blair — recommended that he veto it, on grounds
that the act was in a sense a ratification of secession. Though he could not rec-
oncile their views, Lincoln quickly solved the problem to his own approximate
satisfaction. "The division of a state is dreaded as a precedent," he reasoned.

Secretary of State William H. Seward tendered his resignation after learning that all but one of the thirty-two Republican senators were soon to ask President Lincoln for his removal.

"But a measure made expedient by a war is no precedent for times of peace. It is said that the admission of West Virginia is secession, and tolerated only because it is *our* secession. Well, if we call it by that name, there is still difference enough between secession against the Constitution and secession in favor of the Constitution." On the last day of the year, though he did so with a wry face, he signed the bill. West Virginia would become in June a full-fledged state of the Union, the thirty-fifth, not discounting the eleven who had no representation in Congress pending the settlement of their claim to have abolished their old ties.

Seward and Chase had voted together on the issue, but that was rare. In general they were diametrically opposed, as they had been in the old days when they were rivals for the office which, by a fluke, had gone to Lincoln. Chase, who was jealous of Seward's position as the President's chief adviser, wanted not only the seat closest to the one at the head of the table, but also, as time would show, the principal seat itself. In this connection, noting the way the wind blew, he had aligned himself with the radicals in Congress, the so-called Jacobins who had come to see Seward as the stumbling block in the way of adoption of their notions as to how the war should be fought and the country run, just as Chase had come to see him as a hurdle that would have to be removed or overleaped if he was to fulfill his own ambitions. By way of undoing their common adversary, he fanned the flames of the radicals' hatred by reporting Seward's every private opposition to their aims (the New Yorker, for example, had delayed the promulgation of the Preliminary Emancipation Proclamation by advising Lincoln to wait for a more propitious season before releasing it to the world; than which, indeed, there could be no crime greater in radical eyes) as well as by giving them a blow-by-blow account of every cabinet crisis, omitting nothing that served to thicken the atmosphere of discord and indecision. So it was that at last, on December 17 — four days after the Fredericksburg fiasco, which seemed to them to prove emphatically that the prosecution of the war was in quite the wrong hands — all but one of the thirty-two Republican senators met in secret caucus on Capitol Hill and passed unanimously the following resolution, by way of advice to the leader of their party: "*Resolved,* that . . . the public confidence in the present administration would be increased by a change in and partial reconstruction of the cabinet." It was Seward they were after, Seward alone, and lest there be any doubt on that score a committee of nine was appointed to present the resolution to Lincoln and explain to him just what it was they meant.

The one abstaining senator was New York's Preston King, who went at once to Seward and warned his former senatorial colleague that the Jacobins, "thirsty for a victim" in the wake of recent misfortunes, had selected his neck for the ax. Seward reacted fast when he learned thus of the resolution about to be presented. "They may do as they please about me," he said, "but they shall not put the President in a false position on my account." Accordingly he took a sheet of paper, and having scrawled a few words across it — "Sir, I hereby resign from the office of Secretary of State, and beg that my resignation be accepted immediately" — sent it forthwith to the White House. Lincoln was shocked. "What does this mean?" he asked as he put on his hat and set out for Seward's house, which was just across the street. Seward explained what had happened, along with what was about to happen, and added that he personally would be glad to get from under the burden of official duties and political harassment. "Ah yes, Governor," Lincoln said, shaking his head. "That will do very well for you, but I am like the starling in Sterne's story. 'I can't get out.' " He pocketed the resignation and went sadly back across the White House lawn.

At any rate, next morning when the committee spokesman called, he knew what to expect. He set the time for the presentation at 7 o'clock that evening; he would receive the full committee then. This was a crisis, not only for Lincoln but also for the nation, and he knew it. "If I had yielded to that storm and dismissed Seward," he said later, "the thing would have all slumped over one way, and we should have been left with a scant handful of supporters." Knowing what had to be done was a quite different thing, however, from knowing how to do it. Ben Wade of Ohio, George W. Julian of Indiana, Zachariah Chandler of Michigan: these and others like them were men of power and savage purpose, accomplished haters who would be merciless in revenging even an imagined slight, let alone an outright rebuff. Whatever Lincoln did had better be done without incurring their personal enmity. Besides, he not only had to avoid their anger; he also needed their support. What he required just now was someone to draw their wrath, someone to serve him much as a billygoat serves the farmer who places him in a barnlot to draw fleas. By evening, not without a certain sense of political and even poetical justice, he had chosen the someone. All that remained was to make him serve, and that could be done quite simply by branding him, in the eyes of all, for what he was.

The nine committeemen were prompt; Lincoln received them in his office. By way of a beginning, seventy-one-year-old Jacob Collamer of Vermont, who had been elected spokesman, read the resolution and followed it with a paper which summed up the conclusions reached in caucus the day before. The war should be prosecuted vigorously; cabinet members should be "cordial, resolute, unwavering" in their devotion to the principles of the Republican majority; the cabinet itself, once it had been stripped and rebuilt so as to contain only such stalwarts, should have a larger voice in the running of the government. Wade rose next, a vigorous man with "burning" eyes and bulldog flews, protesting hotly that the President had "placed the direction of our military affairs in the hands of bitter and malignant Democrats." He spoke at length, going somewhat afield from the central issue, and was followed by Fessenden, who agreed that the war was "not sufficiently in the hands of its friends," then brought the discussion back on target by charging specifically "that the Secretary of State [is] not in accord with the majority of the cabinet and [has] exerted an injurious influence upon the conduct of the war." Others had their say along these lines, also at considerable length, but Lincoln kept his temper and said little. After three hours of listening, however, he suggested that the meeting adjourn until the following night. The senators agreed. Alone at last, he saw clearly, as he presently remarked, that if he let these men have their way "the whole government must cave in; it could not stand, could not hold water; the bottom would be out."

He knew what to do and, by now, how to do it; but he was saddened. "What do those men want?" he asked his friend Senator Orville Browning of Illinois next day. "I hardly know, Mr President," Browning replied, "but they are exceedingly violent. . . ." Lincoln knew well enough what they wanted, though, and he said so: "They wish to get rid of me — and I am sometimes half disposed to gratify them." Browning protested, but Lincoln shook his head. "We are now on the brink of destruction," he said. "It appears to me the Almighty is against us, and I can hardly see a ray of hope." Again Browning protested. Though he was not a member of the committee, he had attended the caucus and had voted for the resolution: which, he explained defensively, "was the gentlest thing that could be done. We had to do that, or worse." The trouble he said was Seward. While he personally had a high regard for the Secretary, others were saying that the New Yorker had the President under his thumb. "Why should men believe a lie," Lincoln broke in, "an absurd lie, that could not impose on a child, and cling to it and repeat it in defiance of all evidences to the contrary?" His sadness deepened. "The committee is to be up to see me at 7 o'clock. Since I heard last night of the proceedings of the caucus I have been more distressed than by any event of my life."

If this was so, it did not show in his manner when he welcomed the committeemen that evening for a second round of grievance presentations. Before the discussion got under way, however, he announced to the assembled senators that he had thought it fitting to have the cabinet officers — minus Seward, of course, since even aside from the fact that his resignation was pending, that would have been too indelicate — present to answer the charge that there was discord among them and that the President seldom followed or even asked for their advice. Whereupon the door opened and the six gentlemen in question filed into the room. Lincoln had invited them at the cabinet meeting that morning, after telling them of the matter afoot and of Seward's submission of his resignation. Mostly they had welcomed the chance to confront their accusers, although two of their number — Chase in particular — had protested that they "knew of no good that could come of an interview." In the end, however, the two — the other was Bates — had been obliged to go along with the majority. Now here they were, face to face with critics whose accusations were based, at least in part, on information supplied in private by Chase in order to curry favor with them. Already he was squirming, as if the fleas had jumped at the sight of his large, handsome person: but the worst was still to come.

If Chase and some of the senators were embarrassed by the confrontation, Lincoln certainly was not. He began the proceedings by reading aloud yesterday's bill of particulars, admitting as he went along that he had not consulted the cabinet on all affairs of state or war, and that he had not always followed their advice, even when he had sought it; but in the main, he said, he had valued and used their abilities, individually and collectively. As for discord, he did not think it reasonable to expect seven such independent-minded men to agree on every issue that came before them; but here again, he said, he thought they worked together mainly as a unit, and certainly he himself had no complaint. He paused, then turned to the six cabinet members present, beginning to poll them one by one. Did they or did they not agree with his statement of the case? They did; or so they said, one by one; until he came to Chase. Chase, as it turned out, also agreed, though not without considerable hemming and hawing by way of preamble. He would never have come to the meeting, he said, if he had known he was "to be arraigned." He seemed angry. He seemed to feel that he was being "put upon" — as indeed he was. In the end, with Wade and the others watching balefully, he admitted that matters of prime importance had usually come before the cabinet, though perhaps "not so fully as might be desired," and that there had been "no want of unity in the cabinet, but a general

★

Secretary of the Treasury Salmon P. Chase, trapped in his own web of deceit by Lincoln, nearly lost his own cabinet seat for his behind-the-scenes attacks on William Seward.

acquiescence in public measures." Thus he wound up, and the Jacobins watched him cold-eyed, contrasting what he said now, in the presence of Lincoln and his colleagues, with what he had said in private. The President did not prolong his suffering. Having more or less settled these two points of contention, he shifted the talk to the question of Seward, defending his chief minister against yesterday's charges, and then began to poll the committeemen on their views. At that point Fessenden recoiled. "I do not think it proper," he said, "to discuss the merits or demerits of a member of the cabinet in the presence of his associates." Chase was quick to agree. "I think the members of the cabinet should withdraw," he said. In solemn procession they did so, some amused, some disgruntled, and one, at least, discredited in the eyes of men whose favor he had sought.

Like Simon Cameron a year ago, the Treasury chief had learned the hard way what it meant to tangle with Lincoln. Cameron was in Russia now, a victim of political decapitation, and Chase was determined to avoid such punishment. He would forestall the headsman by submitting, however regretfully, his resignation. This was exactly what Lincoln wanted: as was shown next morning, December 20, when he came into his office and found Chase, Welles, and Stanton grouped around the fire. Chase began to complain of yesterday's damage to his dignity. It had affected him most painfully, he said, for it seemed to indicate a lack of confidence. In fact — he hesitated — he had written out his resignation at home the night before. . . . Lincoln's reaction to this was not at all what the Secretary had expected. His expression was one of downright joy.

"Where is it?" he said eagerly.

★

"I brought it with me," Chase replied, taking a letter from his inside coat pocket.

"Let me have it," Lincoln said, and he put out a long arm.

Chase drew back, but not in time. Lincoln already had hold of the paper, and the Secretary suffered the added shock of having it snatched from his grasp. Reading it quickly through, Lincoln laughed; "a triumphal laugh," Welles called it in his diary. "This cuts the Gordian knot," he exclaimed. "I can dispose of this subject now without difficulty. I see my way clear." Stanton, who had been guilty of some of the same backstairs maneuvers — though he did not know whether the President suspected him, or what he might do if he did — remarked stiffly that he was prepared to tender his resignation, too. But Lincoln already had what he had been working toward. "You may go to your department," he said gaily. "I don't want yours. This" — he held up Chase's letter — "is all I want; this relieves me; the case is clear; the trouble is ended. I will detain neither of you longer."

His satisfaction was obvious, amounting to delight. What he had had in mind all along, and had achieved through skillful handling, was a balance: Chase's resignation against Seward's, which the Jacobins were still urging him to accept. Now, however, with Chase's inseparably included — "If one goes, the other must," he presently notified the senators; "they must hunt in couples" — they would be much less insistent; for, whatever their disgust with the Treasury chief's performance the day before, they still believed that he could be useful to them within the administration's private councils. Lincoln himself described the situation with a metaphor out of his boyhood in Kentucky, where he had seen farmers riding to market with a brace of pumpkins lodged snugly in a bag, one at each end in order to make a balanced load across the horse's withers. "Now I can ride," he said. "I have got a pumpkin in each end of my bag." Accordingly, he sent polite, identical notes to the two ministers, declining to accept their resignations and requesting them to continue as members of his official family. Seward, who had watched the maneuvers with amusement from a seat behind the scene, agreed at once; but Chase held off, still suffering from the fleabites, which were no less painful for being figurative. "I will sleep on it," he said. However, after a day of meditation and prayer — for it was a Sunday and he was intensely religious, spending a good part of each Sabbath on his knees — he agreed to remain at his post, as Lincoln had confidently expected.

Here was a case of double salvation, in more ways than one. Within the confines of his office in the White House, Lincoln had planned and fought a three-day battle as important to the welfare of the nation, and the progress of the war through united effort, as many that raged in the open field with booming guns and casualties by the thousands. In addition to retaining the services of Seward and Chase, both excellent men at their respective posts, he had managed to turn aside the wrath of the Jacobins without increasing their bitterness toward himself or incurring their open hatred, which might well have been fatal. Nor was that all. Paradoxically, because of the way he had gone about it, in avoiding the disruption of his cabinet he had achieved within it a closer harmony than had obtained before. This was partly because of the increased respect his actions earned him, but it was also because of the effect the incident had on the two ministers most intimately concerned. For all his loyalty to Lincoln through the storm, Seward had not previously abandoned the notion that he was the man directly in line for his job. Now, though, with all but one of the senators in his own party having expressed a desire to see him removed from any connection with the executive branch of the government, the presidential itch was cured. From that hour, his devotion to his duties was single-minded and his loyalty acquired an added zeal. So much could hardly be said for Chase, exactly, but he too had been sobered, and his ambition taken down a notch, by the cold-eyed looks the radical leaders had given him while he squirmed. It was no wonder, then, that Lincoln indulged in self-congratulation when he reviewed the three-day maneuver. "I do not see how I could have done better," he remarked.

★ ★ ★ *F*ew would disagree with this assessment, even among the frock-coated politicians he had bested, whether senators or members of his cabinet. In point of fact, whatever shocks they had suffered along the way, there should have been little surprise at the outcome; for the matter had been essentially political, and politics (or statesmanship, if you will, which he once defined as the art of getting the best from men who all too often were intent on giving nothing better than their worst) was a science he had mastered some time back. The military art was something else. Whether Lincoln would ever do as well as Commander in Chief of the nation's armies as he had done as its Chief Executive was more than doubtful — particularly in the light of current testimony as to the condition of the largest of those armies, still on the near bank of the Rappahannock attempting to recover from the shock of its mid-December blood bath.

"Exhaustion steals over the country. Confidence and hope are dying," the Quartermaster General wrote privately this week to its commander. "The slumber of the army since [the attack at Fredericksburg] is eating into the vitals of the nation. As day after day has gone, my heart has sunk and I see greater peril to our nationality in the present condition of affairs than I have seen at any time during the struggle." Complaints were heard from below as well as above, and though these were not addressed to Burnside personally, accusing fingers were leveled in his direction and even higher. "Our poppycorn generals kill men as Herod killed the innocents," a Massachusetts private declared, and a Wisconsin major called this winter "the Valley Forge of the war."

A bitterness was spreading through the ranks. "Alas my poor country!" a New York corporal wrote home. "It has strong limbs to march and meet the foe, stout arms to strike heavy blows, brave hearts to dare. But the brains, the brains — have we no brains to use the arms and limbs and eager hearts with cunning? Perhaps Old Abe has some funny story to tell, appropriate to the occasion. . . . Mother, do not wonder that my loyalty is growing weak," he added. "I am sick and tired of disaster and the fools that bring disaster upon us."

There was a snatch of doggerel, sung to the tune of the old sea chanty "Johnny, Fill up the Bowl," making the rounds:

Abram Lincoln, what yer 'bout?

Hurrah! Hurrah!

Stop this war. It's all played out.

Hurrah! Hurrah!

Abram Lincoln, what yer 'bout?

Stop this war. It's all played out.

We'll all drink stone blind:

Johnny, fill up the bowl!

Veterans in the Army of the Potomac took up the refrain, "all played out," and made it their own. Once they had pretended cynicism as a cover for their greenness and their fears, but now they felt they had earned it and they found the phrase descriptive of their outlook through this season of discontent. "The phrensy of our soldiers rushing to glory or death has, as our boys amusingly affirm, *been played out*," a regimental chaplain wrote. "Our battle-worn veterans go into danger when ordered, remain as a stern duty so long as directed, and leave as soon as honor and duty allow." Case-hardened by their recent experience over the river, particularly in the repeated fruitless assaults on the stone wall at the base of Marye's Heights, they had no use for heroic postures or pretensions nowadays. When they saw magazine illustrations showing mounted officers with drawn sabers leading smartly aligned columns of troops unflinchingly through shellbursts, they snickered and jeered and whooped their motto: "All played out!"

Lincoln already knew something of this, but he learned a good deal more on December 29 when two disgruntled brigadiers hurried from Falmouth to Washington on short-term passes, intending to warn their congressmen of what they believed was imminent disaster. Burnside was planning to recross the Rappahannock any day now, having issued three days' cooked rations the day after Christmas, along with orders for the troops to be held in readiness to move on twelve hours' notice. What alarmed the two brigadiers — John Newton and John Cochrane, the latter a former Republican congressman himself — was that the army, which they were convinced was in a condition of near-mutiny, would come apart at the seams if it was called upon to repeat this soon the tragic performance it had staged two weeks ago in the same arena, and therefore they had come to warn the influential Bay State senator Henry Wilson, chairman of the Senate Military Committee, in hopes that he could get the movement stopped. In the intensity of their concern, as they discovered when they reached the capital, they had failed to take into account the fact that Congress was in recess over the holidays; Wilson had gone home. Undeterred, they went to see the Secretary of State, a former political associate of Cochrane's. When Seward heard their burden of woes he took them straight to the President, to whom — though they were somewhat daunted now, never having intended to climb this high up the chain of command — they repeated, along with hasty assurances that the basis for their admittedly irregular visit was patriotism, not hope for advancement, their conviction that if the Army of the Potomac was committed to battle in its present discouraged state it would be utterly destroyed. Not only would it be unable to hold the line of the Rappahannock; it would not even be able to hold the line of the river from which it took its name. Lincoln, who had known nothing of the pending movement, and scarcely more of the extent of the demoralization Cochrane and Newton claimed was rampant, was infected with their fears and got off a wire to Burnside without delay: "I have good reason for saying that you must not make a general movement without first letting me know of it."

Burnside, though his infantry had already been alerted for a downstream crossing while his cavalry was in motion for a feint upstream — "a risky expedition but a buster," one trooper called the plan — promptly complied with the President's telegram by canceling the movement, but he was angered and saddened by the obvious lack of confidence on the part of his superiors. The army, too — whatever its gladness over the postponement of another blood bath — was aggrieved as it filed back into its camps, feeling mistrusted and mistrustful. "Such checks destroy the enthusiam of any army," the same trooper dolefully protested.

Yet it was at this point, near the apparent nadir of its self-confidence and pride, with disaffection evident in all of its components, from the commander down to the youngest drummer boy, that the only truly imperishable quality of this army first began to be discerned, like a gleam that only shone in darkness. If men could survive the unprofitable slaughter of Fredericksburg — the patent bungling, the horror piled on pointless horror, and the disgust that came with

Brigadier General John Newton (far right) was one of two officers who carried the word to Lincoln of the low morale of the Army of the Potomac and its distrust of Burnside following Fredericksburg.

the conclusion that their comrades had died less by way of proving their love for their country than by way of proving the ineptness of their leaders — it might well be that they could survive almost anything. There were those who saw this. There were those who, unlike Newton and Cochrane, did not mistake the vociferous reaction for near-mutiny, who knew that griping was not only the time-honored prerogative of the American soldier, from Valley Forge on down, but was also, in its way, a proof of his basic toughness and resilience. "The more I saw of the Army of the Potomac," one correspondent wrote from the camps around Falmouth, "the more I wondered at its invincible spirit, which no disaster seemed able to destroy." A *Harper's Weekly* editor perhaps overstated the case — "All played out!" the soldiers who read it doubtless jeered — but was also thinking along these lines in an issue that came out about this time: "Like our forefathers the English, who always began their wars by getting soundly thrashed by their enemies, and only commenced to acheive success when it was thought they were exhausted, we are warming to the work with each mishap."

Lincoln thought so, too, what time he managed to shake off the deep melancholy that was so much a part of his complex nature. He probed and, probing, he considered what emerged. As of the first day of the year which was opening so inauspiciously, the Union had 918,211 soldiers under arms, whereas the Confederacy had 446,622, or a good deal less than half as many. At several critical points along the thousand-mile line of division the odds were even longer — out in Middle Tennessee, for instance, or down along the Rappahannock — and the troubled Commander in Chief found solace in brooding on the figures, even those that reached him from the field of Fredericksburg. "We lost fifty percent more men than did the enemy," a member of the White House staff remarked after hearing his chief discuss the outcome of the fighting there, "and yet there is sense in the awful arithmetic propounded by Mr Lincoln. He says that if the same battle were to be fought over again, every day, through a week of days, with the same relative results, the army under Lee would be wiped out to the last man, [while] the Army of the Potomac would still be a mighty host. The war would be over, the Confederacy gone." There was error here. Northern losses in the battle had exceeded southern losses, not by fifty, but by considerably better than one hundred percent. And yet there was validity in Lincoln's premise as to the end result, and especially was there validity in the conclusion the staff man heard him draw: "No general yet found can face the arithmetic, but the end of the war will be at hand when he shall be discovered."

Scott and McDowell, Pope and McClellan, and now Burnside: none of these was the killer he was seeking. Already he saw that this search was perhaps after all the major problem. All else — while, like Blondin, Lincoln threaded his way, burdened by untold treasures — was, in a sense, a biding of time until the unknown killer could be found. Somewhere he existed, and somewhere he would find him, this unidentified general who could face the grim arithmetic being scrawled in blood across these critical, tragic pages of the nation's history.

★ ★ ★ These and other matters were much on the President's mind when he woke on January 1. After an early-morning conference with Burnside, who had come up from Falmouth to ask in person just what the Commander in Chief's "good reason" had been for not allowing him to handle his own army as he saw fit, Lincoln spent the usual half hour with his barber, then got into his best clothes and went downstairs for the accustomed New Year's White House reception. For three hours, beginning at 11 o'clock, it was "How do you do?" "Thank you." "Glad to see you." "How do you do?" as the invited guests — high government officials, members of the diplomatic corps, and other important dignitaries, foreign and domestic — having threaded their way through the crowd of uninvited onlookers collected on the lawn, alighted from their carriages, came into the parlor, and filed past Lincoln for handshakes and refreshments. At 1 o'clock the long ordeal was over; he went back upstairs to his office for the day's — or, some would say, the century's — most important business, the signing of the Emancipation Proclamation.

Throughout the ninety-nine days since September 23, when the preliminary announcement of intention had been made, there had been much speculation as to whether he would issue or withdraw the final proclamation. Some were for it, some against. His friend Browning, for example, reflecting the view of constituents in the President's home state, thought it "fraught with evil, and evil only." The senator believed that the "useless and mischievous" document would serve "to unite and exasperate" the South, and to "divide and distract us in the North." Lincoln himself, if only by his neglect of the subject while the hundred days ticked off, had seemed to see the point of this objection. In his December message to Congress he had barely mentioned the projected edict, but had reverted instead to his original plan for compensated emancipation, a quite different thing indeed. Alarmed by this apparent failure of nerve, Abolitionists looked to their hero Senator Charles Sumner of Massachusetts, who went to Lincoln three days after Christmas for a straight talk on the matter. He found him hard at work on the final draft of the proclamation, writing it out in longhand. "I know very well that the name connected with this document will never be forgotten," Lincoln said, by way of explanation for his pains, and Sumner returned to his own desk to reassure a qualmish friend in Boston: "The President says he would not stop the Proclamation if he could, and he could not if he would. . . . Hallelujah!"

So it was. Seward brought the official copy over from the State Department, where a skilled penman had engrossed it from Lincoln's final draft, just completed the night before. All it lacked was the President's signature. He dipped his pen, then paused with it suspended over the expanse of whiteness spread out on his desk, and looked around with a serious expression. "I never in my life felt more certain that I was doing right," he said, "than I do in signing this paper. But I have been receiving calls and shaking hands since 9 o'clock this morning, till my arm is stiff and numb. Now this signature is one that will be closely examined, and if they find my hand trembled they will say, 'He had some compunctions.' But anyway it is going to be done." Slowly and carefully he signed, not the usual *A. Lincoln,* but his name in full: *Abraham Lincoln.* The witnesses crowded nearer for a look at the result, then laughed in relief of nervous tension; for the signature, though "slightly tremulous," as Lincoln himself remarked, was bold and clear. Seward signed next, the quick, slanting scrawl of the busy administrator, and the great seal was affixed, after which it went to its place in the State Department files (where it later was destroyed by fire) and in the hearts of men, where it would remain forever, though some of them had doubted lately that it would even be issued.

★

★ ★ ★ *I*t was one thing to claim that by the stroke of a pen the fetters had been struck from the limbs of five million slaves and that their combined worth of more than a billion dollars was thereby automatically subtracted from enemy assets. It was quite another, however, to translate the announcement into fact, especially considering its peculiar limitations. All of Delaware, Maryland, Kentucky, Tennessee, and Missouri were exempt by specific definition within the body of the edict, along with those portions of Virginia and Louisiana already under Federal control. Lincoln himself explained that the proclamation had "no constitutional or legal justification, except as a military measure. The exemptions were made because the military necessity did not apply to the exempted localities." He freed no slave within his reach, and whether those beyond his reach would ever be affected by his pronouncement was dependent on the outcome of the war, which in turn depended on the southward progress of his armies. Just now that progress, East and West — once more with the possible exception of Middle Tennessee, where the issue remained in doubt — was negligible at best and nonexistent for the most part. Nor did the signs in either direction give promise of early improvement. Here in the East, in fact, if this morning's conference with Burnside was any indication of what to expect, the outlook was downright bleak.

The ruff-whiskered general had arrived in a state of acute distress, obviously fretted by more than the discomforts of his all-night ride from Falmouth, and Lincoln was distressed in turn to see him so. He liked Burnside — almost everyone did, personally — for his courage, for his impressive military bearing, and for what one subordinate called his "single-hearted honesty and unselfishness." All these qualities he had, and Lincoln, with a feeling of relief after weeks of trying to budge the balky McClellan, had chosen him in expectation of aggressiveness. The Indiana-born Rhode Islander had certainly given him that at Fredericksburg, in overplus indeed, but with a resolution so little tempered by discretion that critics now were remarking that he waged war in much the same way some folks played the fiddle, "by main strength and awkwardness." He himself was the first to admit his shortcomings. He had done so from the start, and recently in testimony given under oath before a congressional committee he had taken on his shoulders the whole blame for the late repulse. This was in a way disarming; it had the welcome but unfamiliar sound of natural modesty, so becoming in a truly capable man. However, there were those who saw it merely as further proof of his unfitness for the job he had accepted under protest. Burnside, they said, had not only admitted his incompetency; he had sworn to it.

When he opened the New Year's conference by asking what lay behind the telegram advising him not to move against the enemy without notifying Washington beforehand, Lincoln told him of the interview with the two brigadiers, in which they had stated that the army lacked confidence in its commander and was in no fit shape to be committed. Bristling at this evidence of perfidy from below, Burnside demanded to know their names, but Lincoln declined to divulge them for fear of the reprisal which he now saw would be visited upon their heads. This further increased the general's depression. It might well be true, he said, that his army had no faith in him; certainly not a single one of his senior commanders had approved of the movement he had canceled at Lincoln's suggestion. In fact, he added, plunging deeper into gloom, "It is my belief that I ought to retire to private life." When Lincoln demurred, Burnside's spirits rose a bit: enough, at least, to allow a sudden shift to the offensive. However low his own stock might have fallen, he said earnestly, he wanted the President to know that in his opinion neither Stanton's nor Halleck's was any higher. A man was apt to be a poor judge of his own usefulness and the loyalty of his subordinates, but of one thing he was sure. Neither the Secretary of War nor the general-in-chief had the confidence of the army — or of the country either for that matter, he quickly added, though he admitted that Lincoln was probably better informed on this latter point than he was. At any rate it was his belief that they too should be removed. . . . Lincoln expressed no opinion as to whether he could spare Stanton or Halleck, but he assured the unhappy Burnside that he valued his services highly. He urged him to return at once to his command and do the best he could, as he was sure he had done invariably in the past. Burnside replied that his plan was still to cross the Rappahannock, somewhere above or below Fredericksburg, and attack the rebels on their own ground. Lincoln said that was what he wanted, too, but prudence sometimes had to be applied, especially when risky ventures were involved. Whereupon, having secured this approval, however qualified, the general took his leave, apparently in a somewhat better frame of mind.

Still the fact remained that he was returning to his army with the intention of requiring it to pursue a course of action which, by his own admission, did not have the approval of the ranking subordinates who would be charged with its execution. The situation was, to say the least, loaded with possibilities of disaster. Here, Lincoln saw, was where the general-in-chief would fit into the picture; here was where Halleck could begin to perform the principal duty for which he had been summoned to the capital almost six months ago. He could go down to Falmouth for a first-hand look at the lay of the land and a talk with the disaffected corps commanders, then come back and submit his recommendations as to whether Burnside should be given his head or halted and replaced. Accordingly, before going upstairs to dress for the New Year's reception, Lincoln took out a sheet of paper and wrote the owl-eyed general a letter explaining what it was he wanted him to do. "If in such a difficulty as this you do not

★

help," he wrote, "you fail me precisely in the point for which I sought your assistance." The tone was somewhat tart, doubtless because Lincoln was irked at having to ask for what should have been forthcoming as a matter of course, and he added: "Your military skill is useless to me, if you will not do this."

The letter was forwarded through Stanton, who gave it to Halleck that same morning at the reception. "Old Brains," as he was called, was taken aback. Twice already in this war he had ventured into the field — one occasion

This house, used as Burnside's headquarters before and after Fredericksburg, was accidentally set ablaze by troops cooking a meal in the attic in February 1863.

★

was the inchworm advance on Corinth, back in May, when all he got for his pains was an empty town, plus the guffaws that went with being hoodwinked; the other was his trip to see McClellan down on the York-James peninsula, shortly after his arrival East in late July, when he ordered the withdrawal that had permitted Lee to concentrate against Pope with such disastrous results on the plains of Manassas — and he was having no more of such exposure to the jangle of alarums and excursions. He prized the sweatless quiet of his office, where he could scratch his elbows in seclusion and ponder the imponderables of war. Lincoln's letter was a wrench, not so much because of what it said — which was, after all, little more than a definition of Halleck's duties — but because of the way it said it. The fact that his chief had thought it necessary to put the thing on record, in black and white, instead of making the suggestion verbally, which would have left no blot, seemed to him to indicate a lack of confidence. His reaction was immediate and decisive. As soon as the reception was over he went to his office, wrote out his resignation, and sent it at once to the Secretary of War.

Lincoln heard of this development from Stanton late that afternoon, following the signing of the Emancipation Proclamation. Saddened though he was by the general's reaction, which deprived him, as he said, of the professional advice he badly needed at this juncture, he still did not want to lose the services of Old Brains, such as they were. To mollify the offended man he recalled the letter that same day and put it away in his files with the indorsement: "Withdrawn, because considered harsh by General Halleck." He was pleased when the general then agreed to remain at his post, even though he amounted, as Lincoln subsequently remarked, to "little more . . . than a first-rate clerk." The fact was, in spite of his objection to what he called "Halleck's habitual attitude of demur," he valued his opinions highly, especially those on theoretical or procedural matters. "He is a military man, has had a military education. I brought him here to give me military advice." So Lincoln defended him, and added: "However you may doubt or disagree [with] Halleck, he is very apt to be right in the end." Then too, since he knew something of the unfortunate general's sufferings from hemorrhoids, which made him gruff as a sore-tailed bear and caused him to be avoided by all who could possibly stay beyond his reach, Lincoln's sympathy was aroused. Once when he was asked why he did not get rid of so unpleasant a creature, he replied: "Well, the fact is the man has no friends. [He] should be taken care of."

All in all, it had been a wearing day, and as Lincoln went to bed that night (having attended to several other less important matters, such as the complaint made to him by "an old lady of genteel appearance" that, despite previous assurances to the contrary, her boarding house near the corner of Tenth and E Streets was about to be commandeered by the War Department; "I know nothing about it myself," he wrote Stanton, "but promised to bring it to your notice") he might well have slept the sleep of nervous

★

exhaustion: unless, that is, he was kept awake by an aching right hand, which had been squeezed and pumped by more than a thousand people in the course of this busy New Year's, or by the knowledge that from now on — or at any rate until he found the man who, as he said, could "face the arithmetic" — he would have to continue to act as his own general-in-chief, as in fact he had been doing all along, leaving the West Pointer who occupied the post at present to act as little more than a clerk, albeit a first-rate one.

★ ★ ★ *I*n the days that followed hard on this, the one touch of relief in a prevailing military gloom was the news that Bragg had retreated from Stones River and that Rosecrans had taken Murfreesboro. Lincoln would have preferred a bolder pursuit, but he was grateful all the same for what he got. "I can never forget, while I remember anything," he told Rosecrans some months later, looking back, "that at about the end of last year, and beginning of this, you gave us a hard-earned victory which, had there been a defeat instead, the nation could scarcely have lived over." The law of diminishing utility obtained here in reverse; by contrast, this one glimmer swelled to bonfire proportions. All else was blackness — even afloat, where up to now the salt-water navy (so long at least as it had kept to its proper medium and stayed out of the muddy Mississippi) had suffered not a single major check in all the more than twenty months since the opening shots were fired at Sumter. Now suddenly all the news was bad and the checks frequent: not only at Galveston, where Magruder's cotton-clads had wrecked and panicked the Union warships, driving them from the bay, but also at other points along and off the rebel shore, before and after that disaster.

The first of these several naval wounds was self-inflicted, so to speak, or at any rate was not the result of enemy action. This did not make it any less painful or sad, however, for though the loss amounted to only one ship, that one was the most famous in the navy. Under tow off stormy Hatteras, with waves breaking over her deck and starting the oakum from her turret seam, the little ironclad *Monitor* — David to the *Merrimac*'s Goliath in Hampton Roads almost ten months ago — foundered and went to the bottom in the first hour of the last day of the year, taking four of her officers and a dozen of her crew down with her. This was hard news for the North, and close on its heels came word of what happened in Galveston harbor the following day. By way of reaction, the squadron commander at Pensacola ordered the 24-gun screw steamer *Brooklyn* and six gunboats to haul off from the blockade of Mobile and proceed at once to Texas to retrieve the situation. They arrived on January 8, but found there was little they could do except resume the blockade outside the harbor and engage in long-range shelling of the island town, now fast in rebel hands. They kept this up for three days, with little or no profit, until on January 11 they were handed another jolt.

*Lighted by a distress rocket from the Rhode Island, crew-
men of the foundering Monitor (left foreground)
abandon ship in heavy seas off stormy Cape Hatteras.*

About an hour before sundown the *Brooklyn*'s lookout spotted a
bark-rigged vessel, apparently a merchantman, approaching from the south.
When she saw the blockaders she halted as if surprised, and the Union flag officer, finding her manner suspicious, ordered the 10-gun sidewheel steamer *Hatteras* to heave her to for investigation of her papers. As the gunboat approached, she drew off and the chase began. It was a strange business. She ran
awkwardly, despite the trimness of her lines, and though she managed to maintain her distance, on through twilight into a moonless darkness relieved only by
the stars, the blockader had no difficulty in keeping her within sight. At last she
hove to, as if exhausted, her sails furled. The *Hatteras* closed to within a hundred yards, stopped dead, and put a boat out. Before the boarding party
reached her, however, a loud clear voice identified the vessel: "This is the Confederate States steamer *Alabama;* FIRE!" and a broadside lurched her sideways
in the water, striking the *Hatteras* hard amidships so that she too recoiled, as
if in horror. Ten guns to eight, the Federal outweighed her adversary by one

hundred tons, but the advantage of surprise was decisive. Though she promptly returned the fire, the fight was brief. Within thirteen minutes, her walking beam shot away and her magazine flooded, she hoisted the signal for surrender.

"Have you struck?"

"I have."

"Cease fire! Cease fire!"

Within another six minutes she was on the bottom, thirty-fifth on the list of vessels taken, sunk, or ransomed by Captain Raphael Semmes, who would add another thirty-six to the list before the year was out.

He had read in captured Boston newspapers that the 30,000-man expedition under Banks was scheduled to rendezvous off Galveston on January 10 for the conquest of Texas, and he had shown up the following day, intending to get among the transports under cover of darkness, just outside the bar, and sink them left and right. When he saw the gunboats shelling the town, however, he knew it had been retaken, and he seized the opportunity to realize his life's ambition to stage a hand-to-hand fight with an enemy warship, provided he could lure one into pursuit and single combat: which he had done, fluttering just beyond her reach like a wounded bird until, having her altogether to himself, he turned and pounced. He was proud of the outcome of this "first yardarm engagement between steamers at sea," but just now his problem was to get away before his victim's friends, warned of the hoax by the flash and roar of guns, came up to avenge her. Pausing long enough to pick up the 118 survivors — about as many as he had in his whole crew, whose only casualty was a carpenter's mate with a cheek wound — he doused his lights and made off through the night. The *Brooklyn* and the other gunboats, arriving shortly thereafter, saw no sign of the *Hatteras* until dawn showed bits of her wreckage tossed about by the waves. By that time the *Alabama* was nearly a hundred miles away, running hard for Jamaica, where Semmes and his crew — that "precious set of rascals," as he called them, being known in turn as "Old Beeswax" because of the needle-sharp tips to his long black mustache — would parole their captives and celebrate their exploit. Chagrined, the Union skippers turned back to resume their fruitless shelling of the island, bitterly conscious of the fact that instead of redeeming the late Galveston disaster, as they intended, they had enlarged it.

Word of this no sooner reached Washington than it was followed, four days later, by news that was potentially even worse. At Mobile, where the departure of the *Brooklyn* and her consorts had weakened the cordon drawn across the entrance to the bay, the other famous Confederate raider *Florida* had been bottled up since early September, when she slipped in through the blockade with her crew and captain, Commander John N. Maffitt, down with yellow fever. By now they were very much up and about, however: as they proved on the night of January 15, when they steered the rebel cruiser squarely between two of the largest and fastest ships in the blockade squadron and made unscathed for the open sea, leaving her frantic pursuers far behind. Within ten days she had captured and sunk three U.S. merchantmen, the first of more than twenty she would take before midsummer, in happy rivalry with her younger sister the *Alabama*. Secretary Welles had been so furious over her penetration of the cordon, four months back, that he had summarily dismissed the squadron commander from the navy, despite the fact that he was a nephew of Commodore Edward Preble of *Constitution* fame; but this repetition of the exploit, outward bound, was seen by some as a reflection on the Secretary himself and a substantiation of the protest a prominent New Yorker had made to Lincoln, on the occasion of the Connecticut journalist's appointment, that if he would "select an attractive figurehead, to be adorned with an elaborate wig and luxuriant whiskers, and transfer it from the prow of a ship to the entrance of the Navy Department, it would in my opinion be quite as serviceable . . . and less expensive."

Nor was this by any means the last bad news to reach the Department from down on the Gulf before the month was out. On January 21, at the end of the week that had opened with the *Florida*'s escape, John Magruder staged in Texas — apparently, like Browning's thrush, lest it be thought that the first had been no more than a fine careless rapture — a reënactment of the previous descent on the Union flotilla in Galveston harbor. This time the scene was Sabine Pass, eighty miles to the east, and once more two cotton-clad steamboats were employed, with like results. The *Morning Light*, a sloop of war, and the schooner *Velocity,* finding themselves unable to maneuver in all the confusion, struck their flags and surrendered 11 guns and more than a hundred seamen to the jubilant Confederates who had come booming down the pass with a rattle of small arms and a caterwaul of high-pitched rebel yells. Next day the blockade was reëstablished by gunboats sent over from the flotilla cruising off Galveston, but there was little satisfaction in the fact, considering the increase of tension in the wardrooms and on lookout stations. However, a lull now followed, almost as if the crowing rebels were giving the bluejackets time to digest the three bitter pills administered in the course of the past three weeks.

★ ★ ★ **F**or Lincoln there was no such lull, nor did there seem likely to be one so long as the present commander of the Army of the Potomac remained at his post. He had chosen Burnside primarily as a man of action, and however far the ruff-whiskered general had fallen short of other expectations, from the day of his appointment he had never done less than his fervent best to measure up to this one. The Fredericksburg fight, pressed despite a snarl-up of preparatory matters which had turned it into something quite different from what had been intended at the outset, was an instance of that determination to be up and doing, and Lincoln

★

was in constant trepidation that a similar sequence of snarl-ups — the canceled year-end maneuver, for example — presaged a similar disaster. The signs were unmistakably there.

Four days after the New Year's conference Burnside informed the President that he still intended to attempt another Rappahannock crossing, and had in fact alerted his engineers, although his generals practically unanimously remained opposed to the movement. Inclosed with the note was his resignation; Lincoln could either sustain him or let him return to civilian life. Another letter went to Halleck this same day. "I do not ask you to assume any responsibility in reference to the mode or place of crossing," Burnside wrote, "but it seems to me that, in making so hazardous a movement, I should receive some general directions from you as to the advisability of crossing at some point, as you are necessarily well informed of the effect at this time upon other parts of the army of a success or a repulse." However, this attempt to wring a definite personal commitment from the general-in-chief was no more productive than Lincoln's had been. Halleck — described by a correspondent as resembling "an oleaginous Methodist parson in regimentals," with a "large, tabular, Teutonic" face — replied on January 7, administering an elementary textbook strategy lecture. He had always been in favor of an advance, he said, but he cautioned Burnside to "effect a crossing in a position where we can meet the enemy on favorable or even equal terms. . . . If the enemy should concentrate his forces at the place you have selected for a crossing, make it a feint and try another place. Again, the circumstances at the time may be such as to render an attempt to cross the entire army not advisable. In that case theory suggests that, while the enemy concentrates at that point, advantages can be gained by crossing smaller forces at other points, to cut off his lines, destroy his communication, and capture his rear guards, outposts, &c. The great object is . . . to injure him all you can with the least injury to yourself. . . . As you yourself admit, it devolves upon you to decide upon the time, place, and character of the crossing which you may attempt. I can only advise that an attempt be made, and as early as possible. Very respectfully, your obedient servant, H. W. Halleck, General-in-Chief."

Burnside had asked for "general directions." What he got was very general advice. Tacked onto it, however, was a presidential indorsement in which, after urging him to "be cautious, and do not understand that the Government or the country is driving you," Lincoln added: "I do not yet see how I could profit by changing the command of the Army of the Potomac, and if I did, I should not do it by accepting the resignation of your commission." The "yet" might well have given Burnside pause, but at any rate he had a sort of left-handed reply to his ultimatum demanding that the President either fire or sustain him. He prepared therefore to go ahead with his plan for an upstream crossing, beyond Lee's left, and a southward march to some rearward point

★

athwart the Confederate lines of supply and communication. This time he intended to guard against failure by feeling his way carefully beforehand. After originally selecting United States Ford as the bridgehead, a dozen miles above Fredericksburg, he rejected it when a cavalry reconnaissance showed the position well covered by Confederate guns, and selected instead Banks Ford, which was not only less heavily protected but was also less than half as far away. By January 19 his preparations were complete. Next morning his soldiers assembled under full packs for the march, stood there while a general order was read to them, and set out with its spirited phrases ringing in their ears: "The commanding general announces to the Army of the Potomac that they are about to meet the enemy once more. . . . The auspicious moment seems to have arrived to strike a great and mortal blow to the rebellion, and to gain that decisive victory which is due to the country."

It took several hours for so many men to clear their camps, but once this had been done the march went well — indeed, auspiciously — until midafternoon, when a slow drizzle began. For a time it seemed no more than a passing shower, but the sun went down behind a steely curtain of true rain, which was pattering steadily by nightfall. All night it fell; by morning it was drumming without letup. Looking out from their sodden bivouacs, in which they could find not even enough dry twigs for boiling coffee, the soldiers could hardly recognize yesterday's Virginia. "The whole country was an ocean of mud," one wrote. "The roads were rivers of deep mire, and the heavy rain had made the ground a vast mortar bed." Presently, as the troops fell in coffeeless to resume the march in a downpour that showed no sign of slacking, broad-tired wagons loaded with big pontoons (despite all Burnside's precautions against snarl-ups, the pontoniers had been late in getting the word) churned the roads to near-impassability. Their six-mule teams were doubled and even tripled, but to small avail. Then long ropes were attached to the cumbersome things, affording hand-holds for as many as 150 men at a time, but this still did no real good according to a correspondent who watched them strain and fail: "They would flounder through the mire for a few feet — the gang of Lilliputians with their huge-ribbed Gulliver — and then give up breathlessly." Guns were even more perverse. Whole regiments pulled them along with the help of prolonges, leaving deep troughs in the roadbed to mark their progress, but if they stopped for a breather, without first putting brush or logs under the axle, the gun would begin to sink and, what was worse, would keep on sinking until only its muzzle showed, and the men would have to dig it out with shovels. "One might fancy that some new geologic cataclysm had overtaken the world," a reporter declared, surveying the desolation, "and that he saw around him the elemental wrecks left by another Deluge." When Burnside himself, trailing a gaudy kite-tail of staff officers, came riding through this waste of mired confusion, one irrev-

Foiled by an unrelenting winter, Burnside's second attempt to move on Fredericksburg sealed his fate. Days after his mud march, he was relieved of command.

erent teamster whose mules and wagon were stalled like all the rest called out to him across the sea of mud: "General, the auspicious moment has arrived!"

He was undaunted, even in the face of this. Though the rain was still coming down steadily, without a suggestion of a pause, and though most of his soldiers were thinking, as one recalled, that "it was no longer a question of how to go forward, but how to get back," Burnside no more had it in mind to quit now than he had had six weeks ago, when he had kept throwing some of these same men against the fuming base of Marye's Heights. Today was finished but there was still tomorrow, and he gave orders that the march would be resumed at dawn. However, in an attempt to raise the dejected spirits of the troops, he directed that a ration of whiskey be issued to all ranks. Somehow the barrels were brought up in the night and the distribution made next morning. The result, in several cases — for the officers poured liberally and the stuff went into empty stomachs — was spectacular. For example, rival regiments from Pennsylvania and Massachusetts promptly decided the time had come for them to settle a long-term feud, and when a Maine outfit stepped in to try and stop the scuf-

★

fle, the result was the biggest three-sided fist fight in the history of the world. Meanwhile, from grandstand seats on the crests of hills across the way, the rebels were enjoying all of this enormously. Pickets jeered from the south bank of the Rappahannock, and one butternut cluster went so far as to hold up a crudely lettered placard: THIS WAY TO RICHMOND, underlined with an arrow pointing in the opposite direction. Finally, about noon, even Burnside saw the hopelessness of the situation. He gave orders and the long, bedraggled files of men faced painfully about. The Mud March — so called in the official records — was over.

It was over, that is for most of them, except for the getting back to camp and the consequences. For some, though, it was over then and there; they kept slogging northward, right on out of the war. Desertion reached an all-time high. Sick lists had never been so long. Morale hit an all-time low. "I never knew so much discontent in the army before," an enlisted diarist wrote. "A great many say that they 'don't care whether school keeps or not,' for they think there is a destructive fate hovering over our army." This reaction was by no means limited to the ranks, and what was more the men in higher positions were specific in their placement of the blame. "I came to the conclusion that Burnside was fast losing his mind," Franklin was presently saying, and Hooker was even more emphatic in the expression of his views. Without limiting his criticism to the luckless army commander, whom he considered merely inept, he told a newsman that the President was an imbecile, not only for keeping Burnside on but also in his own right, and that the administration itself was "all played out." What the country needed, Fighting Joe declared, and the sooner the better, too, was a dictator.

Much of this reached army headquarters in one form or another, and Burnside's thin-stretched patience finally snapped under the double burden of abuse and ridicule. Early next evening, January 23, while his troops were still straggling forlornly back to their camps, he wired Lincoln: "I have prepared some very important orders, and I want to see you before issuing them. Can I see you alone if I am at the White House after midnight?"

In mud and fog and darkness he left headquarters about 9 o'clock in an ambulance, lost the road, found it, then lost it again, bumping into dead mules, stalled caissons, and other derelicts of the late lamented march. Finally, near midnight, he arrived at the Falmouth railhead, two miles from his starting point, only to learn that the special locomotive he had ordered held had given him up and chuffed away on other business. He took a lantern and set out down the track to meet it coming back, flagged and boarded it, and at last got onto a steamer at Aquia Landing. It was midmorning before he was with Lincoln at the White House, but the orders he brought for his perusal were no less startling for having been delayed. What Burnside was suggesting — in fact *ordering*, "subject to the approval of the President" — was the immediate dismissal of four officers from the service and the relief of six from further duty with the Army of the Potomac. The first group was headed by Joe Hooker, who was referred to as "a man unfit to hold an important commission during a crisis like the present, when so much patience, charity, confidence, consideration, and patriotism are due from every soldier in the field." Next came Brigadier General W.T.H. Brooks, a division commander accused of "using language tending to demoralize his command." The other two, lumped together in one paragraph, were Newton and Cochrane, whose names Burnside had learned simply by checking the morning reports to see what general officers had been on pass at the time of their late-December conference with Lincoln. These four were to be cashiered. The six who were to be relieved were two major generals — Franklin and W. F. Smith, Newton's and Cochrane's corps commander — three brigadiers (including, by some strange oversight, Cochrane, who supposedly had just been cashiered) and one lieutenant colonel, a lowly assistant adjutant who was apparently to be struck by an incidental pellet from the blast that was to bring down all those other, larger birds.

Burnside left the order with the startled President, telling him plainly to make a choice between approving it or accepting its author's resignation from command of an army that included such a set of villains. The order was dated the 23d, a Friday. Lincoln took what was left of Saturday to think the matter over. Then on Sunday, January 25, the ruff-whiskered general got his answer in the form of a general order of Lincoln's own, directing: 1) that Burnside

Joseph Hooker (seated second from right), who had pleaded with Burnside to cease the disastrous assaults on Marye's Heights, was given command of the Army of the Potomac.

★

be relieved of command, upon his own request; 2) that Sumner be relieved, also upon his own request; 3) that Franklin be relieved, period; and 4) "that Maj. Gen. J. Hooker be assigned to the command of the Army of the Potomac."

This last was a hard thing for the departing commander to accept. He had planned to blow up Hooker, but instead he had blown himself up, and Hooker into his place. It was hard, too, for Sumner and for Franklin; the fact that both were the new commander's seniors necessitated their transfer after long association with the eastern army. Lincoln did not so much regret having to sidetrack Franklin, whose lack of aggressiveness at South Mountain and Fredericksburg was notorious, but he was sorry to have to offend the superannuated Sumner, who had saved the day at Fair Oaks and fought well on every field until his soul was sickened by the slaughter at Antietam. Nor had he hurt without regret the normally good-natured Burnside, whose forthright honesty in admission of faults and acceptance of blame was so different from what was ordinarily encountered. However, what there had been of hesitation was mainly based on what Lincoln knew of Fighting Joe himself, who was next in line for the assignment. He had heard from others beside Burnside of Hooker's infidelity to his chief, and also of his excoriation of the Washington authorities. In fact, when the *Times* reporter who had talked recently with Hooker came to Lincoln on this Sunday and told him of what the general had said about the administration's shortcomings and the need for a dictator, Lincoln showed no trace of surprise. "That is all true; Hooker does talk badly," he admitted. But he decided, all the same, that Hooker was what the army and the country needed in the present crisis — a fighter who, unlike Burnside, had self-confidence and a reputation for canniness. "Now there is Joe Hooker," Lincoln had remarked a short time back. "He can fight. I think that is pretty well established."

And so it was. Without consulting Halleck or Stanton or anyone else, and despite the admitted risk to the national cause and the incidental injury to Burnside and Sumner, he made his choice and acted on it. However, before the new commander had been two days at his post, Lincoln sent for him and handed him a letter which was calculated to let him know how much he knew about him, as well as to advise him of what was now expected.

> *General:*
>
> *I have placed you at the head of the Army of the Potomac. Of course I have done this upon what appear to me to be sufficient reasons, and yet I think it best for you to know that there are some things in regard to which I am not quite satisfied with you.*

★

I believe you to be a brave and a skillful soldier, which of course I like. I also believe you do not mix politics with your profession, in which you are right. You have confidence in yourself, which is a valuable if not an indispensable quality. You are ambitious, which, within reasonable bounds, does good rather than harm; but I think that during General Burnside's command of the army you have taken counsel of your ambition and thwarted him as much as you could, in which you did a great wrong to the country and to a most meritorious and honorable brother officer. I have heard, in such way as to believe it, of your recently saying that both the army and the government needed a dictator. Of course it was not for this, but in spite of it, that I have given you the command. Only those generals who gain successes can set up dictators. What I now ask of you is military success, and I will risk the dictatorship. The government will support you to the utmost of its ability, which is neither more nor less than it has done and will do for all commanders. I much fear that the spirit which you have aided to infuse into the army, of criticising their commander and withholding confidence from him, will now turn upon you. I shall assist you as far as I can to put it down. Neither you nor Napoleon, if he were alive again, could get any good out of an army while such a spirit prevails in it.

And now, beware of rashness. Beware of rashness, but with energy and sleepless vigilance go forward and give us victories.

Yours very truly

A. LINCOLN

★ ★ ★

★

179

The Tigress lies moored between two Federal transports. She served as Grant's command boat at the Battle of Shiloh and as McClernand's on the Mississippi River.

SEVEN

Arkansas Post; Transmississippi; Grant

1863 ★ ★ ★ ★ ★ ★ McClernand, conferring with Sherman at Milliken's Bend on the day after his arrival from upriver — it was January 3; the two were aboard the former Illinois politician's headquarters boat, the *Tigress,* tied up to bank twenty-odd miles above Vicksburg — did not blame the red-haired Ohioan for the repulse suffered earlier that week at Chickasaw Bluffs; Sherman, he said in a letter to Stanton that same day, had "probably done all in the present case anyone could have done." The fault was Grant's, and Grant's alone. Grant had designed the operation and then, taking off half-cocked in his eagerness for glory that was rightfully another's, had failed to coöperate as promised, leaving Sherman to hold the bag and do the bleeding. So McClernand said, considerably embittered by the knowledge that a good part of the nearly two thousand casualties lost up the Yazoo were recruits he had been sending down from Cairo for the past two months, only to have them snatched from under him while his back was turned. "I believe I am superseded. Please advise me," he had wired Lincoln as soon as he got word of what was afoot. But permission to go downriver had not come in time for him to circumvent the circumvention; the fighting was over before he got there. He took what consolation he could from having been spared a share in a fiasco. At least he was with his men again — what was left of them, at any rate — and ready to take

★

over. "Soon as I shall have verified the condition of the army," he told Stanton, "I will assume command of it."

He did so the following day. Christening his new command "The Army of the Mississippi" in nominal expression of his intentions, or at any rate his hopes, he divided it into two corps of two divisions each, the first under George Morgan and the second under Sherman — which, incidentally, was something of a bitter pill for the latter to swallow, since he believed a large share of the blame for the recent failure up the Yazoo rested with Morgan, who had promised that in ten minutes he would "be on those hills," but who apparently had forgot to wind his watch. However that might be, McClernand now had what he had been wanting all along: the chance to prove his ingenuity and demonstrate his mettle in independent style. His eyes brightened with anticipation of triumph as he spoke of "opening the navigation of the Mississippi," of "cutting my way to the sea," and so forth. For all the expansiveness of his mood, however, the terms in which he expressed it were more general than specific; or, as Sherman later said, "the *modus operandi* was not so clear."

An ambitious political appointee, General John McClernand, led the Federal attack on Arkansas Post.

In this connection — being anxious, moreover, to balance his recent defeat with a success — the Ohioan had a suggestion. During the Chickasaw Bluffs expedition the packet *Blue Wing,* coming south out of Memphis with a cargo of mail and ammunition, had been captured by a Confederate gunboat that swooped down on her near the mouth of the Arkansas and carried her forty miles up that river to Arkansas Post, an outpost established by the French away back in 1685, where the rebels had constructed an inclosed work they called Fort Hindman, garrisoned by about 5000 men. So long as this threat to the main Federal supply line existed, Sherman said, operations against Vicksburg would be subject to such harassment, and it was his belief that, by way of preamble to McClernand's larger plans — whatever they were, precisely — he ought to go up the Arkansas and abolish the threat by "thrashing out Fort Hindman."

McClernand was not so sure. He had suffered no defeat that needed canceling, and what was more he had larger things in mind than the capture of an obscure and isolated post. However, he agreed to go with Sherman for a discussion of the project with Porter, whose coöperation would be required. They steamed downriver and found the admiral aboard his headquarters boat, the *Black Hawk,* anchored in the mouth of the Yazoo. It was late, near midnight; Porter received them in his nightshirt. He too was not so sure at first. He was short of coal, he said, and the ironclads, which would be needed to reduce the fort, could not burn wood. Presently, though, as Sherman continued to press his suit, asking at least for the loan of a couple of gunboats, which he offered to tow up the river and thus save coal, Porter — perhaps reflecting that he had on his record that same blot which a victory would erase — not only agreed to give the landsmen naval support; "Suppose I go along myself?" he added. Suddenly, on second thought, McClernand was convinced: so much so, indeed, that instead of merely sending Sherman to do the job with half the troops, as Sherman had expected, he decided it was worth the undivided attention of the whole army and its commander, whose record, if blotless, was also blank. With no minus to cancel, this plus would stand alone, auspicious, and make a good beginning as he stepped off on the road that led to glory and the White House.

He took three days to get ready, then (but not until then) sent a message by way of Memphis to notify Grant that he was off — one of his purposes being, as he said, "the counteraction of the moral effect of the failure of the attack near Vicksburg and the reinspiration of the forces repulsed by making them the champions of new, important, and successful enterprises." He left Milliken's Bend that same day, January 8, his 30,000 soldiers still aboard their fifty transports, accompanied by 13 rams and gunboats, three of which were ironclads and packed his Sunday punch. By way of deception the flotilla steamed past the mouth of the Arkansas, then into the White, from which a cutoff led back into the by-passed river. Late the following afternoon the troops began debarking three miles below Fort Hindman, a square bastioned work set on high ground at the head of a horseshoe bend, whose dozen guns included three 9-inch Columbiads, one to each riverward casemate, and a hard-hitting 8-inch rifle. A good portion of the defending butternut infantry, supported by six light pieces of field artillery, occupied a line of rifle-pits a mile and a half below the fort, but these were quickly driven out when the gunboats forged ahead and took them under fire from the flank. Late the following afternoon, when the debarkation had been completed and the four divisions were maneuvering for positions from which to launch an assault, the ironclads took the lead. The *Louisville,* the *De Kalb,* and the *Cincinnati* advanced in line abreast to within four hundred yards of the fort, pressing the attack bows on, one to each casemate, while the thinner-skinned vessels followed close behind to throw in canister and light rifled shell. It was hot work for a time as the

Federal gunboats loose a storm of shot and shell over Confederate Fort Hindman, or Arkansas Post. On shore Union troops march to seize the garrison.

defenders stood to their guns, firing with precision; the *Cincinnati,* for example, took eight hits from 9-inch shells on her pilot house alone, though Porter reported proudly that they "glanced off like peas against glass"; the only naval casualties were suffered from unlucky shots that came in through the ports. When the admiral broke off the fight because of darkness, the fort was silent, apparently overwhelmed. But when Sherman, reconnoitering by moonlight, drew close to the enemy outposts he could hear the Confederates at work with spades and axes, drawing a new line under cover of their heavy guns and preparing to continue to resist despite the long numerical odds. Crouched behind a stump in the predawn darkness of January 11 he heard a rebel bugler sound what he later called "as pretty a reveille as I ever listened to."

Shortly before noon he sent word that he was ready. His corps was on the right, Morgan's on the left; both faced the newly drawn enemy line which extended across the rear of the fort, from the river to an impassable swamp one mile west. McClernand, having established a command post in the woods and sent a lookout up a tree to observe and report the progress of events, passed the word to Porter, who ordered the ironclads forward at 1.30 to renew yesterday's attack. Sherman heard the clear ring of the naval guns, the fire increasing in volume and

★

rapidity as the range was closed. Then he and Morgan went forward, the troops advancing by rushes across the open fields, "once or twice falling to the ground," as Sherman said, "for a sort of rest or pause." As they approached the fort they saw above its parapet the pennants of the ironclads, which had smothered the heavy guns by now and were giving the place a close-up pounding. Simultaneously, white flags began to break out all along the rebel line. "Cease firing! Cease firing!" Sherman cried, and rode forward to receive the fort's surrender.

But that was not to be: not just yet, at any rate, and not to Sherman. Colonel John Dunnington, the fort's commander, a former U.S. naval officer, insisted on surrendering to Porter, and Brigadier General Thomas J. Churchill, commander of the field force, did not want to surrender at all. As Sherman approached, Churchill was arguing with his subordinates, wanting to know by whose authority the white flags had been shown. (He had received an order from Little Rock the night before, while there was still a chance to get away, "to hold out till help arrives or until all dead" — which Holmes later explained with the comment: "It never occurred to me when the order was issued that such an overpowering command would be devoted to an end so trivial.") One brigade commander, Colonel James Deshler of Alabama, a fiery West Pointer in his late twenties — "small but very handsome," Sherman called him — did not want to stop fighting even now, with the Yankees already inside his works. When Sherman, wishing as he said "to soften the blow of defeat," remarked in a friendly way that he knew a family of Deshlers in his home state and wondered if they were relations, the Alabamian hotly disclaimed kinship with anyone north of the Ohio River; whereupon the red-headed general changed his tone and, as he later wrote, "gave him a piece of my mind that he did not relish." However, all this was rather beside the point. The fighting was over and the butternut troops stacked arms. The Federals had suffered 31 navy and 1032 army casualties, for a total of 140 killed and 923 wounded. The Confederates, on the other hand, had had only 109 men hit; but that left 4791 to be taken captive, including a regiment that marched in from Pine Bluff during the surrender negotiations.

McClernand, who had got back aboard the *Tigress* and come forward, was tremendously set up. "Glorious! Glorious!" he kept exclaiming. "My star is ever in the ascendant." He could scarcely contain himself. "I had a man up a tree," he said. "I'll make a splendid report!"

★ ★ ★ *G*rant by now was in Memphis. He had arrived the day before, riding in ahead of the main body, which was still on the way under McPherson, near the end of its long retrogade movement from Coffeeville, northward through the scorched wreckage of Holly Springs, then westward by way of Grand Junction and LaGrange. Having heard no word from Sherman, he knew nothing of his friend's defeat downriver

— optimistic as always, he was even inclined to credit rumors that the Vicksburg defenses had crumbled under assault from the Yazoo — until the evening of his arrival, when he received McClernand's letter from Milliken's Bend informing him of the need for "reinspiration of the forces repulsed."

This was something of a backhand slap, at least by implication — McClernand seemed to be saying that he would set right what Grant had bungled — but what disturbed him most was the Illinois general's expressed intention to withdraw upriver for what he called "new, important, and successful enterprises." For one thing, if Banks was on the way up from New Orleans in accordance with the instructions for a combined assault on Vicksburg, it would leave him unsupported when he got there. For another, any division of effort was wrong as long as the true objective remained unaccomplished, and Grant said so in no uncertain terms next morning when he replied to McClernand's letter: "I do not approve of your move on the Post of Arkansas while the other is in abeyance. It will lead to the loss of men without a result. . . . It might answer for some of the purposes you suggest, but certainly not as a military movement looking to the accomplishment of the one great result, the capture of Vicksburg. Unless you are acting under authority not derived from me, keep your command where it can soonest be assembled for the renewal of the attack on Vicksburg. . . . From the best information I have, Milliken's Bend is the proper place for you to be, and unless there is some great reason of which I am not advised you will immediately proceed to that point and await the arrival of reinforcements and General Banks's expedition, keeping me fully advised of your movements."

He expressed his opinion more briefly in a telegram sent to Halleck that afternoon: "General McClernand has fallen back to White River, and gone on a wild-goose chase to the Post of Arkansas. I am ready to reinforce, but must await further information before knowing what to do." The general-in-chief replied promptly the following morning, January 12: "You are hereby authorized to relieve General McClernand from command of the expedition against Vicksburg, giving it to the next in rank or taking it yourself."

Grant now had what he wanted. Formerly he had moved with caution in the prosecution of his private war, by no means sure that in wrecking McClernand he would not be calling down the thunder on his own head; but not now. Halleck almost certainly would have discussed so important a matter with Lincoln before adding this ultimate weapon to Grant's arsenal and assuring him that there would be no restrictions from above as to its use. In short, Grant could proceed without fear of retaliation except from the victim himself, whom he outranked. However, two pieces of information that came to hand within the next twenty-four hours forestalled delivery of the blow. First, he learned that Port Hudson was a more formidable obstacle than he had formerly supposed, which meant that it was unlikely that Banks's upriver thrust would reach Vicks-

★

burg at any early date. And, second, he received next day from McClernand himself the "splendid report" announcing the fall of Arkansas Post and the capture of "a large number of prisoners, variously estimated at from 7000 to 10,000, together with all [their] stores, animals, and munitions of war." Not only was the urgency for a hookup with Banks removed, but to proceed against McClernand now would be to attack a public hero in his first full flush of victory; besides which, Grant had also learned that the inception of what he had called the "wild-goose chase" had been upon the advice of his friend Sherman, and this put a different complexion on his judgment as to the military soundness of the expedition. All that remained was to play the old army game — which Grant well knew how to do, having had it played against him with such success, nine years ago in California, that he had been nudged completely out of the service. When the time came for pouncing he would pounce, but not before. Meanwhile he would wait, watching and building up his case as he did so.

This did not mean that he intended to sit idly by while McClernand continued to gather present glory; not by a long shot. Four days later, January 17 — McClernand having returned as ordered to the Mississippi, awaiting further instructions at Napoleon, just below the mouth of the Arkansas — Grant got aboard a steamboat headed south from the Memphis wharf. Before leaving he wired McPherson, who had called a halt at LaGrange to rest his troops near the end of their long retreat from Coffeeville: "It is my present intention to command the expedition down the river in person."

★ ★ ★ Banks was going to be a lot longer in reaching Vicksburg than Grant knew, and more was going to detain him than the guns that bristled atop the bluff at Port Hudson. After a sobering look at this bastion he decided that his proper course of action, before attempting a reduction of that place or a sprint past its frowning batteries, would be a move up the opposite bank of the big river, clearing out the various nests of rebels who otherwise would interfere with his progress by harassing his flank as he moved upstream. Brigadier General Godfrey Weitzel, a twenty-eight-year-old West Pointer who already had been stationed in that direction by Ben Butler, was reinforced by troops from the New Orleans and Baton Rouge garrisons and told to make the region west of those two cities secure from molestation. He built a stout defensive work at Donaldsonville, commanding the head of Bayou La Fourche, and threw up intrenchments at Brashear City, blocking the approach from Berwick Bay. Then, crossing the bay with his mobile force on January 13, he entered and began to ascend the Teche, accompanied by three gunboats. This brought him into sudden contact next morning with Richard Taylor, who fought briefly and fell back, sinking the armed steamer *Cotton* athwart the bayou as he did so, corking it against farther penetration. Weitzel, who had lost 33 killed and wounded, including one of the navy skippers picked off by a sniper, reported proudly as he withdrew: "The Confederate States gunboat *Cotton* is one of the things that were. . . . My men behaved magnificently. I am recrossing the bay."

As a successful operation — the first of what he intended would be many — this was unquestionably gratifying to Banks, who made the most of it in reporting the action to Washington as a follow-up to the bloodless reoccupation of the Louisiana capital. Yet even as he tendered his thanks to Weitzel for "the skillful manner in which he has performed the task confided to him," he could also see much that was foreboding in this small-scale expedition up the Teche. For one thing, the rebels were very much there, though in what numbers he did not know, and for another they would fight, but only as it suited them, choosing the time and place that gave them the best advantage, fading back into the rank undergrowth quite as mysteriously as they had appeared, and then moving forward again as the bluecoats withdrew from what Taylor himself, who knew all its crooks and byways, called "a region of lakes, bayous, jungle, and bog."

From the tangled undergrowth along Bayou Teche in Louisiana, Union sharpshooters fire on the gunners of the Confederate gunboat Cotton.

How long it might take to clear such an army of phantoms from the district, or whether indeed it could ever be done, Banks could not tell. By mid-January, however, he had decided that it would have to be done. His expectations, described in mid-December as "most sanguine," were tempered now by prudence and better acquaintance with the peculiar factors involved. He perceived that they would have to be refashioned to conform to a different schedule before he attempted the reduction of Port Hudson and the eventual link-up with Grant in front of Vicksburg, all those devious hundreds of miles up the tawny Mississippi.

★ ★ ★ *I*n Northwest Arkansas and South Missouri things were not going much better for John Schofield, who had risen from a sickbed to resume command of his army on the morrow of Prairie Grove. They could in fact be said to be going a good deal worse, so far at least as personal vexation was concerned. He had won a battle (or anyhow Blunt and Herron had, with the result that they were about to be promoted over his head) and had followed it up with a lunge at Van Buren, resulting in the destruction of Hindman's stores, before withdrawing to Fayetteville; but he had no sooner regained the presumed security of this pro-Union district, where he expected to enjoy in comparative relaxation his belated but welcome promotion to major general, than he was distracted by a series of explosions in his rear. First, Hindman unleashed his cavalry under Brigadier General John S. Marmaduke, a Missouri-born West Pointer, for an all-out raid on the main Federal supply base at Springfield, a hundred miles north of the point where Schofield was in the process of drawing his lines facing south. On New Year's Eve Marmaduke left Lewisburg, on the north bank of the Arkansas River midway across the state, and reached his objective one week later at the head of 2300 horsemen, many of them picked up along the way and added to the original brigade of veterans under Colonel J. O. Shelby, who had led them on every field since Wilson's Creek. Attacking on January 8 the raiders burned the Springfield depot of supplies and withdrew eastward 45 miles to strike at Hartville on the 11th, with similar results after savage fighting, then turned south through a gale of sleet and snow, gobbling up enemy detachments as they went, and recrossed the White River at Batesville on January 25.

Casualties in the two main fights had been about 250 on each side, in addition to which Marmaduke not only had captured and paroled more than 300 of the enemy in the course of the raid, for the most part turning them loose in bitter weather without their outer garments — "In winter," one observer remarked, "the overcoat-bearing Federal was esteemed especially for his pelt" — but also had destroyed vital reserve supplies and refitted his troopers with arms and equipment greatly superior to the ones they had carried northward. All this came out of Schofield's pocket, so to speak, but that was by no means the most painful aftereffect of the operation. Major General Samuel Curtis, promoted to command of the department as a result of his Pea Ridge victory back in March, took alarm and ordered the Army of the Frontier withdrawn from Fayetteville to protect the penetrated region across the state line in its rear, abolishing at a stroke the hard-won gains of Prairie Grove. Schofield protested, to no avail; Missouri soon had greater need than ever for on-the-spot protection, Marmaduke's excursion having served to bring the guerillas out of hiding and onto the highways, along which new recruits hastened to join the bands reassembling under such leaders as George Todd, David Pool, William C. Anderson, called "Bloody Bill," and William C. Quantrill. Enrolling was a simple process. All a recruit had to do was answer "Yes" to the question: "Will you follow orders, be true to your fellows, and kill all those who serve and support the Union?"

In the wake of this sudden activity, in effect not unlike the upsetting of a beehive, came violent dissension in the ranks of the Union leaders. Curtis, a former Iowa Republican congressman and abolitionist, represented the radical faction, while Schofield, with the support of Governor Hamilton R. Gamble, became the champion of conservative views. Militarily, as well, the two generals were divergent in opinion. Curtis wanted to hold all available troops within the borders of the state in order to use them in putting down troublemakers of all sorts, armed or unarmed; Schofield on the other hand believed in taking the offensive against the Confederates to his front in Arkansas. At length, as the situation grew more tense between the two, Lincoln was appealed to as arbitrator. He backed the department commander, ordering Schofield east of the Mississippi and leaving the hero of Pea Ridge in full control. However, the storm of protest which followed this decision gave promise of greater trouble than ever, and caused him to seek a different solution. Transferring Curtis out to Kansas, where his political views would be more in accord with those of the majority of the people, Lincoln appointed as the new commander of the Department of Missouri old Edwin V. Sumner, lately relieved of duty with the Army of the Potomac. But this did not work either; Sumner died en route.

It was March 21. Breaking his journey at Syracuse, New York, the old soldier lay in a coma, as if in belated reaction to the horror of Antietam, where he had begun to lose the grip that had been strong enough to save the day at Fair Oaks. "The Second Corps never lost a flag or a cannon!" he suddenly cried out. When his aide came over he opened his eyes. "That is true; never lost one," he said weakly. At sixty-six he was nearing the end of forty-four years of army service, and except for his long sharp nose he resembled a death's-head. The aide raised him to a more comfortable position on the bed and poured him a glass of wine, prescribed by the doctor to keep up his strength. Sumner took a sip, saying across the rim of the glass by way of a toast: "God save my country, the United States of America," then dropped the glass and died.

★

A veteran of Antietam, the Peninsula campaign, and the Seven Days' Battles, General Edwin V. Sumner was given command of the Union Department of Missouri but died en route.

Lincoln, receiving the news of Sumner's death, decided that Schofield was probably the best man to take charge in Missouri after all. In reassigning him to duty there, however, he thought it proper to give him some advice on how to proceed among people who were engaged in what he called "a pestilent factional quarrel among themselves." It was, he said in the accents of Polonius, "a difficult role, and so much greater will be the honor if you perform it well. If both factions, or neither, shall abuse you, you will probably be about right. Beware of being assailed by one and praised by the other."

The trouble with this, as advice, was that it was the counsel of perfection, since the only way a man could avoid factions, being championed on the one hand and excoriated on the other, was to stay out of Missouri in the first place. Schofield, a rather plump New York West Pointer who wore a long thin growth of curly whiskers in partial compensation for the fact that he was already balding at the age of thirty-two, was quite aware of this, of course, but promised to do his best in that regard. At the same time, however — it was late spring by then, well up in May — he had to forgo his plans for an offensive into Arkansas, not only because of guerilla troubles within his department (they continued to grow worse as time went by, until at last they exceeded in horror the wildest nightmares Curtis or anyone else, except possibly Bill Anderson and Quantrill — not to mention old John Brown — had ever had) but also because he lacked the troops, Missouri having become in effect a recruiting ground for the support of operations far down the big river that laved its eastern flank. Schofield could only give what he had promised, his best, and if this was not a great deal, under the nearly impossible circumstances it was enough.

★ ★ ★ *H*e could take consolation, however, in the fact that the Confederates to the south were quite as bedeviled as he himself was, though in a different way: with the result that throughout this unhappy season, when so much of military importance was moving inexorably toward a climax on the east flank of the theater, they were no more able to assume the offensive than Schofield was. Not only were they suffering from an even more acute shortage of troops, but a sequence of rapid-fire shifts in command, beginning at the very top, quite paralyzed whatever movements they might otherwise have undertaken.

Not that the shifts were avoidable. It had in fact already become apparent that Holmes had been given a good deal more than he could handle. In mid-January, a week after his return to Richmond from his western journey, Davis sent for Kirby Smith, whom he admired, and assigned him to command the newly created Department of West Louisiana and Texas, intending in this way to relieve Holmes of the task of coördinating the efforts of Taylor and Magruder. "Am I thus to be sent into exile?" Smith asked wistfully. Not yet thirty-nine, he ranked second among the nation's seven lieutenant generals, and Lee himself had lately said that he would be pleased to have him as a corps commander, alongside Longstreet and Jackson. Davis explained that the assignment, far from amounting to exile, was as important as any in the whole Confederacy, since his main duty "would be directed to aiding in the defense of the Lower Mississippi and keeping that great artery of the West effectually closed to Northern occupation or trade." Acquiescing, Smith set out in early February, only to learn en route that his command had been enlarged to include the entire Transmississippi. In the light of this he arranged with Pemberton for the transfer of Major General Sterling Price, who was much admired in the Far West and had formerly been governor of Missouri, the scene of his early victories at Wilson's Creek and Lexington. It was hoped that Price would repeat them presently, although a sadly large proportion of the men with whom he had won them were buried now in shallow graves around Corinth and Iuka, and the survivors, few as they were in number, were too badly needed around Vicksburg to be allowed to recross the river. How he would replace them Smith did not know, for the region had been stripped of troops, first by Van Dorn, who had brought them east after his defeat at Elkhorn Tavern, and then by Hindman, who, by stringent enforcement of the conscription laws, had raised the army which he had taken across the Boston Mountains and then returned with no more than a comparative handful. Smith soon found his worst fears confirmed. "The male population remaining are old men, or have furnished substitutes," he reported, "are lukewarm, or are wrapped up in speculation and money-making."

Crossing at Port Hudson, he ascended Red River in a steamboat Richard Taylor had waiting for him by prearrangement, and on March 7 at Alexandria, Louisiana, he assumed command of all troops west of the Mississippi. What he encountered first-off gave his Regular Army nature quite a shock. "There was no general system, no common head," he later reported; "each district was acting independently." It was necessary, he said, to "begin *de novo* in any attempt at a general systematizing and development of the department resources." Accordingly he set out at once on a preliminary tour of inspection, which only served to increase his first dismay. Conferring with Holmes at Little Rock — the North Carolinian now had charge of the subdepartment including Arkansas, Missouri, and Indian Territory — he found him anxiously awaiting the arrival of Price to command the army remnant left by Hindman, who had resigned in a huff at having been superseded by Holmes on the occasion of that officer's step-down from command of the whole theater. Price arrived before the end of the month, yet there was little he could do until he got his men in condition to fight, which obviously would not be soon. Smith meantime established his headquarters at Shreveport. He considered it "a miserable place with a miserable population," but it had the virtue of central location, at the head of navigation of Red River and on the direct route between Texas and Richmond. Here he set to work, laying the groundwork for organization of the enormous region which in time would be known as Kirby-Smithdom. He worked long hours and did not spare himself or his subordinates; but spring had come, and so had Banks and Grant, before his command — which included, in all, about 30,000 soldiers between the Mississippi and the Rio Grande, fewer even than Bragg had in the Duck River Valley or Pemberton had at Vicksburg and Port Hudson — was in any condition to offer them anything more than a token resistance.

★ ★ ★ 　After an all-night boat ride down the Mississippi, from Memphis past the mouth of the Arkansas, Grant reached Napoleon on January 18 to find McClernand, Porter, and Sherman awaiting his arrival with mixed emotions — mixed, that is, so far as McClernand's were concerned; Porter and Sherman were united, if by nothing more than a mutual and intense dislike of the congressman-turned-commander. To them, Grant came as something of a savior, since he outranked the object of their scorn. To McClernand, on the other hand, he seemed nothing of the sort; McClernand plainly suspected another attempt to steal his thunder, if not his army. He had enlarged his Arkansas Post exploit by sending a pair of gunboats up White River to drive the rebels from St Charles and wreck their installations at De Valls Bluff, terminus of the railroad running east from Little Rock toward Memphis. It was smartly done, accomplishing at the latter place the destruction of the depot and some rolling stock, as well as the capture of two 8-inch guns which the flustered garrison was trying to load aboard the cars for a getaway west. Still at Fort Hindman while this was in progress, McClernand received Grant's curt and critical letter ordering him back to the Mississippi at once, and he bucked it along to Lincoln with a covering letter of his own.

"I believe my success here is gall and wormwood to the clique of West Pointers who have been persecuting me for months," he wrote, imploring his friend and fellow-townsman not to "let me be clandestinely destroyed, or, what is worse, dishonored, without a hearing." He asked, "How can General Grant at a distance of 400 miles intelligently command the army with me?" and answered his own question without a pause: "He cannot do it. It

In mid-January 1863, U. S. Grant took personal command of all forces under McClernand and Sherman and began several experiments aimed at taking Vicksburg.

should be made an independent command, as both you and the Secretary of War, as I believe, originally intended."

Grant was about to get in some licks of his own in this regard, if not through out-of-channels access to Lincoln — whom he had not only never met, but had never even seen, despite the fact that both had gone to war from Illinois — then at any rate through Halleck, which was the next-best thing. For the present he merely conferred with the three officers, collectively and singly, and ordered the return of the whole expedition to Milliken's Bend for a renewal of the drive on Vicksburg by the direct route. By now, however, as a result of his talk with these men who had been there, he was beginning to see that the only successful approach, after all, might have to be roundabout. "What may be necessary to reduce the place I do not yet know," he wired the general-in-chief, "but since the late rains [I] think our troops must get below the city to be used effectually."

He spent the night ashore at Napoleon, whose partial destruction by incendiaries the day before caused Sherman to declare that he was "free to admit we all deserve to be killed unless we can produce a state of discipline when such disgraceful acts cannot be committed unpunished." One solution, he decided, would be "to assess the damages upon the whole army, officers included," but no such drastic remedy was adopted. The following morning Grant saw the transports and their escort vessels steam away south, in accordance with his orders, and returned that evening to Memphis. Next day, January 20, he sent Halleck a long dispatch explaining the tactical situation as he saw it and announcing that, by way of a start, he intended to try his hand at redigging the canal across the base of the hairpin bend in front of Vicksburg, abandoned the previous summer by Butler's men when the two Union fleets were sundered and repulsed by the rebel warship *Arkansas,* now fortunately at the bottom of the river. Grant suggested that, in view of the importance of the campaign he was about to undertake, it would be wise to combine the four western departments, now under Banks, Curtis, Rosecrans, and himself, under a single over-all commander in order to assure coöperation. "As I am the senior department commander in the West," he wrote — apparently unaware that Banks was nine months his senior and in point of fact had been a major general before Grant himself was even a brigadier — "I will state that I have no desire whatever for such combined command, but would prefer the command I now have to any other that can be given." From which disclaimer he passed at once to the subject of John McClernand: "I regard it as my duty to state that I found there was not sufficient confidence felt in General McClernand as a commander, either by the Army or Navy, to insure him success. Of course, all would coöperate to the best of their ability, but still with a distrust. This is a matter I made no inquiries about, but it was thrust upon me." (As a later observer pointed out, there was "a touch of artfulness" in this; Grant "elevated Sherman and Porter to speak for entire branches of the service, then sought audiences with them so that the issue might be forced upon him!") However, he continued, "as it is my intention to command in person, unless otherwise directed, there is no special necessity of mentioning this matter; but I want you to know that others besides myself agree in the necessity of the course I had already determined upon pursuing."

His belief that Old Brains was on his side was strengthened the following day by a quick reply to his suggestion that "both banks of the Mississippi should be under one command, at least during the present operations." "The President has directed that so much of Arkansas as you may desire to control be temporarily attached to your department," Halleck wired. "This will give you control of both banks of the river." Pleased to learn of Lincoln's support, even at second hand, Grant kept busy with administrative and logistical matters preparatory to his departure from Memphis at the earliest possible date. McPherson was marching in from LaGrange with two divisions to accompany him downriver; these 14,979, added to the 32,015 already there, would give him an "aggregate present" of 46,994 in the vicinity of Vicksburg, with more to follow, not only from his own Department of the Tennessee, which included a grand total of 93,816 of all arms, but also from the Department of Missouri, now under Curtis and later under Schofield. On January 25 he received further evidence of Lincoln's interest in the campaign for control of the Lower Mississippi, whose whimsical habit of carving itself new channels the Chief Executive knew from having made two flatboat voyages down it to New Orleans as a youth. "Direct your attention particularly to the canal proposed across the point," Halleck urged. "The President attaches much importance to this."

Grant himself was about ready to embark by now, wiring the general-in-chief this same day: "I leave for the fleet . . . tomorrow." Last-minute details held him up an extra day, but on the 27th he was off. "The work of reducing Vicksburg will take time and men," he had told Halleck the week before, "but can be accomplished."

★ ★ ★ *S*herman was already hard at work on the project which had drawn Lincoln's particular attention, and with his present arduous endeavor — in effect a gigantic wrestling match with Mother Nature herself, or at any rate with her son the Father of Waters — added to his previous bloody experience up the Yazoo, he could testify as to the validity of Grant's long-range observation that the conquest of Vicksburg would "take time and men." In fact, he was inclined to think it might require so much of both commodities as to prove impossible. Both were expendable in the ordinary sense, but after all there were limits. He was discouraged, he wrote his senator brother John this week, by the lack of substantial progress by Union arms, East and West, and by the unexpected resilience

★

of the Confederates, civilian as well as military: "Two years have passed and the rebel flag still haunts our nation's capital. Our armies enter the best rebel territory and the wave closes in behind. The utmost we can claim is that our enemy respects our power to do them physical harm more than they did at first; but as to loving us any more, it were idle even to claim it. . . . I still see no end," he added, "or even the beginning of the end."

Perhaps the senseless burning of Napoleon the week before was on his mind or conscience, but the truth was he had enough on his hands to distress him here and now. The rain continued to come down hard — even harder, perhaps, than it was falling along the Rappahannock, where Burnside's Mud March was coming to its sticky close and the soldiers were composing a parody of a bedtime prayer:

> *Now I lay me down to sleep*
>
> *In mud that's many fathoms deep.*
>
> *If I'm not here when you awake*
>
> *Just hunt me up with an oyster rake*

— with the result that Sherman's men, in addition to having to widen and deepen the old canal, which was little more than a narrow ditch across the base of the low-lying tongue of land, had to work day and night at throwing up a levee along its right flank in order not to be washed away by water from the flooded bayous in their rear. Besides, even if the river could be persuaded to scour out a new channel along this line and thus "leave Vicksburg out in the cold," as Sherman said, it would be no great gain so far as he could see. The Confederates would merely shift their guns southward along the bluff to command the river at and below the outlet, leaving the shovel-weary Federals no better off than before. So he told his brother. And Porter, watching his red-haired friend slosh around in the mud and lose his temper a dozen times a day — "half sailor, half soldier, with a touch of the snapping turtle," he called him — once more found it necessary to bolster Sherman's spirits with hot rum and rollicking words. "If this rain lasts much longer we will not need a canal," he ended a note to the unhappy general on January 27. "I think the whole point will disappear, troops and all, in which case the gunboats will have the field to themselves."

Next day, however, Grant arrived, and Porter, reporting the fact to Welles, could say: "I hope for a better state of things."

★　★　★

★

*Oil fields like this one supported
the boom of the early 1860s
as petroleum became the fuel
and lubricant for expanding
northern industry.*

EIGHT

"Shoddy"; Erlanger; Richmond Bread Riot

1863 ★ ★ ★ ★ ★ ★ The word *shoddy* was comparatively new, having originated during the present century in Yorkshire, where it was used in reference to almost worthless quarry stone or nearly unburnable coal. Crossing the ocean to America it took on other meanings, at first being used specifically to designate an inferior woolen yarn made from fibers taken from worn-out fabrics and reprocessed, then later as the name for the resultant cloth itself. "Poor sleezy stuff," one of Horace Greeley's *Tribune* reporters called it, "woven open enough for sieves, and then filled with shearmen's dust," while *Harper's Weekly* used even harsher words in referring to it as "a villainous compound, the refuse and sweepings of the shop, pounded, rolled, glued, and smoothed to the external form and gloss of cloth, but no more like the genuine article than the shadow is to the substance." Thoroughly indignant, the magazine went on to tell how "soldiers, on the first day's march or in the earliest storm, found their clothes, overcoats, and blankets scattering to the wind in rags or dissolving into their primitive elements of dust under the pelting rain."

It followed that the merchants and manufacturers who supplied the government with such cloth became suddenly and fantastically rich in the course of their scramble for contracts alongside others of their kind, the purveyors of tainted beef and weevily grain, the sellers of cardboard haversacks and leaky

★

tents. No one was really discomforted by all this — so far, at least, as they could see — except the soldiers, the Union volunteers whose sufferings under bungling leaders in battles such as Fredericksburg and Chickasaw Bluffs were of a nature that made their flop-soled shoes and tattered garments seem relatively unimportant, and the Confederate jackals who stripped the blue-clad corpses after the inevitable retreat. If the generals were unashamed, were hailed in fact as heroes after such fiascos, why should anyone else have pangs of conscience? The contractors asked that, meanwhile raking in profits that were as long as they were quick. The only drawback was the money itself, which was in some ways no more real than the sleazy cloth or the imitation leather, being itself the shadow of what had formerly been substance. With prosperity in full swing and gold rising steadily, paper money declined from day to day, sometimes taking sickening drops as it passed from hand to hand. All it seemed good for was spending, and they spent it. Spending, they rose swiftly in the social scale, creating in the process a society which drew upon itself the word that formerly had been used to describe the goods they bartered — "shoddy" — and upon their heads the scorn of those who had made their money earlier and resented the fact that it was being debased. One such was Amos Lawrence, a millionaire Boston merchant. "Cheap money makes speculation, rising prices, and rapid fortunes," Lawrence declared, "but it will not make patriots." He wanted hard times back again. Closed factories would turn men's minds away from gain; then and only then could the war be won. So he believed. "We must have Sunday all over the land," he said, "instead of feasting and gambling."

For the present, though, all that was Sunday about the leaders of the trend which he deplored was their clothes. They wore on weekdays now the suits they once had reserved for wear to church, and as they prospered they bought others, fine broadcloth with nothing shoddy about them except possibly what they inclosed. So garbed, and still with money to burn before it declined still further, the feasters and gamblers acquired new habits and pretensions, with the result that the disparaging word was attached by the New York *World* not only to the new society, but also to the age in which it flourished:

The lavish profusion in which the old southern cotton aristocracy used to indulge is completely eclipsed by the dash, parade, and magnificence of the new northern shoddy aristocracy of this period. Ideas of cheapness and economy are thrown to the winds. The individual who makes the most money — no matter how — and spends the most money — no matter for what — is considered the greatest man. To be extravagant is to be fashionable. These facts sufficiently account for the immense and brilliant audiences at the opera and the theatres, and until the final crash comes such audiences undoubtedly will continue. The world has seen its iron age, its silver age, its golden age, and its brazen age. This is the age of shoddy.

The new brown-stone palaces on Fifth Avenue, the new equipages at the Park, the new diamonds which dazzle unaccustomed eyes, the new silks and satins which rustle overloudly, as if to demand attention, the new people who live in the palaces, and ride in the carriages, and wear the diamonds and silks — all are shoddy. . . . They set or follow the shoddy fashions, and fondly imagine themselves à la mode de Paris, when they are only à la mode de shoddy. They are shoddy brokers on Wall Street, or shoddy manufacturers of shoddy goods, or shoddy contractors for shoddy articles for a shoddy government. Six days in the week they are shoddy business men. On the seventh day they are shoddy Christians.

Nor were journalists and previously wealthy men the only ones to express a growing indignation. Wages had not risen in step with the rising cost of food and rent and other necessities of life, and this had brought on a growth of the trade-union movement, with mass meetings held in cities throughout the North to protest the unequal distribution of advantages and hardships. (Karl Marx was even now at work on *Das Kapital* in London's British Museum, having issued with Friedrich Engels *The Communist Manifesto* fifteen years ago, and Lincoln himself had said in his first December message to Congress: "Labor is prior to, and independent of, capital. Capital is only the fruit of labor, and could never have existed if labor had not first existed. Labor is the superior of capital, and deserves much the higher consideration.") One such meeting, held about this time at Cooper Union, filled the building to capacity while hundreds of people waited outside for word to be passed of what was being said within by delegates on the rostrum; whatever it was was being received with cheers and loud applause, along with a sprinkling of hisses and vehement boos. A representative of the hatters, one McDonough Bucklin, believed that the war was being used by the rich as an excuse for increased exploitation of the poor. As Bucklin put it, "The machinery is forging fetters to bind you in perpetual bondage. It gives you a distracted country with men crying out loud and strong for the Union. Union with them means no more nor less than that they want the war prolonged that they may get the whole of the capital of the country into their breeches pocket and let it out at a percentage that will rivet the chain about your neck." It was the old story: "Every day the rich are getting richer, the poor poorer." Apparently at this point Bucklin got carried away, for a *World* reporter noted that "the speaker made some concluding remarks strongly tainted with communism, which did not meet with general approval."

And yet, for all the offense to the sensibilities of the Boston million-aire, who had made his pile in a different time, as well as to those of the New York journalist, whose indignation was one of the tools he used in earning a living, and the labor delegate, who after all was mainly concerned with the fact that he and his hatters were not getting what he considered a large fair slice of the general pie, much of the undoubted ugliness of the era — the Age of Shoddy, if you will — was little more than the manifest awkwardness of national adolescence, a reaction to growing pains. Unquestionably the growth was there, and unquestionably, too — despite the prevalent gaucherie, the scarcity of grace and graciousness, the ap-parent concern with money and money alone, getting and spending — much of the growth was solid and even permanent. The signs were at hand for everyone to read. "Old King Cotton's dead and buried; brave young Corn is king," was the refrain of a popular song written to celebrate the bumper grain crops being gath-ered every fall, of which the ample surpluses were shipped to Europe, where a coincidental succession of drouths — as if the guns booming and growling be-yond the Atlantic had drawn the rain clouds, magnet-like, and then discharged them empty — resulted in poor harvests which otherwise would have signaled the return of Old World famine. More than five million quarters of wheat and flour were exported to England in 1862, whereas the total in 1859 had been less than a hundred thousand. In the course of the conflict the annual pork pack nearly doubled in the northern states, and the wool clip more than tripled. Meanwhile, industry not only kept pace with agriculture, it outran it. In Philadelphia alone, 180 new factories were established between 1862 and 1864 to accommodate labor-saving devices which had been invented on the eve of war but which now came into their own in response to the accelerated demands of the boom economy of wartime: the Howe sewing machine, for example, which revolutionized the gar-ment industry, and the Gordon McKay machine for stitching bootsoles to uppers, producing one hundred pairs of shoes in the time previously required to finish a single pair by hand. All those humming wheels and clamorous drive-shafts needed oil; and got it, too, despite the fact that no such amounts as were now required had even existed before, so far at least as men had suspected a short while back;

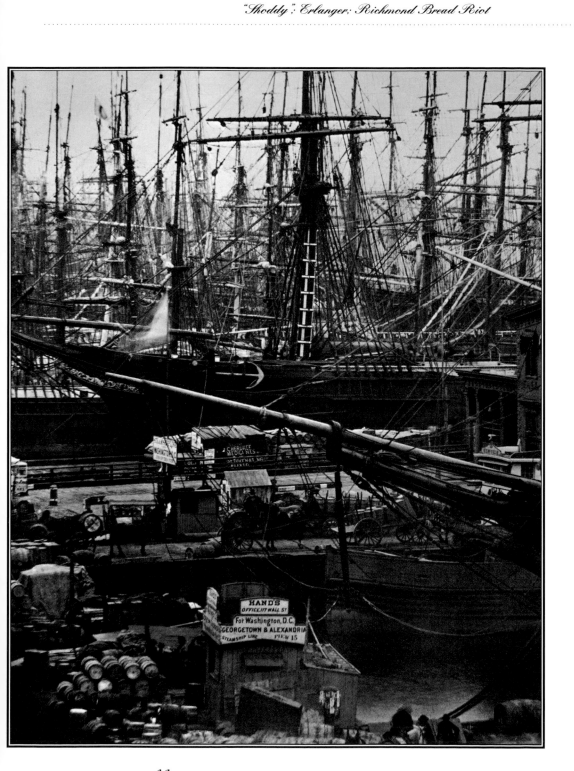

*Merchant ships from around the globe crowd the
docks of New York City's waterfront while cargo in the
foreground awaits shipment to Washington, D.C.*

for within that same brief three-year span the production of petroleum, discovered in Pennsylvania less than two years before Sumter, increased from 84,000 to 128,000,000 gallons. The North was fighting the South with one hand and getting rich with the other behind its back, though which was left and which was right was hard to say. In any case, with such profits and progress involved, who could oppose the trend except a comparative handful of men and women, maimed or widowed or otherwise made squeamish, if not downright unpatriotic, by hard luck or oversubscription to Christian ethics?

A change was coming upon the land, and upon the land's inhabitants; nor was the change merely a dollars-and-cents affair, as likely to pass as to last. Legislation which had long hung fire because of peacetime caution and restraints imposed by jealous Southerners, now departed, came out of the congressional machine about as fast as proponents could feed bills into the hopper. Kansas had become a state and Colorado, Dakota, and Nevada were organized as Territories before the war was one year old, with the result that no part of the national area remained beyond the scope of the national law. Wherever a man went now the law went with him, at least in theory, and this also had its effect. Helping to make room on the eastern seaboard for the nearly 800,000 immigrants who arrived in the course of the conflict — especially from Ireland and Germany, where recruiting agents were hard at work, helping certain northern states to fill their quotas — no less than 300,000 people crossed the prairies, headed west for Pike's Peak or California, Oregon or the new Territories, some in search of gold as in the days of '49 and others to farm the cornlands made available under the Homestead Act of 1862, whereby a settler could stake off a claim to a quarter-section of public land and, upon payment of a nominal fee, call those 160 acres his own; 15,000 such homesteads were settled thus in the course of the war, mostly in Minnesota, amounting in all to some 2,500,000 acres. In this way the development of the Far West continued, despite the distraction southward, while back East the cities grew in wealth and population, despite the double drain in both directions. Nor were the cultural pursuits neglected, and these included more than attendance of the opera as a chance to show off the silks and satins whose rustling had disturbed the *World* reporter. Not only did university enrollments not decline much below what could be accounted for by the departure of southern students, but while the older schools were expanding their facilities with the aid of numerous wartime bequests, fifteen new institutions of higher learning were founded, including Cornell and Swarthmore, Vassar and the Massachusetts Institute of Technology. Campus life was not greatly different as a whole, once the undergraduates and professors grew accustomed to the fact that armies were locked in battle from time to time at various distances off beyond the southern horizon. Interrupted in 1861, for example, the Harvard-Yale boat races were resumed three years later in the midst of the bloodiest season of the war, and not a member of either crew volunteered for service in the army or the navy.

The draft, passed in early January as if in solution of the problem of Fredericksburg losses, hardly affected anyone not willing to be affected or else so miserably poor in these high times as not to be able to scrape up the $300 exemption fee as often as his name or number came up at the periodic drawings, in which case it might be said that he was about as well off in the army as out of it, except for the added discomfort of being drilled and possibly shot at. Large numbers of men from the upper classes, whether recently arrived at that level or established there of old, went to the expense of hiring substitutes (usually immigrants who were brought over by companies newly formed to supply the demand, trafficking thus in flesh to an extent unknown since the stoppage of the slave trade, and who were glad of the chance to earn a nest egg, which included the money they got from the men whose substitutes they were, plus the bounty paid by that particular state to volunteers — minus, of course, the fee that went to the company agent who had got them this opportunity in the first place) not only because it meant that the substitute-hirer was done with the problem of the draft for the duration, but also because it was considered more patriotic. All the same, the parody *We Are Coming, Father Abraham, Three Hundred Dollars More* was greeted with laughter wherever it was heard; for there was no stigma attached to the man who stayed out of combat, however he went about it short of actual dodging or desertion. "In the vast new army of 300,000 which Mr Lincoln has ordered to be raised," one editor wrote, marveling at this gap disclosed in the new prosperity, "there will not be *one* man able to pay $300. Not one! Think of that!"

Washington itself was riding the crest of the wave thrown up by the boom, its ante-bellum population of 60,000 having nearly quadrupled under pressure from the throng of men and women rushing in to fill the partial vacuum created by the departure of the Southerners who formerly had set the social tone. Here the growing pains were the worst of all, according to Lincoln's young secretary John Hay, who wrote: "This miserable sprawling village imagines itself a city because it is wicked, as a boy thinks he is a man when he smokes and swears." In this instance Hay was offended because he and the President, riding back from the Soldiers Home after an interesting talk on philology — for which, he said, Lincoln had "a little indulged inclination" — encountered "a party of drunken gamblers and harlots returning in the twilight from [*erased*]." The fact was, the carousers might have been returning from almost any quarter of the city; for the provost marshal, while unable to give even a rough estimate of the number of houses of prostitution doing business here beside the Potomac, reported 163 gambling establishments in full swing, including one in which a congressman had lately achieved fame by breaking the bank in a single night and leaving with $100,000 bulging his pockets. It was a clutch-and-grab society now, with a clutch-and-grab way of doing business, whether its own or the government's, though it still affected a free and easy manner out of office hours. Nathaniel Hawthorne, in town for a look-round, found that the nation's pulse could be taken better at Willard's Hotel, especially in the bar, than at either the Capitol or the White House. "Everybody may be seen there," he declared. "You exchange nods with governors of sovereign states; you elbow illustrious men, and tread on the toes of generals; you hear statesmen and orators speaking in their familiar tones. You are mixed up with office-seekers, wire pullers, inventors, artists, poets, editors, army correspondents, attachés of foreign journals, long-winded talkers, clerks, diplomats, mail contractors, railway directors, until your own identity is lost among them. You adopt the universal habit of the place, and call for a mint julep, a whiskey skin, a gin cocktail, a brandy smash, or a glass of pure Old Rye; at any hour all these drinks are in request."

Not that there were no evidences of war aside from the uniforms, which were everywhere, and the personal experience of wounds or bereavement. There were indeed. War was the central fact around which life in Washington revolved, and what was more there were constant reminders that war was closely involved with death in its more unattractive forms. Although men with wrecked faces and empty sleeves or trouser-legs no longer drew the attention they once had drawn, other signs were not so easily ignored. Under huge transparencies boasting their skill at embalming, undertakers would buttonhole you on the

By early 1863, uniformed men with empty sleeves or trouser-legs, like those seen here in a Washington crowd, were constant reminders of the horrors of war.

★

street and urgently guarantee that, after receiving payment in advance, they would bring you back from the place where you caught the bullet "as lifelike as if you were asleep," the price being scaled in accordance with your preference for rosewood, pine, or something in between. One section of the city ticked like an oversized clock as the coffinmakers plied their hammers, stocking their shops against the day of battle, the news of which would empty their storerooms overnight and step up the tempo of their hammers in response to the law of supply and demand, as if time itself were hurrying to keep pace with the rush of events. In the small hours of the night, when this cacophonous ticking was stilled, men might toss sleepless on their beds, with dread like a presence in the room and sweat breaking out on the palms and foreheads even of those who knew the horror only by hearsay; but the outward show, by daylight or lamplight, was garish. Pennsylvania Avenue was crowded diurnally, to and beyond its margins of alternate dust and mud, and the plumes and sashes of the blue-clad officers, setting off the occasional gaudy splash of a Zouave, gave it the look of a carnival midway. This impression was heightened by the hawkers of roasted chestnuts and rock candy, and the women also did their part, contributing to the over-all effect the variegated dresses and tall hats that had come into fashion lately, the latter burdened about their incongruously narrow brims "with over-hanging balconies of flowers."

A future historian described them so, finding also in the course of her researches that the ladies "were wearing much red that season." Magenta and Solferino were two of the shades; "warm, bright, amusing names," she called them, derived from far-off battlefields "where alien men had died for some vague cause." Search as she might, however, she could find no shade of red identified with Chickasaw Bluffs, and it was her opinion that the flightiest trollop on the Avenue would have shrunk from wearing a scarlet dress that took its name from Fredericksburg.

★ ★ ★ **A**cross the Atlantic, unfortunately for Confederate hopes of official acceptance into the family of nations, the Schleswig-Holstein problem, unrest in Poland, and the rivalry of Austria and Prussia gave the ministries of Europe a great deal more to think about than the intricacies of what was called "the American question." Aware that any disturbance of the precarious balance of power might be the signal for a general conflagration, they recalled Voltaire's comment that a torch lighted in 1756 in the forests of the new world had promptly wrapped the old world in flames. Russia, by coincidence having emancipated her serfs in the same year the western conflict began, was pro-Union from the start, while France remained in general sympathetic to the South; but neither could act without England, and England could not or would not intervene, being herself divided on the matter. The result, aside from occasional fumbling and inopportune attempts at mediation — mostly on the part of Napoleon III, who had needs and ambitions private and particular to himself — was that Europe, in effect, maintained a hands-off policy with regard to the blood now being shed beyond the ocean.

The double repulse, at Sharpsburg and Perryville, of the one Confederate attempt (so far) to conquer a peace by invasion of the North did not mean to Lord Palmerston and his ministers that the South would necessarily lose the war; far from it. But it did convince these gentlemen that the time was by no means ripe for intervention, as they had recently supposed, and was the basis for their mid-November rejection of a proposal by Napoleon that England, France, and Russia join in urging a North-South armistice, accompanied by a six-month lifting of the blockade. The result, if they had agreed — as they had been warned in no uncertain terms by Seward in private conversations with British representatives overseas — would have been an immediate diplomatic rupture, if not an outright declaration of war: in which connection the London *Times* remarked that "it would be cheaper to keep all Lancashire in turtle and venison than to plunge into a desperate war with the Northern States of America, even with all Europe at our back." No one knew better than Palmerston the calamity that might ensue, for he had been Minister at War from 1812 to 1815, during which period Yankee privateers had sunk about 2500 English ships, almost the entire marine. At that rate, with all those international tigers crouched for a leap in case the head tiger suffered some crippling injury, England not only could not afford to risk the loss of a sideline war; she could not even afford to win one.

Besides, desirable though it was that the flow of American cotton to British spindles be resumed — of 534,000 operatives, less than a quarter were working full time and more than half were out of work entirely; including their dependents, and those of other workers who lost their jobs in ancillary industries, approximately two million people were without means of self-support as a result of the cotton famine — the over-all economic picture was far from gloomy. In addition to the obvious example of the munitions manufacturers, who were profiting handsomely from the quarrel across the way, the linen and woolen industries had gained an appreciable part of what the cotton industry had lost, and the British merchant marine, whose principal rival for world trade was being chased from the high seas by rebel cruisers, was prospering as never before, augmented by more than seven hundred American vessels which transferred to the Union Jack in an attempt to avoid capture or destruction. And though there were those who favored intervention on the side of the South as a means of disposing permanently of a growing competitor, if by no other way then by assisting him to cut himself in two — the poet Matthew Arnold took this line of reason even further, speaking of the

★

INDIAN COTTON DEPÔT

COTTON STORES

OVER THE WAY.
Mr. Bull. "OH! IF YOU TWO LIKE FIGHTING BETTER THAN BUSINESS, I SHALL DEAL AT **THE OTHER SHOP**."

Suffering a cotton famine while the Americans squabble, Great Britain's symbol, a plump John Bull, ponders purchasing the crop from India.

need "to prevent the English people from becoming, with the growth of democracy, *Americanized*" — the majority, even among the hard-pressed cotton operatives, did not. The Emancipation Proclamation saw to that, and Lincoln, having won what he first had feared was a gamble, was quick to press the advantage he had gained. When the workingmen of Manchester, the city hardest hit by the cotton famine, sent him an address approved at a meeting held on New Year's Eve, announcing their support of the North in its efforts to "strike off the fetters of the slave," Lincoln replied promptly in mid-January, pulling out all the stops in his conclusion: "I know and deeply deplore the sufferings which the workingmen at Manchester and in all Europe are called upon to endure in this crisis. . . . Under these circumstances, I cannot but regard your decisive utterance upon the question as an instance of sublime Christian heroism which has not been surpassed in any age or in any country. It is, indeed, an energetic and reinspiring assurance of the inherent power of truth and of the ultimate and universal triumph of justice, humanity, and freedom. I do not doubt that the sentiments you have expressed will be sustained by your great nation, and, on the other hand, I have no hesitation in assuring you that they will excite admiration, esteem, and the most reciprocal feelings of friendship among the American people. I hail this interchange of sentiment, therefore, as an augury that whatever else may happen, whatever misfortune may befall your country or my own, the peace and friendship which now exist between the two nations will be, as it shall be my desire to make them, perpetual."

Palmerston could have made little headway against the current of this rhetoric, even if he had so desired. In point of fact he did not try. Having resisted up to now the efforts of Confederate envoys to rush him off his feet — which they had done their best to do, knowing that it was their best chance to secure European intervention: aside, that is, from such happy accidents as the *Trent* affair, which unfortunately after a great deal of furor had come to nothing — he would have little trouble in keeping his balance from now on. Napoleon, across the Channel, was another matter. Practically without popular objection to restrain him, he continued to work in favor of those interests which, as he saw them, coincided with his own. Through the prominent Paris banking firm, Erlanger et Cie — whose president's son had lately married Matilda Slidell, daughter of the Confederate commissioner — a multi-million-dollar loan to the struggling young nation across the Atlantic was arranged, not in answer to any plea for financial assistance (it had not occurred to the Southerners, including John Slidell, despite the recent matrimonial connection, that asking would result in anything more than a Gallic shrug of regret) but purely as a gesture of good will. So the firm's representatives said as they broached the subject to Secretary of State Judah P. Benjamin in Richmond, having crossed the ocean for that purpose. However, being bankers — and what is more, French bankers — they added that they saw no harm in combining the good-will gesture with the chance to turn a profit, not only for the prospective buyers of the bonds that would be issued, but also for Erlanger et Cie. Then came the explanation, which showed that the transaction, though ostensibly a loan, was in fact little more than a scheme for large-scale speculation in cotton. Each 8% bond, which the firm would obtain at 70 for sale at approximately 100, was to be made exchangeable at face value, not later than six months after the end of the war, for New Orleans middling cotton at 12¢ a pound. There was the catch; for cotton was worth twice that much already, and was still rising. Benjamin, who was quite as sharp as the visiting bankers or their chief — Erlanger was a Jew and so was he; Erlanger was a Frenchman and so was he, after a manner of speaking, being Creole by adoption — saw through the scheme at once, as indeed anyone but a blind man would have done; but he also saw its propaganda value, which amounted at least to financial recognition of the Confederacy as a member of the family of nations. After certain adjustments on which he insisted, though not without exposing himself to charges of ingratitude for having looked a gift horse in the mouth — the original offer of $25,000,000 was scaled down to $15,000,000 and the interest rate to 7%, while the price at which the firm was to secure the bonds was raised to 77 — the deal was closed.

That was in late January, and at first all went well. Issued in early March at 90 — which gave Erlanger a spread of 13 points, plus a 5% commission on all sales — the bonds were enthusiastically oversubscribed and quickly arose to 95½. But that was the peak. Before the month was out they began to fall, and they kept falling, partly because of the influence of U.S. foreign agents who, basing their charge on the fact that Jefferson Davis himself had been a prewar

★

advocate of the repudiation of Mississippi state bonds, predicted vociferously that the Southerners, if by some outside chance they won the war, would celebrate their victory by repudiating their debts. This had its effect. As the price declined, the alarmed Parisian bankers brought pressure on James M. Mason, the Confederate commissioner in London, to bull the market by using the receipts of the first installment for the purchase of his government's own bonds. Reluctantly, with the agreement of Slidell, he consented and, before he was through, put $6,000,000 into the attempt. But even this caused no more than a hesitation. When the artificial respiration stopped, the decline resumed, eventually pausing of its own accord at a depth of 36 before the bonds went off the board entirely. By that time, however, Erlanger et Cie was well in the clear, with a profit of about $2,500,000: which was more than the Confederacy obtained in all from a bond issue for which it had pledged six times that amount in capital and 7% in interest. The real losers, though, were the individual purchasers, mostly British admirers of the Confederacy, who left to their descendants the worthless scroll-worked souvenirs of a curious chapter in international finance.

As a fund-raising device the experiment was nearly a total failure — for the Confederates, that is, if not for the French bankers — but it did provide an additional incentive for Napoleon, who had taken considerable interest in the transaction, to hope for a southern victory. On February 3, after the bond issue

Powerful British prime minister Lord Palmerston kept England from intervening in the American war. He intoned that "those who in quarrels interpose, are apt to get a bloody nose."

had been authorized but before it had begun, the Emperor had his minister at Washington, Henri Mercier by name, present an offer of mediation, suggesting that representatives of the North and South meet on neutral soil for a discussion of terms of peace. The reaction to this was immediate and negative, at least on the part of the North. Seward replied that the Federal government had not the slightest notion of abandoning its efforts to save the Union, and certainly not by any such relinquishment of authority as the French proposal seemed to imply. This was seconded emphatically by Congress on March 3, when both houses issued a joint resolution denouncing mediation as "foreign interference" and reaffirming their "unalterable purpose" to suppress a rebellion which had for its object the tearing of the fabric of the finest government the world had ever known. In short, all that came of this latest effort by Napoleon to befriend the South was a further reduction of his possible influence. And Palmerston, watching the outcome from across the Channel, was more than ever convinced that no good could proceed from any such machinations. Dependent as his people were on U.S. grain to keep them from starvation, with Canada liable to seizure as a hostage to fortune and the British merchant marine exposed to being crippled if not destroyed, it seemed to him little short of madness to step into an argument which was after all a family affair. "Those who in quarrels interpose, Are apt to get a bloody nose," he intoned, falling back on doggerel to express his fears.

A. Dudley Mann, third in the trio of Confederate commissioners in Europe, had opened the year by complaining to his government that "the conduct of [England and France] toward us has been extremely shabby" and deploring their lack of spirit in the face of "the arrogant pretensions of the insolent Washington concern." Now in mid-March, as the third spring of the war began its green advance across the embattled South, all those thousands of miles away, Slidell in Paris was becoming increasingly impatient with Napoleon, whose avowed good will and favors never seemed to lead to anything valid or substantial, and Mason in London was lamenting bitterly that he had "no intercourse, unofficial or otherwise, with any member of the [British] Government." It was his private opinion, expressed frequently to Benjamin these days, that instead of continuing to put up with snubs and rebuffs, he would do better to come home.

* * * If he had come home to Virginia now — as he did not; not yet — he would have done well to brace himself for the shock of finding it considerably altered from what it had been when he left it, a year and a half ago, to begin his aborted voyage on the *Trent*. That was perhaps the greatest paradox of all: that the Confederacy, in launching

a revolution against change, should experience under pressure of the war which then ensued an even greater transformation, at any rate of the manner in which its citizens pursued their daily rounds, than did the nation it accused of trying to foist upon it an unwanted metamorphosis, not only of its cherished institutions, but also of its very way of life.

That way of life was going fast, and some there were, particularly among those who could remember a time when a society was judged in accordance with its sense of leisure, who affirmed that it was gone already. Nowhere was the change more obvious than in Richmond. Though the city was no longer even semi-beleaguered, as it had been in the time of McClellan, the outer fortifications had been lengthened and strengthened to such an extent that wags were saying, "They ought to be called fiftyfications now." Within that earthwork girdle, where home-guard clerks from government offices walked their appointed posts in their off hours, an ante-bellum population of less than 40,000 had mushroomed to an estimated 140,000, exclusive of the Union captives and Confederate wounded who jammed the old tobacco warehouses converted to prisons and hospitals. Yet the discomfort to which the older residents objected was not so much the result of the quantity of these late arrivers as it was of their quality, so to speak, or lack of it. "Virginians regarded the newcomers much as Romans would regard the First Families of the Visigoths," a diarist wrote. In truth, they had provocation far beyond the normal offense to their normal snobbery. Tenderloin districts such as Locust Alley, where painted women helped furloughed men forget the rigors of the field, and Johnny Worsham's gambling hell, directly across from the State House itself, had given the Old Dominion capital a reputation for being "the most corrupt and licentious city south of the Potomac." A Charlestonian administered the unkindest cut, however, by writing home that he had come to Richmond and found an entirely new city erected "after the model of Sodom and New York." According to another observer, an Englishman with a sharper ear for slang and a greater capacity for shock, the formerly decorous streets were crowded now with types quaintly designated as pug-uglies, dead rabbits, shoulder-hitters, "and a hundred other classes of villains for whom the hangman has sighed for many a long year."

Richmond saw and duly shuddered; but there was grimmer cause for shuddering than the wrench given its sense of propriety by the whores and gamblers who had taken up residence within its gates. As new-mounded graves spread over hillsides where none had been before, the population of the dead kept pace with the fast-growing population of the living. Though the Confederates in general lost fewer men in battle than their opponents, the fact that they had fewer to lose gave the casualty lists a greater impact, and it was remarked that "funerals were so many, even the funerals of friends, that none could be more than sparsely attended." Even more pitiful were the dying; Richmonders had come to know what one of them called "the peculiar chant of pain" that went up from a line of springless wagons hauling wounded over a rutted road or a cobbled street. You saw the maimed wherever you looked. For the city's hospitals — including the one on Chimborazo Heights, which had 150 buildings and was said to be the largest in the world — were so congested during periods immediately following battles that men who had lost an arm three days before had to be turned out, white-faced and trembling from shock and loss of blood, to make room for others in more urgent need of medical attention. It was up to the people to take them into their houses for warmth and food, and this they did, though only by the hardest, for both were dear and getting further beyond their means with every day that passed.

A gold dollar now was worth four in Confederate money, and even a despised $1 Yankee greenback brought $2.50 in a swap. Of coined money there was none, and in fact there had never been any, except for four half-dollars struck in the New Orleans mint before the fall of that city caused the government to abandon its plans for coinage. Congress's first solution to the small-change problem had been to make U.S. silver coins legal tender up to $10, along with English sovereigns, French napoleons, and Spanish and Mexican doubloons, but presently a flood of paper money was released upon the country, bills of smaller denominations being known as "shinplasters" because a soldier once had used a fistful to cover a tibia wound. Sometimes, as depreciation continued, that seemed about all they were good for. A War Department official, comparing current with prewar household expenses — flour, then $7, now $28 a barrel; bacon, then 20¢, now $1.25 a pound; firewood, then $3 or $4, now $15 a cord — found, as many others were finding, that he could not make ends meet; "My salary of $3000 will go about as far as $700 would in 1860." Wool and salt, drugs and medicines, nails and needles were scarcely to be had at any price, though the last were often salvaged from sewing kits found in the pockets of dead Federals. Dress muslin was $6 to $8 a yard, calico $1.75, coal $14 a cartload, and dinner in a first-class hotel ran as high as $25 a plate. In addition to genuine shortages, others were artificial, the result of transportation problems. Items that were plenteous in one part of the country might be as rare as hen's teeth in another. Peaches selling for 25¢ a dozen in Charleston, for instance, cost ten, fifteen, even twenty cents apiece in Richmond nowadays. For men perhaps the worst shock was the rising price of whiskey. As low as 25¢ a gallon in 1861, inferior stuff known variously as

Chimborazo Hospital, sprawling on a hill near Richmond, was a complex of 150 single-story buildings that served some 76,000 patients during the war.

bust-head, red-eye, and tangle-foot now sold for as high as $35 a gallon. For women, on the other hand, the main source of incidental distress was clothes, the lack of new ones and the unsuitability of old ones through wear-and-tear and changing styles, although the latter were of necessity kept to a minimum. "Do you realize the fact that we shall soon be without a stitch of clothes?" a young woman wrote to a friend in early January. "There is not a bonnet for sale in Richmond. Some of the girls smuggle them, which I for one consider in the worst possible taste." Apparently ashamed to have let her mind turn in this direction at this time, she hastened to apologize for her flightiness, only to fall into fresh despair. "It seems rather volatile to discuss such things while our dear country is in such peril. Heaven knows I would costume myself in coffee-bags if that would help, but having no coffee, where would I get the bags?"

One provident source of amusement and delivery from care was the theater, which was popular as never before, though it did not escape the censure of the more respectable. "The thing took well, and money flowed into the treasury," a manager afterwards recalled, "but often had I cause to upbraid myself for having fallen so low in my own estimation, for I had always considered myself a gentleman, and I found that in taking control of this theatre and its vagabond company I had forfeited my claim to a respectable stand in the ranks of Society." A prominent Baptist preacher's complaint from his pulpit that "twenty *gentlemen* for the chorus and the ballet" might be more useful to their country in the army, where they could do more than "mimic fighting on the stage," met with the approval of his congregation; but the S.R.O. signs continued to go up nightly beside the ticket windows. When the Richmond Theatre burned soon after New Year's, an entirely new building was promptly raised on the old foundations. Opening night was greeted with an "Inaugural Poem" by Henry Timrod, concluding:

> Bid Liberty rejoice! Aye, though its day
>
> Be far or near, these clouds shall yet be red
>
> With the large promise of the coming ray.
>
> Meanwhile, with that calm courage which can smile
>
> Amid the terrors of the wildest fray
>
> Let us among the charms of Art awhile
>
> Fleet the deep gloom away;
>
> Nor yet forget that on each hand and head
>
> Rest the dear rights for which we fight and pray.

★

If the production itself — Shakespeare's *As You Like It*, "but not as *we* like it," one critic unkindly remarked — left much to be desired in the way of professional excellence, Richmonders were glad to have found release "among the charms," and even the disgruntled reviewer was pleased to note "that the audience evinced a disposition at once to stop all rowdyism." For example, when the callboy came out from behind the curtain to fasten down the carpet, certain ill-bred persons began to yell, "Soup! Soup!" but were promptly shushed by those around them.

An even better show, according to some, was presented at the Capitol whenever Congress was in session, though unfortunately — or fortunately, depending on the point of view — these theatricals were in general unavailable to the public, being conducted behind closed doors. It was not so much what occurred in the regular course of business that was lively or amusing (for, as was usual with such bodies, there was a good deal more discussion of what to do than there was of doing. One member interrupted a long debate as to a proper time for adjournment by remarking, "If the House would adjourn and not meet any more, it would benefit the country." Others outside the legislative assembly agreed, including a Deep South editor who, learning that Congress had spent the past year trying without success to agree on a device for the national seal, suggested "A terrapin *passant*," with the motto "Never in haste"); it was what happened beside the point, so to speak, that provided the excitement. In early February the Alabama fire-eater William L. Yancey, opposing the creation of a Confederate Supreme Court — which, incidentally, never came into being because of States Rights obstructionists — so infuriated Benjamin H. Hill of Georgia, a moderate, that he threw a cutglass inkstand at the speaker and cut his cheek to the bone. As Yancey, spattered with blood and ink, started for him across the intervening desks, Hill followed up with a second shot, this time a heavy tumbler, which missed, and the sergeant-at-arms had to place both men in restraint and remove them from the chamber. Less fortunate was the chief clerk, shot to death on Capitol Square two months later by the journal clerk, who was angry at having been accused of slipshod work by his superior. The killer was sentenced to eighteen years in the penitentiary, but nothing at all was done to a woman who appeared one day on the floor of the House and proceeded to cowhide a Missouri congressman. She too was a government clerk, but it developed that her wrath had been aroused by information that Congress, in connection with enforcement of the Conscription Act, was about to require all clerks to divulge their ages. Deciding that the woman was demented, the House voted its confidence in the unlucky Missourian, who apparently had been selected at random. No such vote was ever given Jefferson Davis's old Mississippi stump opponent Henry S. Foote, who worked hard to deserve the reputation of being the stormiest man in Congress. He fought with his fists, in and out of the chamber, and was always ready to fall back on dueling pistols, with which he had had considerable experience. An altercation with an expatriate Irishman and a Tennessee colleague, who struck Foote over the head with an umbrella and then dodged nimbly to keep from being shot, caused all three to be brought into the Mayor's Court and placed under a peace bond. Another three-sided argument occurred in the course of a congressional hearing in which a Commissary Department witness was so badgered by Foote that the two came to blows. Foote tore off his adversary's shirt bosom, and when Commissary General Lucius B. Northrop came to the witness's assistance Foote knocked him into a corner. According to some who despised Colonel Northrop, asserting that he was attempting to convert the southern armies to vegetarianism, this was Foote's one real contribution to the Confederate war effort. But he was by no means through providing excitement. In the course of a speech by E. S.

Confederate congressman Henry Foote was a brawling, stormy opponent of the Davis administration.

Dargan of Alabama, Foote broke in to call him a "damned rascal," which so infuriated the elderly congressman that he went for the Mississippian with a knife. Foote avoided the lunge, and then — Dargan by now had been disarmed and lay pinned to the floor by colleagues — stepped back within range and, striking an attitude not unworthy of Edwin Booth, whose work he much admired, hissed at the prostrate Alabamian: "I defy the steel of the assassin!"

All this was part and parcel of the revolution-in-progress, and if much of it was scandalous and distasteful, most Confederates could take that too in stride, along with spiraling prices and increasing scarcities. A native inclination toward light-heartedness served them well in times of strain. What the newcomers to Richmond lacked in tone they more than made up for in gaiety. Practically nothing was exempt from being laughed at nowadays, not even the sacred escutcheon of Virginia, whose motto *Sic semper tyrannis,* engraved below the figure of Liberty treading down Britannia, was freely rendered as "Take your foot off my neck!" Officers and men on leave and furlough from the Rappahannock line opened Volume I, "Fantine," of Victor Hugo's *Les Misérables,* which had come out in France the year before, and professed surprise at finding that it was not about themselves, "Lee's Miserables, Faintin'." One whose spirits never seemed to falter was Judah Benjamin, who remarked in this connection that it was "wrong and useless to disturb oneself and thus weaken one's energy to bear what was foreordained." This hedonistic fatalist went his way, invariably smiling, whether in attendance at government councils or at Johnny Worsham's green baize tables across the way. He once assured Varina Davis that with a glass of McHenry sherry, of which she had a small supply, and beaten biscuits made of flour from Crenshaw Mills, spread with a paste made of English walnuts from a tree on the White House grounds, "a man's patriotism became rampant." She found him amusing, an ornament to her receptions, and an excellent antidote to the FFV's who currently were condemning her as "disloyal to the South" because of a rumor that she had employed a white nurse for her baby.

The easy laughter was infectious, though some could hear it for what it was, part of an outward pose assumed at times to hide or hold back tears. What was happening behind the mask — not only Benjamin's, but the public's at large — no one could say for certain. Presently, however, there were signs that the mask was beginning to crack, or at any rate slip, and thus disclose what it had been designed to cover. When the President proclaimed March 5 another "day of fasting and prayer," this too was not exempt from unregenerate laughter; "Fasting in the midst of famine!" some remarked sardonically. Then, just short of one month later, on Holy Thursday — Easter came on April 5, a week before the second anniversary of Sumter — a demonstration staged on the streets of the capital itself gave the authorities cause to question whether all was as well concerning public morale here in the East as they had supposed, especially among those citizens who could not enjoy the relaxations afforded by such places as Johnny Worsham's, where a lavish buffet was maintained for the refreshment of patrons at all hours. The Holy Thursday demonstration, at least at the start, was concerned with more basic matters: being known, then and thereafter, as the Bread Riot.

Apparently it began at the Oregon Hill Baptist church, where Mary Jackson, a huckster with "straight, strong features and a vixenish eye," harangued a group of women who had gathered to protest the rising cost of food. Adjourning to Capitol Square they came under the leadership of a butcher's Amazonian assistant, Minerva Meredith by name. Six feet tall and further distinguished by a long white feather that stood up from her hat and quivered angrily as she tossed her head, she proposed that they move on the shops to demand goods at government prices and to take them by force if this was refused. As she spoke she took from under her apron, by way of emphasis, a Navy revolver and a Bowie knife. Brandishing these she set out for the business section at the head of a mob which quickly swelled to about three hundred persons, including the children some of the women had in tow. "Bread! Bread!" they shouted as they marched. Governor John Letcher, who had watched from his office as the demonstration got under way, had the mayor read the Riot Act to them, but they hooted and surged on past him, smashing plate-glass windows in their anger and haste to get at the goods in the shops on Main and Cary. It was obvious that they were after more than food, for they emerged with armloads of shoes and clothes, utensils and even jewelry, which some began to pile into handcarts they had thought to bring along. Governor Letcher sent for a company of militia and threatened to fire on the looters when it arrived, but the women sneered at him, as they had done at the mayor, and went on with their vandalism. Just then, however, those on the outer fringes of the mob saw a tall thin man dressed in gray homespun climb onto a loaded dray and begin to address them sternly. They could not hear what he was saying, but they saw him do a strange thing. He took money from his pockets and tossed it in their direction. Whereupon they fell silent and his voice came through: "You say you are hungry and have no money. Here is all I have. It is not much, but take it." His pockets empty of all but his watch, he took that out too, but instead of throwing it at them, as he had done the money, he stood with it open in his hand, glancing sidelong at the militia company which had just arrived. "We do not desire to injure anyone," he said in a voice that rang clear above the murmur of the crowd, "but this lawlessness must stop. I will give you five minutes to disperse. Otherwise you will be fired on."

Recognizing the President — and knowing, moreover, that he was not given to issuing idle threats — the mob began to disperse, first slowly, then rapidly as the deadline approached. By the time the five minutes were up, there was no one left for the soldiers to fire at. Davis put his watch back in his pocket, climbed down off the dray, and returned to his office. Outwardly calm, inwardly he was so concerned that he did something he had never done before. He made a special appeal to the Richmond press, requesting that it "avoid all reference directly or indirectly to the affair," and ordered the telegraph company to "permit nothing relative to the unfortunate disturbance . . . to be sent over the telegraph lines in any direction for any purpose." He feared the reaction abroad, as well as in other parts of the South, if it became known that the streets of the Confederate capital had been the scene of a riot that had as its cause, if only by pretense, a shortage of food. Two days later, however, the *Enquirer* broke the story by way of refuting defeatist rumors that were beginning to be spread. Identifying the rioters as "a handful of prostitutes, professional thieves, Irish and Yankee hags, gallows birds from all lands but our own," the paper denounced them for having broken into "half a dozen shoe stores, hat stores and tobacco houses and robbed them of everything but bread, which was just the thing they wanted least."

This one attempt at suggesting censorship was as useless as it was ineffective: Richmond was by no means the only place where such disturbances occurred in the course of Holy Week. Simultaneously in Atlanta a group of about fifteen well-dressed women entered a store on Whitehall Street and asked the price of bacon. $1.10 a pound, they were told: whereupon their man-tall leader, a shoemaker's wife "on whose countenance rested care and determination," pro-

Driven by food shortages and impossibly high prices, hungry women ransack a bakery in Richmond on April 2, 1863, a day of widespread looting in the capital city.

duced a revolver with which she covered the grocer while her companions snatched what they wanted from the shelves, paying their own price or nothing. From there they proceeded to other shops along the street, repeating the performance until their market baskets were full, and then went home. A similar raid was staged at about the same time in Mobile, as well as in other towns and cities throughout the South. Presently countrywomen took their cue from their urban sisters. North Carolina experienced practically an epidemic of demonstrations by irate housewives. Near Lafayette, Alabama, a dozen such — armed, according to one correspondent, with "guns, pistols, knives, and tongues" — attacked a rural mill and seized a supply of flour, while a dozen more came down out of the hills around Abingdon, Virginia, and cowered merchants into handing over cotton yarn and cloth; wagon trains were stopped at gunpoint and robbed of corn near Thomasville and Marietta, Georgia. All these were but a few among the many, and there were those who saw in this ubiquitous manifestation of discontent the first crack in the newly constructed edifice of government. If the Confederacy could not be defeated from without, then it might be abolished from within; for the protests were not so much against shortages, which were by no means chronic at this stage, as they were against the inefficiency which resulted in spiraling prices. These observers saw the demonstrations, in fact — despite the recent successes of southern arms, both East and West — as symptoms of war weariness, the one national ailment which could lead to nothing but defeat. The new government could survive, and indeed had survived already, an assortment of calamities; but that did not and could not include the loss of the will to fight, either by the soldiers in its armies or by the people on its home front.

No one saw the danger more clearly than the man whose principal task — aside, that is, from his duties as Commander in Chief, which now as always he placed first — was to do all he could to avert it. Recently he had undertaken a 2500-mile year-end journey to investigate and shore up crumbling morale, with such apparent success that on his return he could report to Congress, convening in Richmond for its third session on January 12, that the state of the nation, in its civil as well as in its military aspect, "affords ample cause for congratulation and demands the most fervent expression of our thankfulness to the Almighty Father, who has blessed our cause. We are justified in asserting, with a pride surely not unbecoming, that these Confederate States have added another to the lessons taught by history for the instruction of man; that they have afforded another example of the impossibility of subjugating a people determined to be free, and have demonstrated that no superiority of numbers or available resources can overcome the resistance offered by such valor in combat, such constancy under suffering, and such cheerful endurance of privation as have been conspicuously displayed by this people in the defense of their rights and liberties." Moreover, he added, flushed by the confidence his words had generated: "By resolute perseverance in the path we have hitherto pursued, by vigorous efforts in the development of all our resources for defense, and by the continued exhibition of the same unfaltering courage in our soldiers and able conduct in their leaders as have distinguished the past, we have every reason to expect that this will be the closing year of the war."

Since then, despite continued successful resistance by the armies in the field, symptoms of unrest among civilians had culminated in the rash of so-called Bread Riots, the largest of which had occurred in the capital itself and had been broken up only by the personal intervention of the Chief Executive. Two days later — on April 10, just short of three months since his confident prediction of an early end to the conflict — Davis issued, in response to a congressional resolution passed the week before, a proclamation "To the People of the Confederate States." Observing that "a strong impression prevails throughout the country that the war . . . may terminate during the present year," Congress urged the people not to be taken in by such false hopes, but rather to "look to prolonged war as the only condition proffered by the enemy short of subjugation." The presidential proclamation, issued broadcast across the land, afforded the people the unusual opportunity of seeing their President eat his words, not only by revoking his previous prediction, but by substituting another which clearly implied that what lay ahead was a longer and harder war than ever.

Though "fully concurring in the views thus expressed by Congress," he began with the same boldness of assertion as before. "We have reached the close of the second year of the war, and may point with just pride to the history of our young Confederacy. Alone, unaided, we have met and overthrown the most formidable combination of naval and military armaments that the lust of conquest ever gathered together for the subjugation of a free people. . . . The contrast between our past and present condition is well calculated to inspire full confidence in the triumph of our arms. At no previous period of the war have our forces been so numerous, so well organized, and so thoroughly disciplined, armed, and equipped as at present." Then he passed to darker matters. "We must not forget, however, that the war is not yet ended, and that we are still confronted by powerful armies and threatened by numerous fleets. . . . Your country, therefore, appeals to you to lay aside all thoughts of gain, and to devote yourselves to securing your liberties, without which those gains would be valueless. . . . Let fields be devoted exclusively to the production of corn, oats, beans, peas, potatoes, and other food for man and beast; let corn be sown broadcast for fodder in immediate proximity to railroads, rivers, and canals, and let all your efforts be directed to the prompt supply of these articles in the districts where our armies are operating. . . . Entertaining no fear that you will either misconstrue the motives of this address or fail to respond to the call of patriotism, I have placed the facts fully and frankly before you. Let us all unite in the performance of our duty, each in his own sphere, and with concerted, persistent, and well-directed effort . . . we shall maintain the sovereignty and independence of these Confederate States, and transmit to our posterity the heritage bequeathed to us by our fathers."

As usual, the people responded well for the most part to a clear statement of necessity. But there were those who reacted otherwise. The Georgia fire-eater Robert Toombs, for example, who had left the cabinet to join the army on the day of First Manassas and then had left the army to reënter politics after his one big day at Sharpsburg, petulantly announced that he was increasing his plantation's cotton acreage. Nor were opposition editors inclined to neglect the opportunity to launch the verbal barbs they had been sharpening through months of increasing dissatisfaction. "Mr Davis is troubled by blindness," the Mobile *Tribune* told its subscribers, "is very dyspeptic and splenetic, and as prejudiced and stubborn as a man can well be, and not be well."

Thus did the Confederacy enter upon its third year of war.

★　★　★

★

*These officers and men of Sheridan's
division, bivouacked on a farm
in the Tennessee hills, had
been battle tested in the bloody
fighting at Murfreesboro.*

Rosecrans; Johnston; Streight's Raid

1863 ★ ★ ★ ★ ★ ★ **Disenchantment was mainly limited to civilians,** but it was by no means limited to the sphere of civilian activities. Illogically or not — that is, despite the lopsided triumphs at Fredericksburg and Chickasaw Bluffs, the flood-reversing coups at Holly Springs and Galveston, the brilliant cavalry forays into Kentucky and West Tennessee, and the absence of anything resembling a clear-cut defeat east of the Mississippi — there was a growing impression that victory, on field after field, brought little more than temporary joy, which soon gave way to sobering realizations. The public's reaction was not unlike that of a boxer who delivers his best punch, square on the button, then sees his opponent merely blink and shake his head and bore back in. People began to suspect that if the North could survive Fredericksburg and the Mud March, Chickasaw Bluffs and the loss of the *Cairo* to a demijohn of powder, it might well be able to survive almost anything the South seemed able to inflict. A whole season of victories apparently had done nothing to bring peace and independence so much as one day closer. Howell Cobb of Georgia could say, not altogether in jest, "Only two things stand in the way of an amicable settlement of the whole difficulty: the Landing of the Pilgrims and Original Sin," while the Richmond *Examiner* could simultaneously call attention to the chilling fact that, aside from Sumter, "[Lincoln's] pledge once deemed foolish by

★

the South, that he would 'hold, occupy, and possess' all the forts belonging to the United States Government, has been redeemed almost to the letter."

Fredericksburg had been hailed at the outset as the turning point of the war. Presently, however, as Lee and his army failed to find a way to follow it up, the triumph paled to something of a disappointment. In time, paradoxically, the more perceptive began to see that it had indeed been a turning point, though in a sense quite different from the one originally implied; for no battle East or West, whether a victory or a defeat, showed more plainly the essential toughness of the blue-clad fighting man than this in which, judging by a comparison of the casualties inflicted and received, he suffered the worst of his several large-scale drubbings. But this was an insight that came gradually, and only to those who were not only able but also willing to perceive it. Murfreesboro was more immediately disappointing in respect to Confederate expectations, and no such insight was required. Here the contrast between claims and accomplishments was as stark as it was sudden. First it was seen to be a much less brilliant victory than the southern commander had announced before his guns had hushed their growling. Then it was seen to be scarcely a victory at all. It was seen, in fact, to have several of the aspects of a typical defeat: not the least of which was the undeniable validity of the Federal claim to control of the field when the smoke had cleared. "So far the news has come in what may be called the classical style of the Southwest," the *Examiner* observed caustically near the end of the first week in January, having belatedly learned of Bragg's withdrawal. "When the Southern army fights a battle, we first hear that it has gained one of the most stupendous victories on record; that regiments from Mississippi, Texas, Louisiana, Arkansas, &c. have exhibited an irresistible and superhuman valor unknown in history this side of Sparta and Rome. As for their generals, they usually get all their clothes shot off, and replace them with a suit of glory. The enemy, of course, is simply annihilated. Next day more dispatches come, still very good, but not quite as good as the first. The telegrams of the third day are invariably such as make a mist, a muddle, and a fog of the whole affair."

No mist, muddle, or fog could hide Bragg from the ire aroused when the public learned the premature and insubstantial basis for his wire announcing that God had granted him and them a Happy New Year. What saved him from the immediate consequences of their anger was his adversary Rosecrans, who, despite his recent promise to "press [the rebels] to the wall," not only refused to follow up the victory he claimed, but resisted with all his strength — as he had done through the months preceding the march out of Nashville, pleading the need to lay in "a couple of millions of rations" — the efforts by his superiors to prod him into motion. Crittenden, who had commanded the unassailed left wing throughout the first day's fight and then repulsed his fellow-Kentuckian Breckinridge on the second, stated the case as it appeared to many in the Union ranks: "The battle was fought for the possession of Middle Tennessee. We went down to drive the Confederates out of Murfreesboro, and we drove them out. They went off a few miles and camped again. And we, although we were the victors, virtually went into hospital for six months before we could march after them again." He added, by way of developing a theory: "As in most of our battles, very meager fruits resulted to either side from such partial victories as were for the most part won. Yet it was a triumph. It showed that in the long run the big purse and the big battalions — both on our side — must win; and it proved that there were no better soldiers than ours."

Rosecrans disagreed with much of this critique, particularly the remark that the army had gone "into hospital," but he not only subscribed to Crittenden's opinion about the big purse and the big battalions, he also took it a step further by insisting that the last ounce be wrung from the advantage. What good were riches, he seemed to be asking, unless they were at hand?

No mist, muddle, or fog could hide Bragg from the ire aroused when the public learned the premature and insubstantial basis for his wire announcing that God had granted him and them a Happy New Year.

When he swung the purse he wanted it to be heavy. "I believe the most fatal errors of this war have begun in an impatient desire of success, that would not take time to get ready," he protested in mid-February, by way of reply to Halleck's continuous urging. So the general-in-chief changed his tack. "There is a vacant major generalcy in the Regular Army," he wired on March 1, "and I am authorized to say that it will be given to the general in the field who first wins an important and decisive victory." The implication was that Rosecrans had better get to Chattanooga before Grant got to Vicksburg; but Old Rosy did not react at all in the way that had been intended. "As an officer and a citizen, I feel degraded to see such auctioneering of honor," he replied. "Have we a general who would fight for his own personal benefit, when he would not for honor and the country? He would come by his commission basely in that case, and deserve to be despised by men of honor." Halleck in turn resented this show of righteous indignation, and said so, which only served to increase their differences. Rosecrans was convinced by now that all of Washington was against him: especially Stanton, who had promised, in the first flush of excitement over the news of a hard-fought triumph, to withhold "nothing . . . within my power to grant," but who lately had bridled at filling the balky commander's many requisitions and requests, including one that his latest promotion be predated so as to give him rank over Grant and all the other western generals. Finally he protested to the President himself, who gave him little satisfaction beyond assurances of admiration. "I know not a single enemy of yours here," Lincoln wrote, and added: "Truth to speak, I do not appreciate this matter of rank on paper as you officers do. The world will not forget that you fought the battle of Stones River, and it will never care a fig whether you rank Gen. Grant on paper, or he so ranks you."

By then it was mid-March. The bloody contest, ten weeks back, had done much to increase Old Rosy's appreciation of the dangers involved in challenging the rebs on their own ground. The rest of March went by, and all of April. Still he would not budge. May followed. Still he would not move until he was good and ready, down to the final nail in the final horseshoe. As June came

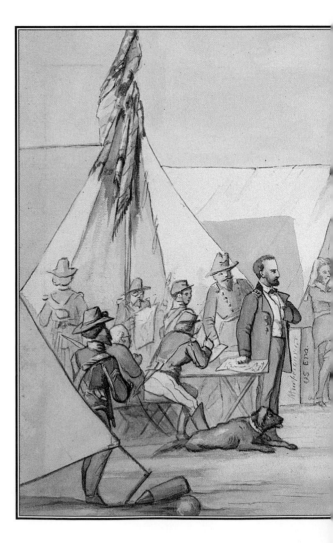

Union general Rosecrans (hatless, left) disciplines a subordinate (hatless, right). The scene depicts one of the administrative chores the general performed daily during his army's long encampment at Murfreesboro.

on, approaching the end of the six-month term which Crittenden said the army spent "in hospital," Rosecrans made a virtue of his immobility, claiming that by refraining from driving Bragg southward he was preventing him from coöperating with Pemberton against Grant. Besides, he added, he had held a council of war at which it had been decided to "observe a great military maxim, not to risk two great and decisive battles at the same time." He thought it best to wait till Vicksburg fell or Grant abandoned the effort to take it, whereupon he himself would advance against Bragg and Chattanooga. Halleck by now was fairly frantic. A master of maxims, he fired one back at Rosecrans: "Councils of war never fight." But this had no more effect than the earlier proddings had done; Old Rosy stayed exactly where he was. If Bragg would only leave him alone, he would gladly return the favor, at any rate until he was good and ready to advance. Just when that would be he would not say.

He might have taken some measure of consolation, amid the prod-dings, from the fact that his opponent's troubles quite overmatched his own. The difference was that Rosecrans' woes came mainly from above, whereas Bragg's came mainly from below. As a result, the latter were not only more widely spread, they were also frequently sharper barbed. His harsh discipline in camp, unbalanced by conspicuous victories in the field, and his reputation as a commander who invariably retreated after battle, whether his troops won or lost, had resulted in bitter censure from all sides, civil as well as military, in and out of the newspapers. Riding one day near his Tullahoma headquarters, soon after his withdrawal behind Duck River, he encountered a man wearing butter-nut garb and requested information about the roads. When this had been given, the general thanked him and, unable to tell from his clothes whether the man was a soldier or a civilian — the kindest thing that could be said about dress in the Army of Tennessee was that it was informal — asked if he belonged to Bragg's army. "Bragg's army?" the countryman replied, scowling at the grim-faced man on horseback. "Bragg's got no army. He shot half of them him-self, up in Kentucky, and the other half got killed at Murfreesboro."

Bragg laughed and rode on, curbing for once his terrible temper. But the experience rankled under pressure of newspaper criticisms leveled at him while his troops were getting settled along their new defensive line: particularly the charge, widely printed and reprinted, that he had pulled out of Murfrees-boro against the advice of his lieutenants. This was patently untrue, as he could prove by the note from Cheatham and Withers, urging immediate retreat, which he had rejected, at least at first, despite Polk's indorsement of their plea. Accord-ingly, he decided to make an issue of it, addressing on January 11 a letter to his chief subordinates. "It becomes necessary for me to save my fair name," he wrote, and "stop the deluge of abuse which [threatens to] destroy my usefulness and demoralize this army." He asked them to acquit him of the fabrication that he had gone against their wishes in ordering a retreat, which in point of fact "was resisted by me for some time after [it was] advised by my corps and divi-sion commanders. . . . Unanimous as you were in council in verbally advising a retrograde movement," he added, "I cannot doubt that you will cheerfully at-test the same in writing." So far, he was on safe ground. Unwilling to let it go at that, however, he closed with something of a flourish: "I desire that you will consult your subordinate commanders and be candid with me. . . . I shall retire without a regret if I find I have lost the good opinion of my generals, upon whom I have ever relied as upon a foundation of rock."

This last was what opened the floodgates. Though none could fail to exonerate him from the specific charge that he had originated the notion of re-treat, his closing statement that he would retire if he found that he had lost their good opinion presented the generals with a once-in-a-lifetime opportunity, which they did not neglect. Hardee, after pointing out that neither he nor his division commanders had proposed a withdrawal, though they had made no objection once the decision had been announced, replied that he had consulted his subordinates, as requested, and found them "unanimous in the opinion that a change in the command of this army is necessary. In this opinion I concur." He had "the highest regard for the purity of your motives, your energy, and your personal character," he told Bragg, but he was "convinced, as you must feel, that the peril of the country is superior to all personal considerations." His lieutenants replied in a similar vein. "I have consulted with my brigade commanders," Cleburne wrote, "and they unite with me in personal regard for yourself . . . but at the same time they see, with regret, and it has also met my observation, that you do not possess the confidence of the army in other respects in that degree necessary to secure success." Breckinridge was as forthright, and what was more — the officers and men of his division having found Bragg's report of the recent battle so disparaging to themselves and their dead comrades that they had urged their chief to challenge him to a duel — took perhaps the greatest satisfaction of all in seizing the present chance to sit in judgment. "Acting with the candor which you invoke," the former Vice President replied, "[my brigade commanders] request me to say that, in their opinion, the conduct of the military operations in front of Murfreesboro made it necessary for our army to retire." Lest the irony of this be lost, he passed at once to a summation. "They also request me to say that while they entertain the highest respect for your patriotism, it is their opinion that you do not possess the confidence of the army to an extent which will enable you to be useful as its commander. In this opinion I feel bound to state that I concur."

Polk was away on leave at the time, visiting his refugee family in North Carolina, and in his absence Cheatham and Withers merely replied with an acknowledgment that they had made the original suggestion to withdraw. When the bishop returned at the end of the month he found the army a-buzz with talk of this latest development. Since there was some difference of opinion as to whether Bragg had really intended to call down all this thunder on his head, Polk wrote to ask whether his chief had meant for him to answer both questions — 1) as to who was responsible for bringing up the subject of retreat, and 2) as to whether the army commander had lost the confidence of his subordinates — or only the first. Bragg by now had had quite enough "candid" responses to the second question, and stated that he had only wanted to get an opinion on the inception of the retreat; "The paragraph relating to my supercedure was only an expression of the feeling with which I should receive your replies." In that case, Polk responded, he believed the original battlefield note would suffice as a documentary answer. He was content to let the matter drop. But learning presently that Hardee and his officers felt that he had dodged the issue, thereby leaving them in the position of insubordinate malcontents, he decided to write directly to his friend the President, attaching the rather voluminous correspondence he had had with Bragg. "I feel it my duty to say to you," he told Davis, "that had I and my division commanders been asked to answer, our replies would have coincided with those of the officers of the other corps. . . . My opinion is he had better be transferred." The best place for him, Polk believed, was Richmond, where "his capacity for organization and discipline, which has not been equaled among us, could be used by you at headquarters with infinite advantage to the whole army. I think, too," he added, "that the best thing to be done in supplying his place would be to give his command to General Joseph E. Johnston. He will cure all discontent and inspire the army with new life and confidence. He is here on the spot, and I am sure will be content to take it."

Davis was quite aware that Johnston was at Tullahoma, having ordered him there two weeks ago, when Bragg's circular, together with the replies of Hardee and his lieutenants, first landed on the presidential desk. "Why General Bragg should have selected that tribunal, and have invited its judgment upon him, is to me unexplained; it manifests, however, a condition of things which seems to me to require your presence." So Davis wrote Johnston, who was engaged at the time in an inspection of the Mobile defenses, instructing him to proceed at once to Bragg's headquarters and determine "whether he had so far lost the confidence of the army as to impair his usefulness in his present position. . . . You will, I trust, be able, by conversation with General Bragg and others of his command, to decide what the best interests of the service require, and to give me the advice which I need at this juncture. As that army is part of your command," the President added, knowing the Virginian's meticulosity in such matters, "no order will be necessary to give you authority there, as, whether present or absent, you have a right to direct its operations and do whatever else belongs to the general commanding."

However, Johnston's squeamishness went further than Davis reckoned. He found much that was improper in the conduct of an inquiry which might result in the displacement of the officer under investigation by the one who was doing the investigating. Besides, he had a high regard for the grim-faced North Carolinian's abilities. "Bragg has done wonders, I think," he wrote privately. "No body of troops has done more in proportion to numbers in the same time." Accordingly on February 3, ten days after his arrival, although "incessant rain has permitted me to see but a fourth of the troops as yet," he reported them "in high spirits, and as ready as ever for fight." He found his confidence in Bragg not only unshaken but "confirmed by his recent operations, which, in my opinion, evince great vigor and skill." In short: "It would be very unfortunate to remove him at this juncture, when he has just earned, if not won, the gratitude of the country." He would report more fully, Johnston said, when he had complet-

★

ed his inspection. Meanwhile, "I respectfully suggest that, should it appear to you necessary to remove General Bragg, no one in this army or engaged in this investigation ought to be his successor." Nine days later, his final report buttressed his first impression. He had found the men "well clothed, healthy, and in good spirits," which gave "positive evidence of General Bragg's capacity to command. . . . To me it seems that the operations of this army in Middle Tennessee have been conducted admirably. I can find no record of more effective fighting in modern battles than that of this army in December, evincing great skill in the commander and courage in the troops." He had heard, he said in closing, that Polk and Hardee had advised their present chief's removal and his own appointment to the command; but "I am sure that you will agree with me that the part I have borne in this investigation would render it inconsistent with my personal honor to occupy that position. . . . General Bragg should not be removed."

With that, he left for Chattanooga. Davis replied that he was "truly gratified at the language of commendation which you employ in relation to General Bragg," but he considered it "scarcely possible," in the light of Polk's and Hardee's formal disapproval, "for [Bragg] to possess the requisite confidence of the troops." He still thought Johnston should take over, and he could not see that this involved any breach of military etiquette. Johnston was already in command, by rank and title,

Braxton Bragg poses with the sword (below) he carried during the war. The city of Mobile presented the sword to him for his heroic service in the Mexican War.

whenever he was on the scene; "The removal of General Bragg would only affect you so far as it deprived you of his services." However, Davis assured him, "You shall not be urged by me to any course which would wound your sensibility of views of professional propriety." In early March, Johnston having made no reply to this, the Secretary of War added his pleas to those of the Commander in Chief. It was his opinion that Bragg should be "recalled altogether," but if Johnston's conscience would not permit this, then he suggested that he keep him at hand, "as an organizer and disciplinarian," in the post of assistant commander. "Let me urge you, my dear general," Seddon wrote, "to think well, in view of all the great interests to our beloved South . . . and, if possible, make the sacrifice of your honorable delicacy to the importance of the occasion and the greatness of our cause." When Johnston still did not reply — he was back in Mobile by now, though Davis and Seddon supposed he was still in Chattanooga — the matter was taken out of his hands by a wire from Richmond, which reached him on March 12: "Order General Bragg to report to the War Department here for conference. Assume yourself direct charge of the army in Middle Tennessee."

Perhaps Davis and Seddon had decided that what Johnston had been wanting all along, and even hinting at, was for them to *order* him to the post in spite of his objections; that way, the conditions of honor would be met, since he would have done all he could to avoid the outcome. If so, they were wrong. Johnston really did not want the command. The fact was, he did not want the larger one he had already — his duties, he said disparagingly, were those of an "inspector general" — despite the President's and the Secretary's insistence that it was the most important post in the Confederacy. If that was the case, Lee should have it as a reward for his recent accomplishments; then "with great propriety," Johnston wrote in confidence to a friend, he himself could return to his native Virginia and resume command of the army he had lost at Seven Pines, "where the Yankee bullets found me." Now it looked as if that hope was going up in smoke. He was ordered to Middle Tennessee, with no alternative to compliance except submission of his resignation.

So it seemed. When he returned to Tullahoma on March 19, however, he found a way — still on grounds of sparing offense to what Seddon had called his "honorable delicacy" — at least to delay what he had sought all this time to avoid. Bragg's wife was down with typhoid, despaired of by the doctors, and her husband had given over his official duties in order to be at her bedside round the clock. It was therefore no more than normal courtesy, under the circumstances, for Johnston to carry out that portion of the orders which required him to take command of the army; but as for increasing the distracted general's present woes by instructing him to report at once to Richmond, that was manifestly impossible, Johnston wired the authorities, "on account of Mrs Bragg's critical condition." Besides, he added, the country was "becoming practicable" now that the rains had slacked and the roads were drying; "Should the enemy advance, General Bragg will be indispensable here." Apparently he intended to take the Secretary's earlier suggestion that he keep the unpopular general at hand as his assistant. But presently even this went by the board. By the time Mrs Bragg had recovered sufficiently from her illness to permit her husband's return to active duty, Johnston himself was bedridden, suffering from a debility brought on by a flare-up of his wounds. "General Bragg is therefore necessary here," he notified Richmond on April 10. "If conference with him is still desirable, might not a confidential officer visit him, for the purpose, in Tullahoma?"

* * *

★ ★ ★ That was that; Bragg remained at his post by default, so to speak. Meanwhile — principally by courtesy of Rosecrans, who, though the methods employed to avoid compliance were quite different in each case, would no more be budged by his superiors than Johnston would be influenced by his — the Army of Tennessee enjoyed, throughout the opening half of the year, the longest period of inaction afforded any considerable body of Confederates in the whole course of the war. Polk's corps was on the left at Shelbyville, Hardee's on the right at Wartrace, with cavalry extending the long defensive line westward to Columbia and eastward to McMinnville, seventy air-line miles apart. Breastworks protected by abatis were thrown up along the critical center, and behind them, once the countryside emerged from the quagmires created by the late winter and early spring rains — which had afforded one self-styled etymologist the opportunity to remark that the name of the little railroad town where Bragg had his headquarters was derived from the conjunction of two Greek words: *tulla,* meaning "mud," and *homa,* meaning "more mud" — the infantry enjoyed the foison of the lush Duck River Valley and indulged in such diversions as attending church services and revival meetings (Bragg set an example here by allowing himself to be baptized in an impressive ceremony) or chuck-a-luck games and cockfights, depending on individual inclinations. The army's effective strength had risen by now to almost 50,000 of all arms, including better than 15,000 cavalry, who passed the time in a quite different manner by probing at Rosecrans' flanks and rear and harassing his front.

Joe Wheeler got things off to a rousing start on January 13 with a strike at Harpeth Shoals, midway between Nashville and Clarksville, where he captured or sank four loaded packets and one lightly armored gunboat, taking them under fire from the bank, and thus effectively suspended the flow of goods up the Cumberland River, the main Federal supply line. But this accomplishment was more than offset, another fifty miles downstream, by the repulse

★

he suffered on February 3 when he launched an ill-conceived and poorly coördinated assault on an outnumbered but stout blue garrison at Dover, two weeks short of the anniversary of the fall of adjacent Fort Donelson to Grant. Bedford Forrest, who had not only lost some of his best men but had also had two fine horses shot from under him in the course of attacks which he had advised against making in the first place, was so incensed by Wheeler's handling of the affair that he bluntly told the young commander that he would resign from the army before he would fight again under his direction. The discouraged graybacks limped back to Columbia, the western tip of Bragg's long crescent. Meanwhile, far out the opposite horn, Morgan was doing no better, if indeed as well. With two of his regiments detached to stir up excitement in Kentucky, he too suffered a bloody repulse at the hands of an inferior force on March 20 at Milton, fifteen miles northeast of Murfreesboro, and still another, two weeks later, at nearby Liberty, which resulted in his being driven in some confusion back on his base at McMinnville. Perhaps the best that could be said for all these various affairs, at any rate from the Confederate point of view, was that

*R*ebel cavalryman Joe Wheeler
was characterized by one friend as
"the gamest little banty I ever seen."

they all occurred within the Union lines and therefore served, victories and defeats alike, to keep Rosecrans off balance by increasing his native caution and apprehensiveness. "Their numerous cavalry goads and worries me," he had informed Washington at the outset, "but I will try to be equal to them."

This was going to be more difficult than he knew. Even as he wrote, Earl Van Dorn, the South's ranking major general — ordered north by Johnston over Pemberton's frantic protest at thus being practically stripped of cavalry despite the skill he recently had shown in handling that arm — was on the way from Mississippi with two divisions of horsemen, all thirsty for more of the glory they lately had tasted when they threw a whole Yankee army into retreat from Holly Springs. In this respect, their leader was the thirstiest man among them. After the Transmississippi disasters and the Corinth fiasco, which had resulted, amid wholesale condemnation, in his being superseded as commander of his home-state forces, his bad luck had suddenly turned good, and he was eager to take further advantage of the switch. Presently, soon after his arrival on February 22 at Columbia, where he assumed responsibility for protecting the left horn of Bragg's crescent while Wheeler protected the right, Rosecrans gave the diminutive Mississippian just the chance he had been seeking ever since his return to his first love, cavalry. The Federal plan was for a convergence of two infantry columns, one out of Murfreesboro under Phil Sheridan, the other out of Franklin, directly south of Nashville, under Colonel John Coburn; they would unite at Spring Hill, a dozen miles north of Columbia, then move together against that place, foraging as they went. Coburn set out on March 4, with just under 3000 of all arms. Van Dorn was waiting for him next morning at Thompson's Station, just above the intended point of convergence, with twice as many men — including Forrest, who had been transferred in consideration of his vow to serve no more under Wheeler. The result was a sudden and stunning victory, cinched by Forrest, who came in on the flank and rear while Van Dorn maintained pressure against the front, and a bag of 1221 prisoners, including Coburn, whose artillery and cavalry, along with one of his infantry regiments assigned to guard the forage train, had fled at the first detection of the odds. His thirst unslaked, Van Dorn sent his captives south and turned east to tackle Sheridan, intending thus to sweep the board of all available opponents, but found that the other column had taken warning from the boom of guns and pulled back out of danger.

Rosecrans too had taken alarm, and though his present-for-duty strength now stood at 80,124, as compared to Bragg's 49,068, he began to suspect that he was outnumbered. "I am not, as you know, an alarmist," he wired Halleck on the day after Coburn's defeat, "but I do not think it will do to risk as we did before." He reinforced the threatened quarter, causing the rebel horsemen to pull back. But when the blue tide once more receded, Van Dorn returned again, cutting and slashing, left and right, and playing all the while on Rosecrans' fears. On March 24, having leapfrogged his headquarters to Spring Hill, he sent Forrest against Brentwood (ten miles north of Federal-held Franklin) where a garrison of about 800 Wisconsin and Michigan infantry protected army stores and a stockaded railroad bridge across the Little Harpeth River. Forrest appeared before the place next morning, demanding an unconditional surrender. "Come and take us," Colonel Edward Bloodgood replied stoutly, until he saw the graybacks preparing to do just that: whereupon he changed his mind and hauled down his flag. Setting fire to the stockade and packing the stores for removal along with his captives, Forrest sent one regiment up the Nashville pike to spread the scare in that direction — which it did, penetrating the southern environs of the city and riding within plain sight of the capitol tower — while the main body, after pausing to fight a confused rear-guard action provoked by a blue column that moved up from Franklin, made its getaway eastward before turning south to safety. In a general order issued on the last day of the month, Bragg expressed the "pride and gratification" he felt as a result of the "two brilliant and successful affairs recently achieved by the forces of the cavalry of Major General Van Dorn."

Unwilling to rest on his laurels now that fortune's smile was broadening still further, Van Dorn moved on April 10 against Franklin itself. A forced reconnaissance, he called it afterwards, though the defenders insisted that it had been an all-out attempt to take the place by storm. In support of the former contention was the fact that casualties were fewer than a hundred on each side; anyhow, he disengaged and withdrew when he found that the Union commander, Major General Gordon Granger, had been reinforced to a strength of about 8000. Back at Spring Hill, he continued to design projects for the discomfiture of the enemy, assisting Bragg to hold onto the fruitful region despite the odds which favored a Federal advance. On through April he labored, and into May, though apparently not so exclusively as to require him to abandon other pursuits; for at 10 o'clock on the morning of May 7, Dr George B. Peters, a local citizen, walked into headquarters, where Van Dorn was hard at work at his desk, and shot him in the back of the head with a pistol. He died about 2 o'clock that afternoon, by which time the assassin was safe within the Union lines, having ridden off in the buggy he had left parked outside while he stepped indoors to carry out his project. The accepted explanation was that the doctor had chosen this emphatic means to protest the general's attention to his young wife, though there were some who claimed that he had done the shooting for political reasons. At any rate, that was the end of the saga of Buck Van Dorn. Fortune's smile had turned out fickle after all, and they buried him in Columbia next day.

After Earl Van Dorn was assassinated, his personal flag was returned to Miss Constance Cary of Richmond, who had made the banner. It bore the name "Constance" on the reverse side.

heeler had got back in stride by then with a double blow at Rosecrans' rail supply lines on April 10, the day Van Dorn tested the Franklin defenses and found them strong. The first was scored northeast of Nashville, beyond Andrew Jackson's Hermitage, by secretly posting guns along the near bank of a bend that took the Cumberland River within 500-yard range of the Louisville & Nashville tracks. After a wait of two hours, Wheeler reported, "a very large locomotive came in view, drawing eighteen cars loaded with horses and other stock." Though the target was moving his marksmanship was excellent, according to a Federal brigadier. "The first shot knocked off the dome of the locomotive, the next went through the boiler, one shot broke out a spoke in one of the driving-wheels." When the engine stalled in a cloud of steam, the gunners continued to pump shells into the cars, scattering bluecoats, horses, and cattle in all directions. Meanwhile, on the Nashville & Chattanooga side of the Tennessee capital, another group of Wheeler's men rode into Antioch, where they ambushed and derailed a train by spreading the tracks and took from the wreckage about seventy Union captives — including twenty officers, three of whom were members of Rosecrans' staff — along with some forty Confederates en route to Ohio prison camps, $30,000 in greenbacks, and a large mail containing much useful information. Loaded with booty, the raiders got away eastward to join their friends, who by now had ridden back past the Hermitage after their shooting-gallery fun on the Cumberland. Wheeler's total cost for both accomplishments was one man wounded.

He was cheered all round and greeted with smiles on his return, for both actions had a somewhat comic tinge. But the loudest cheers and the broadest smiles were reserved for Bedford Forrest, who began to win his *nom de guerre* "the Wizard of the Saddle" with an exploit which took him, through the closing days of April and the opening days of May, into parts of three states and across the northern width of Alabama. He was drawn in that direction by a Federal project which got under way, by coincidence on that same April 10, with the embarkation at Nashville of an expedition designed to sever Bragg's main supply line, the Western & Atlantic Railroad, between Atlanta and Chattanooga. This had been attempted once before, a year ago this week, but had resulted in the Great Locomotive Chase and the capture of the twenty-two spies who tried it. The new plan, while perhaps equally daring, was of a quite different nature. Taking a page from the book the rebel cavalry fought by — particularly John Morgan and Forrest himself — Colonel Abel D. Streight, New-York-born commander of a regiment of Hoosier infantry, proposed to Rosecrans that a large body of men, say 2000, be mounted for a quick but powerful thrust, into and out of the South's vitals. Rosecrans, who so often had been on the receiving end of this kind of thing, was delighted at the prospect of turning the tables, and his delight increased when Streight removed his final objection by agreeing to mount the men on mules instead of horses, of which there was a shortage; mules, he said, were not only more sure-footed, they were also more intelligent. (Which was true, so far as it went, though that was by no means all of the story. Mules had other, less admirable qualities: as he would presently discover.) At any rate, Rosecrans gave his approval to the project, designated Streight as commander, and assigned him three more regiments of Ohio, Indiana, and Illinois infantry, together with two companies of North Alabama Unionists — a breed of men who were known to their late compatriots as "homemade Yankees," but who were expected to prove invaluable as guides through a region unfamiliar to everyone else in the flying column — and a requisition for some nine hundred quartermaster mules. This would mount only about half of the troops, but Rosecrans explained that the rest could secure animals by commandeering them from rebel sympathizers while on the way to their starting point in the northeast corner of Mississippi.

So Streight got his men and mules aboard the transports and steamed next morning down the Cumberland to unload at Palmyra, on the left bank just around the bend from Clarksville, for a stock-gathering march to Fort Henry, where they again met the transports for the long ride south up the Tennessee to Eastport, Mississippi. That was the true starting point, tactically speaking, but Streight — a broad-chested man of soldierly appearance, just past forty, with a tall forehead, light-colored eyes, a fleshy, powerful-looking nose, and a dark, well-trimmed beard framing a wide, determined mouth exposed below a clean-shaven upper lip — had already encountered complications well outside the original margin he had allowed for error. For one thing, after waiting to pick up rations and forage on the Ohio, the navy did not turn up at Fort Henry on time, with the result that he did not reach Eastport until April 19, three days behind schedule. For another, a delayed check disclosed that a large proportion of the quartermaster mules were sadly afflicted with distemper, while many others were unbroken colts, not over two years old. This last exposed a further drawback; for he found that his converted infantrymen, as one of them remarked, "were at first very easily dismounted, frequently in a most undignified and unceremonious manner." Practice might improve the men's equestrian skill, but the mules were going to remain a problem. About five hundred had been commandeered on the course of the overland march, which more than made up for the hundred-odd who died of sickness and exhaustion while en route; but this gain was canceled on the evening of his arrival at Eastport. Returning to headquarters about midnight from a conference with Brigadier General Grenville M. Dodge, who had brought a 7500-man column over from Corinth to serve as a screen for the raiders' departure, he learned that some four hundred of the creatures — naturally the most intelligent of the lot — had escaped from their crudely built corrals and now were scattered about the countryside, disrupting

★

the stillness of the night and mocking his woes with brays that had the sound of fiendish laughter. Two more days were spent here in rounding them up; half of them, that is, for the rest were never recovered. However, Dodge made up the difference with animals out of his pack train, and Streight at last got started in earnest, moving eastward across Bear Creek on the morning of April 22.

Five days behind schedule, but still protected from inquisitive eyes by the screen Dodge's troops had drawn along the south bank of the Tennessee River, he reached Tuscumbia late on the 24th and called a final two-day rest halt before resuming the march at 11 p.m. of the 26th, his force reduced to 1500 by a rigid inspection in which the surgeons culled such men as they judged unfit for the rigorous work ahead. All next day, and the next, as the column moved south to Russellville, then eastward to Mount Hope, rain and mud held its progress to a crawl and 300 of the fledgling troopers were reconverted to infantry because their mounts were too weak to carry anything heavier than a saddle. On the 29th, however, the sun broke through, giving "strong hopes of better times," as Streight declared in his last rearward message, and he began to pick up speed, along with replacements for his ailing mules. Thirty-five miles he made that day, clearing Moulton to make camp that night at the western foot of Day's Gap, a narrow defile piercing a lofty ridge that signaled the advent of the Appalachians.

An engineer and surveyor for western railroads before the war, Grenville Dodge entered the war as colonel of an Iowa regiment. He was promoted to brigadier after being wounded at the Battle of Pea Ridge.

At this point, with the tactically dangerous flatlands left behind, he was about halfway to his first objective: Rome, Georgia, where the Confederacy had a cannon foundry and machine shops for the Western & Atlantic, whose main line was barely a half-day's ride beyond. Starting early next morning, the last day of April, Streight rode at the head of the column toiling upward through the gap. "The sun shone out bright and beautiful as spring day's sun ever beamed," his adjutant later recalled, "and from the smouldering campfires of the previous night the mild blue smoke ascended in graceful curves and mingled with the gray mist slumbering on the mountain tops above." There was in fact much that was dreamlike and idyllic about the scene — "well calculated to inspire and refresh the minds of our weary soldiers," the admiring lieutenant phrased it — until suddenly, without previous intimation of a transition, as Streight and the forward elements of the column neared the crest, the dream shifted kaleidoscopically into nightmare. From downhill, in the direction of last night's camp, the deep-voiced booms of guns, mixed in with the tearing rattle of musketry, abruptly informed him that he was under attack.

It was Forrest. A week ago today — the day after Streight left Eastport — he had received at Spring Hill, Tennessee, orders from Bragg to proceed south to the Florence-Tuscumbia region and assist the inadequate local defense units to oppose the force moving eastward under Dodge. He left next morning, April 24, and thirty-six hours later had his 1577-man brigade at Brown's Ferry, Alabama, ninety miles away. Leaving one of his three regiments to guard the north bank of the Tennessee in case Dodge decided to strike in that direction, he ferried the others across on the 26th and moved west through Courtland to Town Creek, which he reached in time to challenge a Federal crossing. The long-range skirmish continued until dusk of the following day, when Forrest received word from a scout that a mounted column estimated at 2000 men had left Mount Hope that morning, headed east. This was the first he had heard of Streight's existence, but he decided at once that this was the major threat, not the larger force immediately to his front. Accordingly, leaving Dodge to the local defenders and the regiment already posted beyond the river, he took off southward at dawn of the 29th for Moulton, which Streight had cleared six hours before. At midnight, having covered fifty miles of road with just over a thousand horsemen and eight guns, he went into bivouac, four miles short of Streight's camp at Day's Gap, in order to give his saddle-weary troopers some rest for tomorrow, and soon after sunrise was banging away at the Federal rear.

In the course of the three-day running fight which followed, the pursued had certain definite advantages. The first was a superiority of numbers; although Streight's enjoyment of this was considerably diminished by the fact that he did not know he had it. All the same, the numerical odds were with him, three to two, whether he knew it or not, and what was more they grew as he

★

moved eastward past well-stocked farms untouched by war till now. When his mules gave out, as they frequently did, he could remount his men by seizing others; whereas for Forrest, coming along in the raiders' clean-swept wake, a broken-down horse meant a lost rider. Another tactical advantage accruing to the blue commander was that whenever he chose to make a stand he could not only select the terrain best suited for defensive fighting, he could also lay small-scale ambushes by which a rear-guard handful could shock the pursuers with surprise fire, forcing them to halt and deploy, then hurry ahead to rejoin the main body before the attack was delivered. Streight was altogether aware of this advantage, and used it first within three miles of the point where he heard the opening boom of guns. Selecting a position along a wooded ridge, with a boggy creek protecting his left and a steep ravine his right, he sent back word for the rear-guard Alabama Unionists, still skirmishing in Day's Gap, to retreat on the run through the newly drawn line and thus draw the graybacks into ambush. It worked to perfection. As the pursuers rode fast to overtake the homemade Yankees, the waiting bluecoats rose from the underbrush and shattered the head of the column with massed volleys. When reinforcements came up to repeat the attempt, this time advancing a section of artillery to counterbalance the two 12-pounder mountain howitzers firing rapidly from the ridge, the defenders followed up a second repulse with a counterattack and captured both of the guns, then drew off, leaving the rebels rocked back on their heels.

Forrest was thrown into a towering rage by the loss of his guns and the fact that the raiders had won first honors and drawn first blood — including that of his brother, Captain William Forrest, who had led his company of scouts in the charge and had been unhorsed by a bullet that broke his thigh — but by the time he got his troopers back into line for a third attack, the bluecoats had pulled out. He pushed on, closing again on their rear at Crooked Creek, where Streight again formed line of battle, six miles beyond the first. Here, from about an hour before dark until 10 o'clock that night, the two forces engaged in a fire fight. Determined to give the raiders no rest, Forrest kept forcing the issue by moonlight, and his orders, though brief, were conclusive: "Shoot at everything blue and keep up the scare." Finally, with one flank about to crumple, Streight "resumed the march," leaving the two captured guns behind him, spiked. At midnight, then again two hours later, he laid ambushes, but Forrest kept crowding him and did not call a halt till daylight, when he paused long enough to water and feed the horses and give the weaker ones an opportunity to catch up. Streight meanwhile pushed on to the outskirts of Blountsville, which he reached about midmorning of May Day, having covered forty-three miles over mountain roads since the skirmishing began soon after sunrise yesterday. However, before his men could finish feeding their weary mounts, Forrest once more was driving in the pickets, and the two commands went through the town in a whirl of dust and gunsmoke, shooting at one another over the ears of their horses or the cruppers of their mules.

So it went, all that day and the next, eastward another fifty miles, then northeastward along the near bank of the Coosa River, with Streight making stands behind the east fork of the Black Warrior River and Big Will's Creek, laying ambushes in the heavily wooded valley off the southern end of Lookout Mountain, and burning the only bridge across Black Creek, just short of Gadsden. Forrest kept the pressure on, however. He got over the last-named obstacle by using a ford that was shown him, under fire from the opposite bank, by a sixteen-year-old farm girl, Emma Sanson — in appreciation of whose courage he took time and pains to leave an autograph note of thanks:

> *Hed Quaters in Sadle*
>
> *May 2 1863*
>
> *My highest regardes to miss Ema Sanson for hir Gal-*
> *lant conduct while my posse was skirmishing with the*
> *Federals across Black Creek near Gadesden Allabama.*
>
> *N. B. Forrest*
>
> *Brig Genl Comding N. Ala —*

and pressed on after the blue raiders, engaging them in another running fight through Gadsden and beyond, where they soon were forced to make another stand. He had the advantage of singleness of purpose, plus the chance to give his men a breather when he chose, pursuing as it were in shifts, some resting while others kept up the chase; whereas Streight not only had to keep fending off the myriad and apparently inexhaustible graybacks hot on his trail — a profitless business at best — but also had to keep pushing on toward the accomplishment of his mission in North Georgia. After nearly three days of riding and fighting, and two nights without rest, his men were falling asleep on muleback and even in line of battle whenever he called a halt to lay another ambush or defend another opportune position, and now that his pursuers had avoided delay at Black Creek, thanks to Emma Sanson, he faced another sleepless night. "It now became evident to me," he later reported, "that our only hope was in crossing the river at Rome and destroying the bridge, which would delay Forrest a day or two and give us time to collect horses and mules and allow the command a little time to sleep, without which it was impossible to proceed."

Accordingly, when he reached Turkeytown, eight miles beyond Gadsden, he selected two hundred of the best-mounted men and sent them ahead to seize the bridge across the Oostanaula River at Rome and hold it until the main body came up. At sunset, four miles farther along, he formed again for battle "as it was impossible to continue the march through the night without feeding and resting." In the course of the preliminary skirmish, however, he discovered that much of the men's ammunition had been ruined by dampness and abrasion. Instead of risking another general engagement under these circumstances, he decided to disengage — "unobserved, if possible" — and lay another ambush in a thicket half a mile ahead. When Forrest detected the ruse and began to move out on the flank, Streight had to pull back and make a run for it in the dusk, beginning another horrendous night march with men who by now had the look of somnambulists and mules that were "jaded, tender-footed, and worn out." But the worst development, so far, was encountered when they reached the Cedar Bluff ferry across the Chattooga River, just above its confluence with the Coosa. The 200-man detail had passed this way a short while back, headed for Rome, but had neglected to post a guard: with the result that some citizens had spirited the ferryboat away, leaving Streight with the sort of problem he had been leaving Forrest all along.

Yet he was nothing if not persevering. Turning left, he plodded wearily through the darkness along the west bank of the Chattooga, intent on reaching a bridge near Gaylesville, half a dozen miles upstream. Whereupon — while Forrest was giving his troopers a few hours' sleep: all but one squadron, which he instructed to stay on the trail of the raiders and "devil them all night" — Streight and his muleback soldiers entered the worst of their several Deep South nightmares. The way led through extensive "choppings" where the timber had been cut and burned to furnish charcoal for nearby Round Mountain Furnace, which in turn supplied the Rome foundry with pig iron. Though the raiders succeeded in wrecking part of the smelting plant — the one substantial blow they struck in the course of their long ride across Alabama — they paid a high price in the extra miles they covered in order to bring it within reach. Lost in a maze of wagon trails, segments of the blue column were scattered about the choppings until daylight showed them the way back to the river and then to the bridge, which they crossed and burned in their wake. Wobbly with fatigue, animals and men alike, they staggered along the opposite bank, again to the vicinity of Cedar Bluff, then turned eastward five more miles to the Lawrence plantation, which they reached about 9 a.m. The Georgia line was only five miles ahead, with Rome barely another fifteen miles beyond, but Streight had no choice except to drop from exhaustion or halt for rest and food. He had no sooner begun the distribution of rations, however, than the graybacks once more were driving in his pickets.

Forrest had swum the Chattooga at sunup, using long ropes to drag two of his guns across, submerged on the sandy bottom. Down to six hundred men by now, he was outnumbered worse than two to one and knew it, even if

Union general Abel D. Streight led mule-mounted infantry on a daring raid deep into Confederate territory but was eventually captured by Forrest's more experienced horse-mounted cavalry.

Streight did not. All along he had had to avoid the obvious maneuver of circling the flank of the blue column in order to block its path; for in that case, goaded by desperation, the Federals might have run right over him, swamping his line with the sheer weight of numbers. Even now, in fact, though his troopers were considerably refreshed by the sleep they had enjoyed while the bluecoats were stumbling around in the choppings south of Gaylesville, he preferred not to risk a pitched battle if he could accomplish his purpose otherwise. So he did as he had done before, in similar circumstances: sent forward, under a flag of truce, an officer with a note demanding immediate surrender "to stop the further and useless effusion of blood."

Streight, who had had to wake his men to put them into line of battle — where they promptly fell asleep again, with bullets whistling overhead — replied that he was by no means ready to give up, but that, sharing Forrest's humane views as to unnecessary bloodshed, he was willing to parley. He insisted further, when the guns fell silent and the two commanders met between the lines, that he would not even consider laying down his arms unless his opponent would prove that he had an overwhelming superiority of numbers. Forrest declined to show his hand in any such manner; but all the while, acting under previous instructions, the officer in charge of the section of artillery kept bringing his two guns over a distant rise in the road, then back under cover and over the rise again, producing for the benefit of Streight, who had been placed so as to

★

watch all this over Forrest's shoulder, the appearance of a stream of guns arriving at intervals to bolster the rebel line. "Name of God!" Streight cried at last. "How many guns have you got? There's fifteen I've counted already." Forrest looked around casually. "I reckon that's all that has kept up," he said. So Streight went back to his own lines for a conference with his regimental commanders, most of whom, as he later reported, "had already expressed the opinion that, unless we could reach Rome and cross the river before the enemy came up with us again, we should be compelled to surrender." At this juncture, a messenger arrived from the 200-man detail sent ahead the night before and reported that the bridge across the Oostanaula was strongly held by rebel troops in Rome. That did it; Streight returned and announced his willingness to surrender. Forrest replied, "Stack your arms right along there, Colonel, and march your men away down that hollow."

The total bag, including the 200-man detail picked up on the way into Rome that same Sunday afternoon as it returned from its fruitless mission, was 1466 bluecoats, and though they had been feared as would-be conquerors — a fear which had thrown the Rome citizenry into such a panic of feverish activity that the Federal scouts, observing from across the Oostanaula, had mistaken the milling for preparedness — they were welcomed and fed generously as captives. Forrest's own entrance was the occasion for the presentation of a horseshoe wreath of flowers, hailing him as the town's deliverer, and a fine saddle horse, which helped to make up for the two that had been shot from under him in the course of the long chase. Then began a famous celebration, attended by what one matron called "just a regular wholesale cooking of hams and shoulders and all sorts of provisions" to relieve the hunger pangs of the gray heroes. Nor were the prisoners excluded from this bounty; "We were quite willing to feed the Yankees when they had no guns," she added. But the Roman holiday was cut short on the night of May 5 by the arrival of word that another column of blue raiders had left Tuscumbia that afternoon, headed southeast for Jasper and possibly Montgomery. Forrest and his men were back in the saddle next morning. Riding once more through Gadsden the following day, they learned that the rumor was groundless, Dodge having returned to Corinth; so they swung north, recovering the third regiment en route, to resume their accustomed work in Tennessee. On May 10, however — another Sunday — Forrest was handed orders from Bragg, instructing him to have his brigade continue its present march but for him to report in person to army headquarters, where he would receive, along with a recommendation for promotion to major general, appointment to the command Van Dorn had vacated three days ago, when he came under the Spring Hill doctor's pistol.

★ ★ ★

★

Shelby Foote

As part of General Ulysses S.
Grant's strategy to by-pass
Vicksburg, Union soldiers dredge
a canal across a bend in the
Mississippi River.

TEN

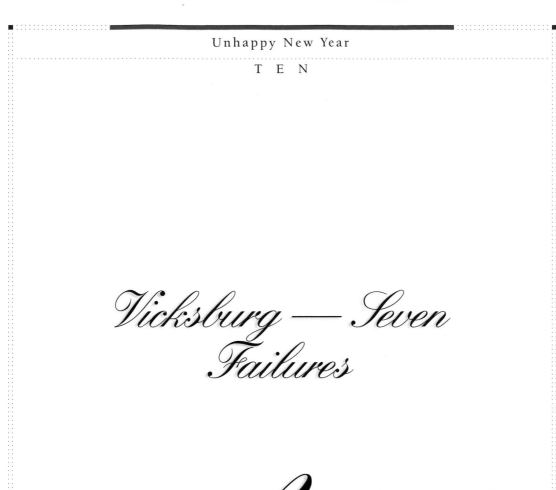

Vicksburg — Seven Failures

1863 ★ ★ ★ ★ ★

Along toward sunset of January 28, completing a 400-mile overnight trip from Memphis down the swollen, tawny, mile-wide Mississippi, a stern-wheel packet warped in for a west-bank landing at Young's Point, just opposite the base of the long hairpin bend in front of Vicksburg and within half a dozen air-line miles of the guns emplaced along the lip of the tall clay bluff the city stood on. First off the steamboat, once the deck hands had swung out the stageplank, was a slight man, rather stooped, five feet eight inches in height and weighing less than a hundred and forty pounds, who walked with a peculiar gait, shoulders hunched "a little forward of the perpendicular," as one observer remarked, so that each step seemed to arrest him momentarily in the act of pitching on his face. He had on a plain blue suit and what the same reporter called "an indifferently good 'Kossuth' hat, with the top battered in close to his head." Forty years old, he looked considerably older, partly because of the crow's-feet crinkling the outer corners of his eyes — the result of intense concentration, according to some, while others identified them as whiskey lines, plainly confirming rumors of overindulgence and refuting the protestations of friends that he never touched the stuff — but mainly because of the full, barely grizzled, light brown beard, close-cropped to emphasize the jut of a square jaw and expose a mouth described as being "of the letterbox shape," clamped firmly shut below a nose that surprised by contrast, being delicately chiseled, and blue-gray eyes that gave the face a somewhat out-of-balance look because one was set a trifle lower than the other. Wearing neither sword nor sash, and indeed no trappings of rank at all, except for the twin-starred straps of a major general tacked to the weathered shoulders of his coat, he was reading a newspaper as he came down the plank to the Louisiana shore, and he chewed the unlighted stump of a cigar, which not only seemed habitual but also appeared to be a more congruous facial appendage than the surprisingly aquiline nose.

"There's General Grant," an Illinois soldier told a comrade as they stood watching this unceremonious arrival.

"I guess not," the other replied, shaking his head. "That fellow don't look like he has the ability to command a regiment, much less an army."

It was not so much that Grant was unexpected; he had a habit of turning up unannounced at almost any time and place within the limits of his large department. The trouble was that he bore such faint resemblance to his photographs, which had been distributed widely ever since Donelson and which, according to an acquaintance, made him look like a "burly beef-contractor." In person he resembled at best a badly printed copy of one of those photos, with the burliness left out. Conversely, the lines of worry — if his friends were right and that was what they were — were more pronounced, as was perhaps only natural when he had more to fret about than the discomfort of holding still for a camera. Just now, for instance, there was John McClernand, who persisted in considering the river force a separate command and continued to issue general orders under the heading, "Headquarters, Army of the Mississippi." Before Grant had been downriver two days he received a letter from McClernand, noting "that orders are being issued directly from your headquarters directly to army corps commanders, and not through me." This could only result in "dangerous confusion," McClernand protested, "as I am invested, by order of the Secretary of War, indorsed by the President, and by order of the President communicated to you by the General-in-Chief, with the command of all the forces operating on the Mississippi River. . . . If different views are entertained by you, then the question should be immediately referred to Washington, and one or the other, or both of us, relieved. One thing is certain; two generals cannot command this army, issuing independent and direct orders to subordinate officers, and the public service be promoted."

Grant agreed at least with the final sentence — which he later paraphrased and sharpened into a maxim: "Two commanders on the same field are always one too many" — but he found the letter as a whole "more in the nature of a reprimand than a protest." The fact was, it approached outright insubordination, although not quite close enough to afford occasion for the pounce

Grant was crouched for. "I overlooked it, as I believed, for the good of the serv-ice," he subsequently wrote. By way of reply, instead of direct reproof, he is-sued orders announcing that he was assuming personal command of the river expedition and instructing all corps commanders, including McClernand, to re-port henceforth directly to him; McClernand's corps, he added by way of a stinger, would garrison Helena and other west-bank points well upriver. Out-raged at being the apparent victim of a squeeze play, the former congressman responded by asking whether, "having projected the Mississippi River expedi-tion, and having been by a series of orders assigned to the command of it," he was thus to be "entirely withdrawn from it." Grant replied to the effect that he would do as he saw fit, since "as yet I have seen no order to prevent my tak-ing command in the field." McClernand acquiesced, as he said, "for the purpose of avoiding a conflict of authority in the presence of the enemy," but requested that the entire matter be referred to their superiors in Washington, "not only in respect for the President and Secretary, under whose authority I claim the right to command the expedition, but in justice to myself as its author and actual pro-moter." Grant accordingly forwarded the correspondence to Halleck, saying that he had assumed command only because he lacked confidence in McClernand. "I respectfully submit the whole matter to the General-in-Chief and the Presi-dent," he ended his indorsement. "Whatever the decision made by them, I will cheerfully submit to and give a hearty support."

In bucking all this up to the top echelon Grant was on even safer ground than he supposed. Just last week McClernand had received, in reply to a private letter to Lincoln charging Halleck "with wilful contempt of superior au-thority" because of his so-far "interference" in the matter, "and with incompe-tency for the extraordinary and vital functions with which he is charged," a note in which the President told him plainly: "I have too many *family* controversies (so to speak) already on my hands to voluntarily, or so long as I can avoid it, take up another. You are now doing well — well for the country, and well for yourself — much better than you could possibly be if engaged in open war with General Halleck. Allow me to beg that for your sake, for my sake, and for the country's sake, you give your whole attention to the better work." So it was: McClernand already had his answer before he filed his latest appeal. Lincoln would not interfere. The army was Grant's, and would remain Grant's, to do with as he saw fit in accomplishing what Lincoln called "the better work."

His problem was how best to go about it. Now that he had inspect-ed at first hand the obstacles to success in this swampy region, much of which was at present under water and would continue to be so for months to come, he could see that the wisest procedure, from a strategic point of view, "would have been to go back to Memphis, establish that as a base of supplies, fortify it so that the storehouses could be held by a small garrison, and move from there along the line of the [Mississippi & Tennessee] railroad, repairing as we advanced to the Yalobusha," from which point he would have what he now so gravely lacked: a straight, high-ground shot at the city on the rebel bluff. So he wrote, years later, having gained the advantage of hindsight. For the present, however, he saw certain drawbacks to the retrograde movement, which in his judgment far outweighed the strictly tactical advantages. For one thing, the November elections had gone against the party that stood for all-out prosecution of the war, and this had turned out to be a warning of future trouble, with the croakers finding encouragement in the reverse. There was the question of morale, not only in the army itself, but also on the home front, where even a temporary withdrawal would be considered an admission that Vicksburg was too tough a nut to crack. At this critical juncture, both temporal and political, with voluntary enlistment practically at a standstill throughout much of the North and the new conscription laws already meeting sporadic opposition, such a discouragement might well prove fatal to the cause. "It was my judgment at the time," Grant subsequently wrote, "that to make a backward movement as long as that from Vicksburg to Memphis, would be interpreted, by many of those yet full of hope for the preservation of the Union, as a defeat, and that the draft would be resisted, desertions ensue, and the power to capture and punish deserters lost. There was nothing left to be done but to *go forward to a decisive victory*. This was in my mind from the moment I took command in person at Young's Point."

In his own mind at least that much was settled. He would stay. But this decision only brought him face to face with the basic problem, as he put it, of how "to secure a footing upon dry ground on the east side of the river, from which the troops could operate against Vicksburg . . . without an apparent retreat." Aside from a frontal assault, either against the bluff itself or against the heights flanking it on the north — which Sherman, even if he had done nothing more last month, had proved would not only be costly in the extreme but would also be fruitless, and which Grant said "was never contemplated; certainly not by me" — the choice lay between whether to cross upstream or down, above or below the rebel bastion. One seemed about as impossible as the other. Above, the swampy, fifty-mile-wide Delta lay in his path, practically roadless and altogether malarial. Even if he were able to slog his foot soldiers across it, which was doubtful, it was worse than doubtful whether he would be able to establish and maintain a vital supply line by that route. On the other hand, to attempt a crossing below the city seemed even more suicidal, since this would involve a run past frowning batteries, not only at Vicksburg itself, but also at Warrenton and Grand Gulf, respectively seven and thirty-five miles downriver. Armored gunboats — as Farragut had demonstrated twice the year before, first up, then down, with his heavily gunned salt-water fleet — might run this fiery gauntlet, taking their losses as they went, but brittle-skinned transports and sup-

0 10 20 30 40 50
Scale in Miles

Moon Lake

Yazoo Pass

Coldwater R.

Tallahatchie River

White River

MISSISSIPPI & TENNESSEE RAILROAD

Arkansas River

ARKANSAS POST
(FORT HINDMAN)

Mississippi River

Yalobusha River

• Grenada

ARKANSAS

YAZOO PASS ROUTE

FORT PEMBERTON

Greenwood

MISSISSIPPI CENTRAL RAILROAD

Rolling Fork

Sunflower River

Lake Providence

STEELE'S BAYOU ROUTE

Black Bayou

• Yazoo City

Yazoo River

Bayou Macon

Deer Creek

Steele's Bayou

Big Black River

LAKE PROVIDENCE ROUTE

Milliken's Bend •

• Haynes' Bluff

VICKSBURG, SHREVEPORT & TEXAS RR

CANAL

• Vicksburg

SOUTHERN

MISSISSIPPI RAILROAD

Jackson •

Tensas River

Washita River

• Grand Gulf
• Port Gibson

MISSISSIPPI

Mississippi River

• Natchez

NEW ORLEANS, JACKSON & GREAT NORTHERN RAILROAD

Pearl River

Red River

LOUISIANA

Grant foresaw failure for a series of expeditions aimed at Vicksburg, but as he later wrote, "I let the work go on, believing employment was better than idleness."

ply boats would be quite another matter, considering the likelihood of their being reduced to kindling in short order, with much attendant loss of life and goods. . . . In short, the choice seemed to lie between two impossibilities, flanking a third which had been rejected before it was even considered.

Two clear advantages Grant had, however, by way of helping to offset the gloom, and both afforded him comfort under the strain. One was the unflinching support of his superiors; the other was an ample supply of troops, either downstream with him or else on call above. "The eyes and hopes of the whole country are now directed to your army," Halleck presently would tell him. "In my opinion, the opening of the Mississippi River will be to us of more advantage than the capture of forty Richmonds. We shall omit nothing which we can do to assist you." Already, before Grant left Memphis, Old Brains had urged him: "Take everything you can dispense with in Tennessee and [North] Mississippi. We must not fail in this if within human power to accomplish it." His total effective strength within his department, as of late January, was approximately 103,000 officers and men, and of these, as a result of abandoning railroads and other important rear-area installations, Grant had been able to earmark just over half for the downriver expedition: 32,000 in the two corps under McClernand and Sherman, already at hand, and 15,000 in McPherson's corps, filing aboard transports southbound from Memphis even now. In addition to these 47,000 — the official total, "present for duty, equipped," was 46,994 — another 15,000 were standing by under Hurlbut, who commanded the fourth corps, ready to follow McPherson as soon as they got the word. Just now, though, there not only was no need for them; there actually was no room. Because of the high water and the incessant rain overflowing the bayous, there was no place to camp on the low-lying west bank except upon the levee, with the result that the army was strung out along it for more than fifty miles, north and south, under conditions that were anything but healthy. As morale declined, the sick-lists lengthened; desertions were up; funerals were frequent. "Go any day down the levee," one recruit wrote home, "and you could see a squad or two of soldiers burying a companion, until the levee was nearly full of graves and the hospitals still full of sick. And those that were not down sick were not well by a considerable." Pneumonia was the chief killer, with smallpox a close second. Some regiments soon had more men down than up. The food was bad. Paymasters did not venture south of Helena, which increased the disaffection, and the rumor mills were grinding as never before. When the mails were held up, as they frequently were, it was reported from camp to camp, like a spark moving along a fifty-mile train of powder, that the war was over but that the news was being kept from the troops "for fear we could not be held in subjection if we knew the state of affairs." They took out at least a share of their resentment on such rebel property as came within their reach. "Farms disappear, houses are burned and plundered, and every living animal killed and eaten," Sherman informed his senator brother. "General officers make feeble efforts to stay the disorder, but it is idle." Then when the mail came through at last they could read in anti-administration newspapers of the instability and incompetence of the West Pointers responsible for their welfare, including Sherman — "He hates reporters, foams at the mouth when he sees them, snaps at them; sure symptoms of a deep-seated mania" — and the army commander himself: "The confidence of the army is greatly shaken in General Grant, who hitherto undoubtedly depended more upon good fortune than upon military ability for success."

The wet season would continue for months, during which all these problems would be with him. As Grant said in retrospect, "There seemed to be no possibility of a land movement before the end of March or later." Yet "it would not do to lie idle all this time. The effect would be demoralizing to the troops and injurious to their health. Friends in the North would have grown

---

"In my opinion, the opening of the Mississippi River will be to us of more advantage than the capture of forty Richmonds. We shall omit nothing which we can do to assist you."

— Henry W. Halleck

---

more and more insolent in their gibes and denunciations of the cause and those engaged in it." So he launched (or rather, continued) what he called "a series of experiments," designed not only "to consume time," but also to serve the triple purpose of diverting "the attention of the enemy, of my troops, and of the public generally." Two failures were already behind him in his campaign against Vicksburg: the advance down the Mississippi Central and the assault on the Chickasaw Bluffs, both of which had ended in retreat. Now there followed five more failures, bringing the total to seven. Looking back on them later he was to say — quite untruthfully, as the record would show — that he had "never felt great confidence that any of the experiments resorted to would prove successful," though he had always been "prepared to take advantage of them in case they did."

The third of these seven "experiments" — the attempt, by means of a canal across the base of the tongue of land in front of Vicksburg, to divert the channel of the river and thus permit the column of warships, transports, and supply boats to by-pass the batteries on the bluff — had been in progress ever

since the return of the army from Arkansas Post, but Sherman, who had assigned a thousand men a day to the digging job, was not sanguine of results.
"The river is about full and threatens to drown us out," he was complaining as
he sloshed about in a waste of gumbo, with the rain coming down harder every
week. "The ground is wet, almost water, and it is impossible for wagons to haul
stores from the river to camp, or even horses to wallow through." Conversely, as
if to preserve a balance of optimism, Grant's expectations rose with the passage
of time. In early March he wired Halleck: "The canal is near completion. . . .
I will have Vicksburg this month, or fail in the attempt." But this was the signal
for disaster. "If the river rises 8 feet more, we would have to take to the trees,"
Sherman had said, and presently it did. The dam at the upper end of the cut
gave way, and the water, instead of scouring out a channel — as had been
expected, or anyhow intended — spread all over the lower end of the peninsula,
forcing the evacuation of the troops from their flooded camps, with the resultant sacrifice of many horses and much equipment. "This little affair of ours here
on Vicksburg Point is labor lost," Sherman reported in disgust, announcing the
unceremonious end of the third experiment.

But Grant already had a fourth in progress. Fifty-odd miles above
Vicksburg, just west of the river and south of the Arkansas line, lay Lake Providence, once a bend of the Mississippi but long since abandoned by the Old Man
in the course of one of his cataclysmic whims. Though the lake now was
land-locked, separated moreover from the river by a levee, Bayou Baxter drained
it sluggishly westward into Bayou Macon, which in turn flowed into the Tensas
River, just over a hundred winding miles to the south. Still farther down, the
Tensas joined the Ouachita to form the Black, and the Black ran into the Red,
which entered the Mississippi a brief stretch above Port Hudson. Despite its
roundabout meandering, a distance of some 470 miles, this route seemed to
Grant to offer a chance, once the levee had been breached to afford access to
Lake Providence and the intricate system of hinterland bayous and rivers, for a
naval column to avoid not only the Vicksburg batteries but also those below at
Warrenton and Grand Gulf. Accordingly, two days after his arrival at Young's
Point, he sent an engineer detail to look into the possibilities indicated on the
map, and the following week, in early February, he went up to see for himself. It
seemed to him that "a little digging" — "less than one-quarter," he said, of what
Sherman had done already on the old canal — "will connect the Mississippi and
Lake, and in all probability will wash a channel in a short time." If so, the way
would be open for a bloodless descent, at the end of which he would join Banks
for a combined attack on Port Hudson, and once that final bastion had been reduced the Confederacy would have been cut in two and the Great Lakes region
would have recovered its sorely missed trade connection with the Gulf. Impressed
by this vista, Grant sent at once for McPherson to come down with a full division

★

and get the project started without delay. "This bids fair to be the most practicable route for turning Vicksburg," he told him in the body of the summons.

He could scarcely have assigned the task to an officer better prepared to undertake it. McPherson, who was thirty-three and a fellow Ohioan, had been top man in the West Point class of '53 and had returned to the academy as an engineering instructor; he also had worked on river and harbor projects in the peacetime army, and had served at the time of Shiloh, when he was a lieutenant colonel, as chief engineer on Grant's staff. His advancement since then had been rapid, though not without some grousing, on the part of line officers he had passed on his way up the ladder, that a man who had never led troops in a major action should be given command of a corps. Sherman, on the other hand, considered him the army's "best hope for a great soldier," not excepting Grant and himself; "if he lives," he added. A bright-eyed, pleasant-faced young man, alternately bland and impulsive, McPherson came quickly down from Memphis with one of his two divisions and set to work at once. Without waiting for the levee to be cut, he horsed a small towboat overland, launched it on the lake, and got aboard for a reconnaissance — with the result that his high hopes took a sudden

This eyewitness sketch of Lake Providence accurately depicts the sodden, desolate terrain through which the Federals tried to cut a channel to circumvent Vicksburg.

★

drop. The Bayou Baxter outlet led through an extensive cypress brake, and what could be found of its channel, which was but little at the present flood stage, was badly choked with stumps and snags that threatened to knock or rip the bottom out of whatever came their way. He put his men to work with underwater saws, but it was clear that at best the job would be a long one, if not impossible. Besides, Grant now saw that, even if a passage could be opened in time to be of use, he would never be able to get together enough light-draft boats to carry his army down to the Red River anyhow. McPherson and his staff meanwhile enjoyed something of a holiday, taking a regimental band aboard the little steamer for moonlight excursions, to and from the landing at one of the lakeside plantation houses which turned out to have a well-stocked cellar. Soldiers too found relaxation in this quiet backwater of the war, mainly in fishing, what time they were not taking turns on the underwater saws. By early March it was more or less obvious that nothing substantial was going to come of this fourth attempt to take or by-pass Vicksburg, but Grant declared, later and rather laconically: "I let the work go on, believing employment was better than idleness for the men."

★ ★ ★ All seven of these experiments, four of which by now had gone by the board, anticipated some degree of coöperation from the navy. For the most part, indeed, they were classically amphibious, depending as much on naval as on army strength and skill. But if Porter, whatever his other shortcomings — one acquaintance called him "by all odds the greatest humbug of the war" — was not the kind of man to withhold needed help, neither was he the kind to be satisfied with a supporting role if he saw even an outside chance at stardom. And he believed he saw one now: had seen it, in fact, from the outset, and had already made his solo entrance on the stage. One of the two main reasons for attempting the reduction of Vicksburg and Port Hudson — in addition, that is, to opening a pathway to New Orleans and the Gulf — was to choke off rebel traffic along and across the nearly three hundred miles of river that flowed between them, particularly that segment of it tangent to the mouth of Red River, the main artery of trade connecting the goods-rich Transmississippi's far-west region with the principal Confederate supply depots in Georgia and Virginia. To accomplish this, the admiral perceived, it would not be absolutely necessary to capture either of the two bastions anchoring opposite ends of the long stretch of river. All that was needed, really, was to control what lay between them, and this could be done by sending warships down to knock out whatever vestiges of the rebel fleet remained and to establish a sort of internal blockade by patrolling all possible crossings. In early February, accordingly, while Sherman's men were still digging their way across soggy Vicksburg Point and Grant was steaming upriver for a preliminary look at cypress-choked Lake Providence, Porter gave orders which put his plan in the way of execution.

★

First off, this would require a run past the batteries on the bluff, and he gave the assignment to the steam ram *Queen of the West*, which had done it twice before, back in July, in an unsuccessful attempt to come to grips with the *Arkansas*. She was one of the navy's best-known vessels, having led the ram attack at the Battle of Memphis, where she had been commanded by her designer and builder, Colonel Charles Ellet, Jr., who had died of the only wound inflicted on a Northerner in that one-sided triumph. His son, nineteen-year-old Colonel Charles R. Ellet — who, as a medical cadet, had gone ashore in a rowboat, accompanied by three seamen, to complete the Memphis victory by raising the Stars and Stripes over the post office — had succeeded his uncle, Brigadier General A. W. Ellet, who had succeeded the first Ellet as commander of the ram fleet, as skipper of the *Queen*. Patched up from the two poundings she had taken from Vicksburg's high-perched guns, and fitted out now with guns of her own for the first time — previously she had depended solely on her punch — she made her run at daybreak, February 4, taking an even dozen hits, including two in the hull but none below the water line, and pulled up at a battery Sherman had established on the west bank, just around the bend, for the protection of his diggers. Above the town, two nights later, Porter set adrift a barge loaded with 20,000 bushels of coal, which made it downstream on schedule and without mishap, apparently not having been spotted by the lookouts on the bluff. "This gives the ram nearly coal enough to last a month," the admiral proudly informed Secretary Welles, "in which time she can commit great havoc, if no accident happens to her."

Though at first it seemed an unnecessary flourish — he knew the rebels had nothing afloat to match the *Queen* — that final reservation was prophetic. Setting out on the night of February 10, accompanied by an ex-Confederate steamboat, the *DeSoto*, which had been captured by the army below Vicksburg, Ellet began his career as a commerce raider in fine style, slipping past the Warrenton batteries undetected and going to work at once on enemy shipping by destroying skiffs and flatboats on both banks. He burned or commandeered hundreds of bales of cotton, taking some aboard for "armoring" the wheelhouse, destroyed supply trains heavily loaded with grain and salt pork being sent to collection points, and in reprisal for a sniper bullet, which struck one of his sailors in the leg, burned no less than three plantation houses, together with their outbuildings, apparently undismayed even when one planter's daughter sang "The Bonny Blue Flag" full in his face as the flames crackled. His greatest single prize, however, was the corn-laden packet *Era No. 5*, which he captured after passing Natchez and entering the Red River. But at that point, or just beyond it — seventy-five miles from the mouth of the river and with Alexandria in a turmoil less than half that far ahead — he and the *Queen* ran out of luck. On Valentine's Day, approaching Gordon's Landing, where a battery of guns had been reported, the ram stuck fast on a mud flat and was taken sudden-

*The Queen of the West fires on a rebel gunboat during a
12-day raid in which she destroyed $200,000 worth of
food and cotton on boats supplying Vicksburg.*

ly under fire by enemy gunners who yelled with delight at thus being offered a stationary target at a range of four hundred yards. In short order the boat's engine controls were smashed, her escape-pipe shot away, her boiler fractured. As she disappeared in hissing clouds of steam — one survivor later claimed to have avoided scalding his lungs because "I had sufficient presence of mind to cram the tail of my coat into my mouth" — officers and men began to tumble bales of cotton over the rail, then leap after them into the river, clinging to them in hope of reaching the *DeSoto* or the *Era*, a mile below. By now it was every man for himself, including the wounded, and the youthful skipper was not among the last to abandon the *Queen* in favor of a downstream ride astride a bale of cotton.

Picked up by the *DeSoto*, Ellet and the others were alarmed to discover that in the excitement she had unshipped both rudders and become unmanageable; so they set her afire and abandoned her, too, in favor of the more recently captured *Era*. Their career as raiders had lasted just four days. From now on, their only concern was escape, which seemed unlikely because of reports that the Confederates had at Alexandria a high-speed steamboat, the *William H. Webb,* which would surely be after them as soon as the news arrived upriver. She mounted only one gun, they had heard, and would never have dared to tackle the *Queen,* but now the tables were more or less turned; the pursuers became the pursued. "With a sigh for the poor fellows left behind, and a hope that our enemies would be merciful," a survivor wrote, "the prow of the *Era* was turned toward the Mississippi." They made it by daylight, after a race through stormy darkness unrelieved except for blinding flashes of lightning, and started north up the big river, heaving overboard all possible incidentals, including rations, in an attempt to coax more speed from their unarmed boat. Next morning, February 16, just below Natchez, with the *Webb* reportedly closing fast on their stern, they were startled to see an enormous, twin-stacked vessel bearing down on them from dead ahead. Their dismay at the prospect of being ground between two millstones was relieved, however, when the lookout identified her as the *Indianola.* The latest addition to the ironclad fleet and the pride of the Federal inland-waters navy, she mounted two great 11-inch smoothbores forward and a pair of 9-inch rifles amidships, casemated between her towering sidewheel-boxes, while for power she boasted four engines, driving twin screws in addition to her paddles, and she had brought two large barges of coal along, one lashed to starboard and one to port, to insure a long-term stay on the previously rebel-held 250-mile stretch of river above Port Hudson. Porter had sent her down past the Vicksburg batteries three nights ago, intending for her to support the *Queen* and thus, as he said, "make matters doubly sure."

Learning from Ellet that the *Queen* had been lost, Lieutenant Commander George Brown, captain of the *Indianola,* decided at once to proceed downriver, accompanied by the *Era.* Presently they sighted the *Webb,* in hot pursuit, and once more the tables were turned; for the *Webb* took one quick look at the iron-clad monster and promptly made use of her superior speed to withdraw before coming within range of those 11-inch guns, two short-falling shots from which only served to hurry her along, as one observer said, "for all the world like a frightened racehorse." Brown gave chase as far as the mouth of Red River, up which the rebel vessel disappeared, but there he called a halt, Porter having warned him not to venture up that stream without an experienced pilot, which he lacked. While Brown continued on patrol, guarding against a reëmergence of the *Webb,* Ellet took off northward in the *Era* with the unpleasant duty of informing Porter that he had lost the *Queen.* Two days later, still on patrol at the mouth of the Red, Brown received astounding news. The Confederates had resurrected the *Queen of the West,* patching up her punctured hull and repairing her fractured steam drum. Even now, in company with the skittish *Webb* and two cottonclad boats whose upper decks were crowded with sharpshooters, she was preparing to come out after the *Indianola.* Brown thought it over and decided to retire.

He would have done better to leave without taking time to think it over; the fuze was burning shorter than he knew. However, he was in for a fight in any event because of the two coal barges, which he knew would decrease his upstream speed considerably, but which he was determined to hold onto, despite the fact that the *Indianola*'s bunkers were chock-full. Partly this decision was the result of his ingrained peacetime frugality, but mostly it was because he wanted to have plenty of fuel on hand in case Porter complied with his request, forwarded by Ellet, that another gunboat be sent downriver as a replacement for the *Queen*. Brown left the mouth of the Red on Saturday, February 21, and stopped for the night at a plantation landing up the Mississippi to take on a load of cotton bales, which he stacked around the ironclad's low main deck to make her less vulnerable to boarders. Next morning he was off again in earnest, all four engines straining to offset the drag of the two barges lashed alongside. He did not know how much of a head start he had, but he feared it was not enough. In point of fact, it was even less than he supposed; for the four-boat Confederate flotilla, including the resurrected *Queen*, set out after him at about the same hour that Sunday morning, ninety miles astern of the landing where the *Indianola* had commandeered the cotton. The race was on.

It was not really much of a race. Major Joseph L. Brent, commanding the quartet of rebel warships, each of which was in the charge of an army captain, could have overtaken Brown at almost anytime Tuesday afternoon, the 24th, but he preferred to wait for darkness, which would not only make the aiming of the ironclad's big guns more difficult but would also give the Grand Gulf batteries a chance at her as she went by. Held to a crawl though she was by the awkward burden of her barges, the *Indianola* got past that danger without mishap; but Brown could see the smoke from his pursuers' chimneys drawing closer with every mile as the sun declined, and he knew that he was in for a fight before it rose again. He also knew by now that no reinforcing consort was going to join him from the fleet above Vicksburg, in spite of which he held doggedly to his barges, counting on them to give him fender protection from ram attacks. As darkness fell, moonless but dusky with starlight, he cleared for action and kept half of his crew at battle stations: "watch and watch," it was called. At 9.30 he passed New Carthage, which put him within thirteen miles of the nearest west-bank Union battery, but by that time the rebel boats were in plain sight. Abreast of Palmyra Island, heading into Davis Bend — so called because it flowed past the Confederate President's Brierfield Plantation — Brown swung his iron prow around to face his pursuers at last, thus bringing his heavy guns to bear and protecting his more vulnerable stern.

As the *Queen* and the *Webb* came at him simultaneously, the former in the lead, he fired an 11-inch shell point-blank at each. Both missed, and the *Queen* was on him, lunging in from port with such force that the barge on that

★

side was sliced almost in two. Emerging unscathed from this, except for the loss of the barge, which was cut adrift to sink, the *Indianola* met the *Webb* bows on, with a crash that knocked most of both crews off their feet and left the Confederate with a gash in her bow extending from water line to keelson, while the Federal was comparatively unhurt. Nevertheless the *Webb* backed off and struck again, crushing the remaining barge so completely as to leave it hanging by the lashings. Meanwhile the *Queen,* having run upstream a ways to gain momentum, turned and came charging down, striking her adversary just abaft the starboard wheelhouse, which was wrecked along with the rudder on that side, and starting a number of leaks along the shaft. Likewise the *Webb,* having gained momentum in the same fashion, brought her broken nose down hard and fair on the crippled ironclad's lightly armored stern, starting the timbers and causing the water to pour in rapidly. All this time the *Indianola* had kept throwing shells into the smoky darkness, left and right, but had scored only a single hit on the *Queen,* which did no considerable damage to the boat herself though it killed two and

---

As darkness fell, moonless but dusky with starlight, he cleared for action and kept half of his crew at battle stations: "watch and watch," it was called.

---

wounded four of her crew. Brown, having done his worst with this one shot, was now in a hopeless condition, scarcely able to steer and with both of his starboard engines flooded. After waiting a while in midstream until the water had risen nearly to the grate-bars of the ironclad's furnaces, planning thus to avoid her capture by making sure that she would sink, he ran her hard into the more friendly west bank and hauled down his colors just as the two cottonclads came alongside, crowded with yelling rebels prepared for boarding. Quickly they leaped down and attached two ropes by which the steamers could haul the *Indianola* across the river to the Confederate-held east bank, barely making it in time for her to sink in ten feet of water. As soon as they got their prisoners ashore they went to work on the captured dreadnought, intending to raise her, as they had raised the *Queen of the West* the week before, for service under the Stars and Bars.

  Though he had heard the heavy nighttime firing just downriver, Porter did not know for certain what had happened until two days later, when a seaman who had escaped from the *Indianola* during her brief contact with the western bank came aboard his flagship *Black Hawk* and gave him an eyewitness account of the tragedy. Coming as it did on the heels of news of the loss of the

Queen — which in turn had been preceded, two months back, by the destruction of the *Cairo* — the blow was hard, especially since it included the information that the *Queen* had been taken over by the enemy and had played a leading part in the defeat of her intended consort, which was now about to be used in the same manner as soon as the rebels succeeded in getting her afloat. What made it doubly hard, for Porter at any rate, was the contrast between his present gloom and his recent optimism. "If you open the Father of Waters," Assistant Navy Secretary G. A. Fox had wired the acting rear admiral in response to reports of his progress just two weeks ago, "you will at once be made an admiral; besides we will try for a ribboned star. . . . Do your work up clean," Fox had added, "and the public will never be in doubt who did it. The flaming army correspondence misleads nobody. Keep cool, be very modest under great success, as a contrast to the soldiers." At any rate, such strain as there had been on Porter's modesty was removed by the awareness that all he had really accomplished so far — aside from the capture of Arkansas Post, which had had to be shared with the army — was the loss of three of his best warships, two of which were now in enemy hands. What filled his mind just now was the thought of what this newest-model ironclad, the former pride of the Union fleet, could accomplish once she went into action on the Confederate side. Supported as she would be by the captured ram, she might well prove invincible in an upstream fight. In fact, any attempt to challenge her en masse would probably add other powerful units to the rebel flotilla of defected boats, since any disabled vessel would be swept helplessly downstream in such an engagement. Far from opening the Father of Waters, and gaining thereby a ribboned star and the permanent rank of admiral, Porter could see that he would be more likely to lose what had been won by his predecessors. Besides, even if he had wanted to launch such an all-out attack, he had no gunboats in the vicinity of Vicksburg now; they had been sent far upriver to coöperate in another of Grant's ill-fated amphibious experiments.

Porter was inventive in more ways than one, however, and his resourcefulness now stood him in good stead. If he had no available ironclad, then he would build one — or anyhow the semblance of one. Ordering every man off the noncombatant vessels to turn to, he took an old flat-bottomed barge, extended its length to three hundred feet by use of rafts hidden behind false bulwarks, and covered it over with flimsy decking to support a frame-and-canvas pilot house and two huge but empty paddle-wheel boxes. A casemate was mounted forward, with a number of large-caliber logs protruding from its ports, and two tall smokestacks were erected by piling barrels one upon another. As a final realistic touch, after two abandoned skiffs were swung from unworkable davits, the completed dummy warship was given an all-over coat of tar. Within twenty-four hours, at a reported cost of $8.63, the navy had what appeared, at least from a distance, to be a sister ship of the *Indianola*. Belching smoke from pots of burning tar and

★

*A*drift in the Mississippi, Porter's counterfeit Federal
gunboat — made by transforming a coal barge with scrap
wood, canvas, and tar — floats past Vicksburg.

oakum installed in her barrel stacks, she was set adrift the following night to make her run past the Vicksburg batteries. They gave her everything they had, but to no avail; her black armor seemingly impervious to damage, she glided unscathed past the roaring guns, not even deigning to reply. At daybreak she grounded near the lower end of Sherman's canal, and the diggers pushed her off again with a cheer. As she resumed her course downriver, the *Queen of the West,* coming up past Warrenton on a scout, spotted the dark behemoth in the distance, bearing down with her guns run out and her deck apparently cleared for action. The ram spun on her heel and sped back to spread the alarm: whereupon — since neither the *Queen* nor the broken-nosed *Webb* was in any condition for another fight just yet — all four of the Confederate vessels made off southward to avoid a clash with this second ironclad. Aboard the *Indianola,* still immobile and now deserted by her new friends, the lieutenant in charge of salvage operations was for holding onto her and fighting it out, despite repeated orders for him to complete her destruction before she could be recaptured. At a range of about two miles, the dreadnought halted as if to look the situation over before closing in for the bloody work she was bent on. Still the lieutenant held his ground until nightfall, when he decided to comply with the instructions of his superiors. After heaving the 9-inch rifles into the river, he laid the 11-inch smoothbores muzzle to muzzle and fired them with slow matches. When the smoke from this had cleared, he came back and set fire to what was left, burning the wreckage to the water line and ending the brief but stormy career of the ironclad *Indianola*.

Next morning, seeing the black monster still in her former position, some two miles upriver — one observer later described her as "terrible though inert" — a party of Confederates went out in a rowboat to investigate. Drawing closer they recognized her for the hoax she was, and saw that she had come to rest on a mudbank. Nailed to her starboard wheelhouse was a crudely lettered sign. "Deluded people, cave in," it read.

★ ★ ★ "Then, too," Grant added, continuing the comment on his reasons for keeping McPherson's men sawing away at the underwater stumps and snags clogging the Bayou Baxter exit from Lake Providence even after he knew that, in itself, the work was unlikely to produce anything substantial, "it served as a cover for other efforts which gave a better prospect of success." What he had in mind — in addition, that is, to Sherman's canal, which was not to be abandoned until March — was a fifth experimental project, whose starting point was four hundred tortuous miles upriver from its intended finish atop the Vicksburg bluff. In olden days, just south of Helena and on the opposite bank, a bayou had afforded egress from the Mississippi; Yazoo Pass, it was called, because it connected eastward with the Coldwater River, which flowed south into the Tallahatchie, which in turn combined with the Yalobusha, farther down, to form the Yazoo. Steamboats once had plied this route for trade with the planters of the Delta hinterland. In fact, they still steamed up and down this intricate chain of rivers, but only by entering from below, through the mouth of the Yazoo River; for the state of Mississippi had sealed off the northern entrance, five years before the war, by constructing across the mouth of Yazoo Pass a levee which served to keep the low-lying cotton fields from going under water with every rise of the big river. Now it was Grant's notion that perhaps all he needed to do, in order to utilize this old peacetime trade route for his wartime purpose, was cut the levee and send in gunboats to provide cover for transports, which then could be unloaded on high ground — well down the left bank of the Yazoo but short of Haines Bluff, whose fortifications blocked an ascent of that river from below — and thus, by forcing the outnumbered defenders to come out into the open for a fight which could only result in their defeat, take Vicksburg from the rear. Accordingly, at the same time he ordered McPherson down from Memphis to Lake Providence, he sent his chief topographical engineer, Lieutenant Colonel James H. Wilson, to inspect and report on the possibility of launching such an attack by way of Yazoo Pass.

Wilson, described by a contemporary as "a slight person of a light complexion and with rather a pinched face," was enthusiastic from the start. An Illinois regular, only two years out of West Point and approaching his twenty-sixth birthday, he recently had been transferred from the East, where he had served as an aide to McClellan at Antietam, and he had approached his western assignment with doubts, particularly in regard to Grant, whose "simple and unmilitary bearing," as the young man phrased it, made a drab impression by contrast with the recent splendor of Little Mac, whose official family had included an Astor and two genuine French princes of the blood. But in this case familiarity bred affection; Wilson soon was remarking that his new commander was "a most agreeable companion both on the march and in camp." What drew him more than anything, however, was the trust Grant showed in sending him to take charge of the opening phase of this fifth and latest project for the reduction of the Gibraltar of the West. After a bit of preliminary surveying and shovel work, he wasted no time. On the evening of February 3 — while Ellet prepared to take the *Queen* past the Vicksburg bluff at daybreak and Grant himself was about to head upriver for a first-hand look at Lake Providence — Wilson mined and blew the levee sealing the mouth of Yazoo Pass. The result was altogether spectacular, he reported, "water pouring through like nothing else I ever saw except Niagara." After waiting four days for the surface level to equalize, east and west of the cut, he boarded a gunboat, steamed "with great ease" into Moon Lake, a mile beyond, and "ran down it about five miles to where the Pass leaves it." Hard work was going to be involved, he wrote Grant's adjutant, but he was confident of a large return on such an investment. Grant was infected at once with the colonel's enthusiasm. Wilson already had with him a 4500-man division from Helena; now a second division was ordered to join him from there. Presently, when he reported that he had got through to the Coldwater, McPherson was told to be prepared to follow with his whole corps. "The Yazoo Pass expedition is going to prove a perfect success," Grant informed Elihu B. Washburne, his home-state Representative and congressional guardian angel.

Hard work had been foreseen, and that was what it took. Emerging from Moon Lake, Wilson found the remaining twelve-mile segment of the pass sufficiently deep but so narrow in some places that the gunboat could not squeeze between giant oaks and cypresses growing on opposite banks. These had to be felled with axes, a patience-testing business but by no means the most discouraging he encountered. Warned of his coming, the Confederates had brought in working parties of slaves from surrounding plantations and had chopped down other trees, some of them more than four feet through the bole, so that they lay athwart the bayou, ponderous and apparently immovable. Undaunted, Wilson borrowed navy hawsers long enough to afford simultaneous handholds for whole regiments of soldiers, whom he put to work snaking the impediments out of the way. They did it with such ease, he later remarked, that he never afterwards wondered how the Egyptians had lifted the great stones in place when they built the Pyramids; enough men on a rope could move anything, he decided. Still, he had no such span of time at his disposal as the Pharaohs had had, and this was at best a time-consuming process. February was almost gone before he reached the eastern end of the pass. South of there, however, he expected to find clear sailing. The Coldwater being "a considerable stream," he reported, vessels of almost any length and draft could be sent from the Mississippi into the Tallahatchie in just four days. And so it proved when a ten-boat flotilla, including two ironclads, two steam rams, and six tinclads — the 22 light transports were to come along behind — tried it during the first week in March. In fact, it was not until the warships were more than a hundred miles down the winding Tallahatchie, near its junction with the Yalobusha, that Wilson realized he was in for a great deal more trouble, and of a kind he had not encountered up to now.

The trouble now was the rebels themselves, not just the various obstructions they had left in his path before fading back into the swamps and woods. Five miles above Greenwood, a hamlet at the confluence of the rivers, they had improvised on a boggy island inclosed by a loop of the Tallahatchie a fort whose parapets, built of cotton bales and reinforced with sandbags, were designed not only to deflect heavy projectiles but also to keep out the river itself, which had gone well past the flood stage when the Yankees blew the levee far upstream. Fort Pemberton, the place was called, and it had as its commander a man out of the dim Confederate past: Brigadier General Lloyd Tilghman, who had fought against Grant and the ironclads under similar circumstances at Fort Henry, thirteen months ago. Exchanged and reinstated, he was determined to wipe out that defeat, though the odds were as long and the tactical situation not much different. His immediate superior, Major General W. W. Loring, was also a carry-over from the past, and as commander of the Delta subdepartment he intended to give the Federals even more trouble than he had given Lee and Jackson in Virginia the year before, which was considerable. A third relic on the scene was the former U.S. ocean steamer *Star of the West,* whose name had been in the scareheads three full months before the war, when the Charleston batteries fired on her for attempting the relief of Sumter. Continuing on to Texas, she had been captured in mid-April by Van Dorn at Indianola and was in the rebel service as a receiving-ship at New Orleans a year later, when Farragut provoked her flight up the Mississippi and into the Yazoo to avoid recapture. Here above Greenwood she ended her days afloat, but not her career, for she was sunk in the Tallahatchie alongside Fort Pemberton, blocking the channel and thus becoming an integral part of the outer defenses of Vicksburg. Three regiments, one from Texas and two from Mississippi, were all the high command could spare for manning the breastworks and the guns, which included one 6.4-inch rifle and half a dozen smaller pieces. This was scarcely a formidable armament with which to oppose 11-inch Dahlgrens housed in armored casemates, but on March 11 — while northward a long column of approaching warships and transports sent up a winding trail of smoke, stretching out of sight beyond the heavy screen of woods — the graybacks were a determined crew as they sighted their guns up the straight stretch of river giving down upon the fort.

Lieutenant Commander Watson Smith, who had charge of the ten-boat Union flotilla, was by now in a state of acute distress; he had never experienced anything like this in all his years afloat. Coming through Yazoo Pass into the Coldwater and down the Tallahatchie, all of which were so narrow in places that the gunboats had to be warped around the sharper bends with ropes, one tinclad had shattered her wheel and was out of action, while another had lost both smokestacks. All the rest had taken similar punishment in passing over rafts of driftwood or under projecting limbs that came sweeping and crashing along their upper works. The most serious of these mishaps was suffered when the *Chillicothe,* one of the two ironclads, struck a snag and started a plank in her bottom, which had to be held in place by beams shored in from the deck above. Smith's distress was greatly increased this morning, however, when this same unlucky vessel, at the head of the column, rounded the next-to-final bend leading down to the Yazoo and was struck hard twice on the turrets by high-velocity shells from dead ahead. She pulled back to survey the damage and fortify with cotton bales, then came on again that afternoon, accompanied by the other ironclad, the *De Kalb.* She got off four rounds at 800 yards and was about to fire a fifth — the loaders had already set the 11-inch shell in the gun's muzzle and were stripping the patch from the fuze — when a rebel shell came screaming through the port; both projectiles exploded on contact, killing 2 and wounding 11 of the gun crew. The two ironclads withdrew under urgent orders from Smith, whose distress had increased to the point where, according to Porter's subsequent report, he was showing "symptoms of aberration of mind."

Twice more, on the 13th and the 16th — without, however, attempting to close the range — the ironclads tried for a reduction of the fort at the end of that tree-lined stretch of river, as straight and uncluttered as a bowling alley:

Admiral David Dixon Porter preferred to operate alone, yet worked in perfect harmony with Grant.

with similar results. Unable to maneuver in the narrow stream, the two boats took a terrible pounding, but could do little more than bounce their big projectiles off the resilient enemy parapet. The infantry, waiting rearward in the transports, gave no help at all; for the flooded banks made debarkation impossible, and any attempt at a small-boat attack — even if such boats had been available, which they were not — would have been suicidal. By the time the third day's bombardment was over, both ironclads were badly crippled; the *De Kalb* had lost ten of her gun-deck beams and her steerage was shot to pieces, while the luckless *Chillicothe* had more of her crew felled by armor bolts driven inward, under the impact of shells from the hard-hitting enemy rifle, to fly like bullets through the casemate. On March 17, in an apparent moment of lucidity, Smith ordered the flotilla to withdraw. Everyone agreed that this was the wisest course: everyone but Wilson, who complained hotly to Grant that the issue had not been pressed. "To let one 6½-inch rifle stop our navy. Bah!" he protested, and put the blame on "Acting Rear Admiral, Commodore, Captain, Lieutenant-Commander Smith" and the other naval officers. "I've talked with them all and tried to give them backbone," he said, "but they are not confident."

Returning up the Coldwater two days later — while Loring and Tilghman were celebrating the repulse in victory dispatches sent downriver to Vicksburg — the disconsolate Federals met the second Helena division on its way to reinforce them under Brigadier General Isaac Quinby, who outranked all the brass at hand and was unwilling to retreat without so much as a look at what stood in the way of an advance. So the expedition turned around and came back down again. Stopping short of the bend leading into the bowling alley, the men aboard the transports and gunboats slapped at mosquitoes and practiced their marksmanship on alligators, while Quinby conducted a boggy twelve-day reconnaissance which finally persuaded him that Smith had been right in the first place. Besides, even Wilson was convinced by now that the game was not worth the candle, for the rebels had brought up another steamboat which they were "either ready to sink or use as a boarding-craft and ram," and it seemed to the young colonel that they were "making great calculations 'to bag us' entire." He agreed that the time had come for a final departure. This began on April 5 and brought the Yazoo Pass experiment to a close. Being, as he said, "solicitous for my reputation at headquarters," Wilson ended a letter to Grant's adjutant with a request for the latest staff gossip, and thought to add: "Remember me kindly to the general."

His fears, though natural enough in an ambitious young career officer who had failed in his first independent assignment, were groundless. For unlike Porter, who no sooner learned the details of the Tallahatchie nightmare than he relieved Watson Smith of duty with the fleet and sent him North — where presently, by way of proving that his affliction had been physical as well as mental, he died in a delirium of fever and chagrin — Grant did not hold the collapse of

★

this fifth experiment against his subordinate, but rather, when Wilson returned at last to Young's Point after an absence of more than two months, welcomed him back without reproach into the fold. By then the army commander had a better appreciation of the problems that stood in the way of an amphibious penetration of the Delta, having been involved simultaneously in a not unsimilar nightmare of his own. In point of fact, however, no matter how little he chose to bring it to bear, Porter had even greater occasion for such charity, since he had been more intimately involved, not only as the author but also as the on-the-scene director of this latest fiasco, the sole result of which had been the addition of a sixth to the sequence of failures designed for the reduction of Vicksburg.

Left with time more or less on his hands after the downriver loss of two of his best warships, and being anxious moreover to offset the damage to his reputation with an exploit involving something less flimsy than a dummy iron-clad, the admiral pored over his charts and made various exploratory trips up and down the network of creeks and bayous flowing into the Yazoo River below Haines Bluff, whose guns he had learned to respect back in December. Five miles upstream from its junction with the Mississippi, the Yazoo received the sluggish waters of Steele Bayou, and forty miles up Steele Bayou, Black Bayou connected eastward with Deer Creek, which in turn, at about the same upstream distance and by means of another bayou called Rolling Fork, connected eastward with the Sunflower River. That was where the payoff came within easy reach; for the Sun-flower flowed into the Yazoo, fifty miles below, offering the chance for an uncon-tested high-ground landing well above the Haines Bluff fortifications, which then could be assaulted from the rear or by-passed on the way to the back door of Vicksburg. Though the route was crooked and the distance great — especially by contrast; no less than two hundred roundabout miles would have to be tra-versed by the column of gunboats and transports in order to put the troops ashore no more than twenty air-line miles above their starting point — Porter was so firmly convinced he had found the solution to the knotty Vicksburg prob-lem that he called at Young's Point and persuaded Grant to come aboard the *Black Hawk* for a demonstration. Steaming up the Yazoo, the admiral watched the tree-fringed north bank for a while, then suddenly to his companion's amaze-ment signaled the helm for a hard turn to port, into brush that was apparently impenetrable. So far, high water had been the curse of the campaign, but now it proved an asset. As the boat swung through the leafy barrier, which parted to ad-mit it, the leadsman sang out a sounding of fifteen feet — better than twice the depth the ironclads required. Formerly startled, Grant was now convinced, espe-cially when Porter informed him that they were steaming above an old road once used for hauling cotton to the river. Practically all the lower Delta was sub-merged, in part because of the seasonal rise of the rivers, but mostly because of the cut Wilson had made in the levee, four hundred miles upstream at Yazoo

Pass; a tremendous volume of water had come down the various tributaries and had spread itself over the land. It was Porter's contention, based on limited reconnaissance, that as a result all those creeks and bayous would be navigable from end to end by vessels of almost any size, including the gunboats and transports selected to thread the labyrinth giving down upon the back-door approach to Vicksburg. Infected once more with contagious enthusiasm, Grant returned without delay to Young's Point, where he issued orders that same night for the army's share in what was known thereafter as the Steele Bayou expedition.

Sherman drew the assignment, along with one of his two divisions of men who just that week had been flooded out of their pick-and-shovel work on the doomed canal, and went up the Mississippi to a point where a long bend swung eastward to within a mile of Steele Bayou. On the afternoon of March 16, after slogging across this boggy neck of land, he made contact with the naval units, which had come up by way of the Yazoo that morning. As soon as he got

Infected once more with contagious enthusiasm, Grant returned without delay to Young's Point, where he issued orders that same night for the army's share in what was known thereafter as the Steele Bayou expedition.

his troops aboard the waiting transports the column resumed its progress northward, five ironclads in the lead, followed by four all-purpose tugs and a pair of mortar boats which Porter, not knowing what he might encounter in the labyrinth ahead, had had "built for the occasion." With his mind's eye fixed on permanent rank and the ribboned star Fox had promised to try for, the admiral was taking no chances he could avoid. All went well — as he had expected because of his preliminary reconnaissance — until the gunboats approached Black Bayou, where the unreconnoitered portion of the route began. This narrow, four-mile, time-forgotten stretch of stagnant water was not only extremely crooked, it was also filled with trees. Porter used his heavy boats to butt them down, bulldozer style, and hoisted them aside with snatch blocks. This was heavy labor, necessarily slow, and as it progressed the column changed considerably in appearance. Overhead branches swept the upper decks of the warships, leaving a mess of wreckage in the place of boats and woodwork. Occasionally, too, as Porter said, "a rude tree would throw Briarean arms" around the stacks of the slowly passing vessels, "and knock their bonnets sideways." After about a mile of this, Sherman's men were put to work with ropes and axes, clearing a broader passage for the transports, while the sturdier ironclads forged ahead, thumping and bumping their way into Deer Creek, where they resumed a northward course next morning.

But this was worse in several ways, one of them being that the creek was even narrower than the bayou. If the trees were fewer, they were also closer together, and vermin of all kinds had taken refuge in them from the flood; so that when one of the gunboats struck a tree the quivering limbs let fall a plague of rats, mice, cockroaches, snakes, and lizards. Men were stationed about the decks with brooms to rid the vessels of such unwelcome boarders, but sometimes the sweepers had larger game to contend with, including coons and wildcats. These last, however, "were prejudiced against us, and refused to be comforted on board," the admiral subsequently wrote, "though I am sorry to say we found more Union feeling among the bugs." To add to the nightmare, Deer Creek was the crookedest stream he had ever encountered: "One minute an ironclad would apparently be leading ahead, and the next minute would as apparently be steering the other way." Along one brief stretch, less than half a mile in length, the five warships were steaming in five quite different directions. Moreover, this was a region of plantations, which meant that there were man-made obstacles such as bridges, and though these gave the heavy boats no real trouble — they could plow through them as if they were built of matchsticks — other impediments were more disturbing. For example, hearing of the approach of the Yankees, the planters had had their baled cotton stacked along both creekbanks and set afire in order to keep it out of the hands of the invaders: with the result that, from time to time, the gunboats had to run a fiery gauntlet. The thick white smoke sent the crews into spasms of coughing, while the heat singed their hair, scorched their faces, and blistered the paint from the vessels' iron flanks.

So far, despite the crowds of field hands who lined the banks to marvel at the appearance of ironclads where not even flat-bottomed packets had ventured before, Porter had not seen a single white man. He found this odd, and indeed somewhat foreboding. Presently, however, spotting one sitting in front of a cabin and smoking a pipe as if nothing unusual were going on around him, the admiral had the flagship stopped just short of another bridge and summoned the man to come down to the landing; which he did — a burly, rough-faced individual, in shirt sleeves and bareheaded; "half bulldog, half bloodhound," Porter called him. When the admiral began to question him he identified himself as the plantation overseer. "I suppose you are Union, of course?" Porter said. "You all are so when it suits you." "No, by God, I'm not, and never will be," the man replied. "As to the others, I know nothing about them. Find out for yourself. I'm for Jeff Davis first, last, and all the time. Do you want any more of me?" he added; "for I am not a loquacious man at any time." "No, I want nothing more with you," Porter said. "But I am going to steam into that bridge of yours across the stream and knock it down. Is it

*A soldier high in a tree clears the way for a Federal transport
through the dense vegetation of Steele Bayou during the last
of Grant's experiments around Vicksburg.*

strongly built?" "You may knock it down and be damned," the overseer told
him. "It don't belong to me." Catching something in his accent, Porter remarked: "You're a Yankee by birth, are you not?" "Yes, damn it, I am," the man
admitted. "But that's no reason I should like the institution. I cut it long ago."
And with this he turned on his heel and walked away. Porter had the skipper
ring "Go ahead fast," and the ironclad smashed through the bridge about as
easily as if it had not been there. When he looked back, however, to see what
impression this had made on the overseer, he saw him seated once more in front
of the cabin, smoking his pipe, not having bothered even to turn his head and
watch. Deciding that the fellow "was but one remove from a brute," Porter was
disturbed by the thought that "there were hundreds more like him" lurking

★

somewhere in the brush. At any rate, he fervently hoped that Sherman's men — particularly one regiment, which had the reputation of being able to "catch, scrape, and skin a hog without a soldier leaving the ranks" — would "pay the apostate Yankee a visit, if only to teach him good manners."

Under the circumstances, even aside from the necessary halts, half a mile an hour was the best speed the ironclads could make on this St Patrick's Day. Nightfall overtook them a scant eight miles from the morning's starting point. Twelve miles they made next day, but the increased speed increased the damage to the boats, including the loss of all the skylights to falling debris, and when they stopped engines for the night, Porter heard from up ahead the least welcome of all sounds: the steady chuck of axes, informing him that the rebels were warned of his coming. He wished fervently for Sherman, whose men were still at work in Black Bayou, widening a pathway for their transports, and consoled himself with the thought that the red-haired general would be along eventually; "there was only one road, so he couldn't have taken the wrong one." For the present, however, he did what he could with what he had, sending the mortar boats forward in the darkness; and when their firing stopped, so had the axes. Next morning, March 19, he pushed on. Despite the delay involved in hoisting the felled trees aside, he made such good progress that by nightfall he was within half a mile of the entrance to Rolling Fork. At daybreak he steamed north again, but the flagship had gone barely two hundred yards when, just ahead and extending all the way across the creek, the admiral saw "a large green patch . . . like the green scum on ponds." He shouted down from the bridge to one of the admiring field hands on the bank: "What is that?" "It's nuffin but willers, sah," the Negro replied, explaining that in the off season the plantation workers often went out in skiffs and canoes to cut the willow wands for weaving baskets. "You kin go through dat lak a eel."

That this last was an overstatement — based on a failure to realize that, unlike skiffs and canoes, the gunboats moved *through* rather than *over* the water, and what was more had paddle wheels and overlapping plates of armor — Porter discovered within a couple of minutes of giving the order to go ahead. Starting with a full head of steam, the ironclad made about thirty yards before coming to a dead stop, gripped tightly by the willow withes, not unlike Gulliver when he woke to find himself in Lilliputian bonds. The admiral called for hard astern; but that was no good either; the vessel would not budge. Here was a ticklish situation. The high creekbanks rendered the warships practically helpless, for their guns would not clear them even at extreme elevation. Not knowing what he would do if the Confederates made a determined boarding attack, Porter fortified a nearby Indian mound with four smoothbore howitzers and put the flagship's crew over the side with knives and hooks and orders to cut her loose, twig by twig. It was slow work; "I wished ironclads were in Jericho," he later declared. Just then his wish seemed about to be fulfilled. The shrill shrieks of two rifle shots, which he recognized as high-velocity Whitworths, were followed at once by a pair of bursts, abrupt as blue-sky thunder and directly over the mound. Suddenly, in the wake of these two ranging shots — within six hundred yards of Rolling Fork and less than ten miles from clear sailing down the broad and unobstructed Sunflower River — two six-gun rebel batteries were firing on the outranged smoothbores from opposite directions, and the naval commander was shocked to see his cannoneers come tumbling down the rearward slope of the mound, seeking cover from the rain of shells. Continuing to hack at the clinging willows, he got his mortars into counterbattery action and, with the help of half a dollar, persuaded a "truthful contraband" (so Porter termed him later, but just then he called him Sambo; which drew the reply, "My name aint Sambo, sah. My name's Tub") to attempt to get a message through to Sherman and his soldiers, wherever downstream they might be by now. "Dear Sherman," the note began: "Hurry up, for Heaven's sake."

Tub reached Sherman on Black Bayou late that night, having taken various short cuts, and Sherman started northward before daylight, accompanied by all the troops on hand. Retracing the messenger's route through darkness, they carried lighted candles in their hands as they slogged waist-deep through swamps and canebrakes. "The smaller drummer boys had to carry their drums on their heads," the general afterwards recalled, "and most of the men slung their cartridge boxes around their necks." All the following day they pushed on, frequently losing their way, and into darkness again. At dawn Sunday, March 22, they heard from surprisingly close at hand the boom of Porter's mortars, punctuated by the sharper crack of the Whitworths. Presently they encountered rebels who had got below the ironclads and were felling trees to block their escape downstream. Sherman chased them from their work and pushed on. Soon he came within sight of the beleaguered flotilla, but found it woefully changed in appearance. After finally managing to extricate the willow-bound flagship with winches, Porter had unshipped the rudders of all five gunboats and was steaming backward down the narrow creek, fighting as he went. He had not only heard the sound of axes in his rear; what was worse, he had suddenly realized that the Confederates might dam the creek upstream with cotton bales and leave him stranded in the mud. The arriving bluecoats ran the snipers off — they were not actually so numerous as they seemed; just industrious — and came up to find the admiral on the deck of the flagship, directing the retreat from behind a shield improvised from a section of smokestack. "I doubt if he was ever more glad to meet a friend than he was to see me," Sherman later declared. For the present, though, he asked if Porter wanted him to go ahead and "clean those fellows out" so the navy could resume its former course. "Thank you, no," the admiral said. He had had enough, and so had Sherman, who complained hotly that this was

★

"the most infernal expedition I was ever on." As Porter subsequently put it, "The game was up, and we bumped on homeward."

All the way downstream, from Deer Creek through Black Bayou, the sailors took a ribbing from the soldiers who stood along the banks to watch them go by, in reverse and rudderless. "Halloo, Jack," they would call. "How do you like playing mud turtle?" "Where's all your masts and sails, Jack?" "By the Widow Perkins, if Johnny Reb hasn't taken their rudders away and set them adrift!" But an old forecastleman gave as good as he got. "Dry up!" he shouted back at them. "We wa'n't half as much used up as you was at Chickasaw Bayou." So it went until the gunboats regained Steele Bayou and finally the mouth of the Yazoo, where they dropped anchor — those that still had them — and were laid up for repairs. Within another week they were supplied with new chimneys and skylights and woodwork; they glistened with fresh coats of paint, and according to Porter, "no one would have supposed we had ever been away from a dock-yard." By then, too, the officers had begun to discuss their share in this sixth of Grant's Vicksburg failures with something resembling nostalgia. There was an edge of pride in their voices as they spoke of the exploit, and some even talked of being willing to go again. But they did so, the admiral added, much "as people who have gone in search of the North Pole, and have fared dreadfully, wish to try it once more."

★ ★ ★ *D*espite the high hopes generated during the preliminary reconnaissance up Steele Bayou, Grant was no more discouraged by this penultimate failure, reported in no uncertain terms by a disgusted Sherman, than he had been by the preceding five. Now as before, he already had a successive experiment in progress, which served to distract the public's attention and occupy his mind and men. Besides, for once, he had good news to send along to Washington with the bad — the announcement of the first real success achieved by Federal arms on the river since his arrival in late January — although his pleasure in reporting it was considerably diminished by the fact that it had been accomplished not in his own department but in Banks's, not by the army but by the navy, and not by Porter but by Farragut.

Banks himself had been having troubles that rivaled Grant's, if not in number — being limited by a lack of corresponding ingenuity and equipment in his attempts to come to grips with the problem — then at any rate in thorniness. Port Hudson was quite as invulnerable to a frontal assault as Vicksburg, so that here too the solution was restricted to two methods: either to attack the hundred-foot bluff from the rear or else to go around it. He worked hard for a time at the latter, seeking a route up the Atchafalaya, into the Red, and thence into the Mississippi, fifty miles above the Confederate bastion. At first this appeared to be ready-made for his use, but it turned out to be impractical on three counts. 1) He had only one gunboat designed for work on the rivers; 2) a large portion of the Atchafalaya basin was under water as a result of breaks in the neglected levees; and 3) he became convinced that to leave the rebel garrison alive and kicking in his rear would be to risk, if not invite, the recapture of New Orleans. This last was so unthinkable that it no sooner occurred to him than he abandoned all notion of such an attempt. As for attacking Port Hudson from the rear, he perceived that this would be about as risky as attacking it from the front. Knowing nothing of Grant's success or failure upriver, except the significant fact that something must have happened to delay him, Banks did not know but what the Confederates would be free to concentrate against him from all directions, including the north, as soon as he got his troops ashore; which would mean, at best, that he would lose his siege train in a retreat from superior numbers, and at worst that he would lose his army. Thus both methods of approaching a solution to the problem seemed to him likely to end in disaster; he did not know what to do, at least until he could get in touch with Grant upstream. Consequently, he did nothing.

This reverse approach, with its stress on what the enemy might do to him, rather than on what he intended to do to the enemy, had not been Grant's way of coming to grips with the similar problem, some three hundred miles upstream; nor was it Farragut's. The old sea dog — approaching sixty-two, he was Tennessee-born and twice married, both times to Virginians, which had caused some doubt as to his loyalty in the early

Admiral Farragut hoped to expand Union control of the Mississippi River by steaming past Port Hudson.

months of the war — had surmounted what had seemed to be longer odds below New Orleans the year before, and he was altogether willing to try it again, "army or no army." In early March, when he received word that the rebels, by way of reinforcing their claim to control of the whole Red River system, along with so much of the Mississippi as ran between Vicksburg and Port Hudson, had captured the steam ram *Queen of the West,* he took the action as a challenge to personal combat; especially when they emphasized it by sinking and seizing the ironclad

Indianola, which for all he knew was about to join the *Queen* in defying the flag she once had flown. He promptly assembled his seven wooden ships off Profit's Island, seven miles below Port Hudson, intending to take them past the fortified heights for a showdown with the renegade boats upriver. He had with him the three heavy sloops-of-war *Hartford, Richmond,* and *Monongahela,* the old side-wheeler *Mississippi,* and three gunboats. All were ocean-going vessels, unarmored but mounting a total of 95 guns, mostly heavy — the flagship *Hartford* alone carried two dozen 9-inch Dahlgrens — with which to oppose the 21 pieces manned by the Confederates ashore. This advantage in the weight of metal would be offset considerably, however, by the plunging fire of the guns on the hundred-foot bluff and by the five-knot current, which would hold the ships to a crawl as they rounded the sharp bend at its foot. In an attempt to increase the speed and power of his slower and larger ships, Farragut gave instructions for the three gunboats to be lashed to the unengaged port sides of the three sloops; the *Mississippi,* whose paddle boxes would not allow this, would have to take her chances unassisted. It was the admiral's hope that the flotilla would steam past undetected in the moonless darkness, but a greenhorn chaplain, watching the gun crews place within easy reach "little square, shallow, wooden boxes filled with sawdust, like the spittoons one used to see in country barrooms," was shocked to learn that the contents were to be scattered about the deck as "an absorbent" to keep the men from slipping in their own blood, when and if the guns began to roar and hits were scored. At 9.30 p.m. March 14, the prearranged signal — two red lights described by the same impressionable chaplain as "two distinct red spots like burning coals" — appeared just under the stern of the flagship in the lead, and the run began.

At first it went as had been planned and hoped for. Undetected, unsuspected, the *Hartford* led the way up the long straight stretch of river leading due north into the bend that would swing the column west-southwest; she even cleared the first battery south of town, her engines throbbing in the darkness, her pilot hugging the east bank to avoid the mudflat shallows of the point across the way. Then suddenly the night was bright with rockets and the glare of pitch-pine bonfires ignited by west-bank sentinels, who thus not only alerted the gun crews on the bluff, but also did them the service of illuminating their targets on the river down below. The fight began as it were in mid-crescendo. Still holding so close to the east bank that the men on her deck could hear the shouts of the enemy cannoneers, the flagship opened a rolling fire which was taken up in turn by the ships astern. The night was misty and windless; smoke settled thick on the water, leaving the helmsmen groping blindly and the gunners with nothing to aim at but the overhead muzzle flashes. In this respect the *Hartford* had the advantage, steaming ahead of her own smoke, but even she had her troubles, being caught by the swift current and swept against the enemy bank as she turned into the bend. Helped by her gunboat tug, she backed off

The Monongahela, heavily damaged in Farragut's run under the guns of Port Hudson, failed to pass the bastion and remained downriver for repairs.

and swung clear, chugging upstream at barely three knots, much damaged about her top and spars, but with only three men hit. Attempting to follow, the *Richmond* was struck by a plunging shot that crashed into her engine room and caromed about, cracking both port and starboard safety valves and dropping her boiler pressure below ten pounds. Too weak to make headway, even with the assistance of the gunboat lashed to her flank, she went with the current and out of the fight, leaking steam from all her ports, followed presently by the *Monongahela,* which suffered the same fate when her escort's rudder was wedged by an unlucky shot, one of her own engines was disabled by an overheated crankpin, and her captain was incapacitated by a shell that cut the bridge from under him and pitched him headlong onto the deck below. Between them, the two sloops and their escorts lost 45 killed and wounded before they veered out of range downriver. But the veteran frigate *Mississippi* — Commodore Matthew Perry's flagship, ten years ago, when he steamed into Tokyo Bay and opened Japan to the Western world — took the worst beating of the lot, not only from the Confederates on the bluff, but also from the gunners on the *Richmond,* who, not having gotten the word that the sloop had turned in the opposite direction, fired at the flashes of the side-wheeler's guns as they swept past her. Blind in the smoke, pounded alike by friend and foe, the pilot went into the bend and put the ship hard to larboard all too soon: with the result that she ran full tilt onto the mudflats across the way from the fuming bluff. Silhouetted against the glare of bonfires and taking hit after hit from the rebel guns, she tried for half an hour to pull loose by reversing her engines, but to no avail. Her captain ordered her set afire as soon as the crew — 64 of whom were casualties by now — could be taken off in boats, and it was only through the efforts of her executive, Lieutenant George Dewey, that many of her wounded were not roasted, including a badly frightened ship's boy he found hiding under a pile of corpses. Burning furiously, the *Mississippi* lightened before dawn and drifted off the flats of her own accord, threatening to set the other repulsed vessels afire as she passed unmanned among them and piled up at last on the head of Profit's Island, where she exploded with what an observer called "the grandest display of fireworks I ever witnessed, and the costliest."

It had been quite a costly operation all around. Thirty-five of the flotilla's 112 casualties were dead men — only two less than had been killed in the venture below New Orleans by a force almost three times as large — and of the seven ships that had attempted to run Port Hudson, one was destroyed and four had been driven back disabled. As a box score, this gave the Confederates ample claim to the honors of the engagement; but the fact remained that, whatever the cost, Farragut had done what he set out to do. He had put warships north of the bluff on the Mississippi, and he was ready to use them to dispute the rebel claim to control of the 250 miles of river below Vicksburg. Dropping down at dawn to just beyond range of Port Hudson's upper batteries, he fired the prearranged three-gun signal to let the rest of the flotilla know that he was still afloat, then set out upriver and anchored next morning off the mouth of the Red, up which he learned that the renegade *Queen* and the fast-steaming *Webb* had taken refuge after their flight from Porter's dummy ironclad. Both were too heavily damaged, as a result of their ram attacks on the *Indianola,* to be able to fight again without extensive repairs. So he heard; but he was taking no chances. Lowering the *Hartford*'s yards to the deck, he lashed them there and carried a heavy anchor chain from yard tip to yard tip, all the way round, to fend off attackers. Still unsatisfied, he improvised water-line armor by lashing cypress logs to the sides of the vessel and slung hawsers from the rigging, thirty feet above the deck, with heavy netting carried all the way down to the rail to frustrate would-be boarders. Then, accompanied by her six-gun escort *Albatross,* the *Hartford* — whose own builders would scarcely have recognized her, dressed out in this manner — set out northward, heading for Vicksburg in order to open communications with the upper fleet.

Passing Grand Gulf on March 19 the two ships came under fire that cost them 2 more killed and 6 more wounded, almost three times the number they had lost five nights ago; otherwise they encountered no opposition between Port Hudson and the point where they dropped anchor next morning, just beyond range of the lower Vicksburg batteries. Porter was up Steele Bayou, but

★

conferring that afternoon with Grant and A. W. Ellet, the ram fleet commander, Farragut asked that he be reinforced by units from the upper flotilla. Ellet volunteered to send two of his boats, the *Switzerland* and the *Lancaster,* respectively under C. R. Ellet, the former captain of the *Queen,* and his uncle Lieutenant Colonel J. A. Ellet. They made their run at first light, March 25. The *Lancaster* was struck repeatedly in her machinery and hull, but she made it downstream, where a week's patchwork labor would put her back in shape to fight again. Not so the *Switzerland;* she received a shell in her boilers and others which did such damage to her hull that she went to pieces and sank, affording her nineteen-year-old skipper another ride on a bale of cotton. Unperturbed, Grant reported her loss as a blessing in disguise, since it served to reveal her basic unfitness for combat: "It is almost certain that had she made one *ram* into another vessel she would have closed up like a spy-glass, encompassing all on board."

In point of fact, whatever the cost and entirely aside from his accustomed optimism, he and all who favored the Union cause had much to be joyful

---

"It is almost certain that had she made one ram into another vessel she would have closed up like a spy-glass, encompassing all on board."

— Ulysses S. Grant

---

about. As a result of this latest naval development, which would establish a blockade of the mouth of the Red and deny the rebels the use of their last extensive stretch of the Mississippi, Farragut had cut the Confederacy in two. The halves were still unconquered, and seemed likely to remain so for no one knew how long, but they were permanently severed one from the other. When the *Hartford* and the *Albatross* passed Port Hudson and were joined ten days later below Vicksburg by the steam ram *Lancaster,* the cattle and cereals of the Transmississippi, together with the goods of war that could be smuggled in through Mexico from Europe, became as inaccessible to the eastern South as if they were awaiting shipment on the moon.

This was not to say, conversely, that the Mississippi was open throughout its length to Federal commerce or even to Federal gunboats; that would not be the case, of course, until Vicksburg and Port Hudson had been taken or abolished. Continuing his efforts to accomplish this end, or anyhow his half of it, Grant was already engaged in the seventh of his experiments — which presently turned out to be the seventh of his failures. Work on the canal across the base of

★

Vicksburg Point having been abandoned, he sent an engineering party out to find a better site for such a project close at hand. Receiving a report that a little digging south of Duckport, just above Young's Point, would give the light-draft vessels access to Roundaway Bayou, which entered the main river at New Carthage, well below the Vicksburg and Warrenton batteries, Grant gave McClernand's men a turn on the picks and shovels. For once, however, he had no great hope that much would come of the enterprise, even if it went as planned — only the lightest-draft supply boats would be able to get through; besides, there would still be the Grand Gulf batteries to contend with — and for once he was right. Even this limited success depended on a rise of the river; whereupon the river, perverse as always, began to fall, leaving Grant with a seventh failure on his hands.

★ ★ ★ "This campaign is being badly managed," Cadwallader Washburn, a brigadier in McPherson's corps, informed his congressman brother Elihu in Washington. "I am sure of it. I fear a calamity before Vicksburg. All Grant's schemes have failed. He knows that he has got to do something or off goes his head. My impression is that he intends to attack in front." (Washburn's fears were better founded than he knew. Grant had just written a long letter to Banks, reviewing his lack of progress up to now, and in it he had stated flatly: "There is nothing left for me but to collect my strength and attack Haines Bluff. This will necessarily be attended with much loss, but I think it can be done." On April Fools' Day, however, accompanying Porter up the Yazoo for a reconnaissance of the position, he decided that such an attack "would be attended with immense sacrifice of life, if not defeat," and abandoned the notion, adding: "This, then, closes out the last hope of turning the enemy by the right.") Nor were others, farther removed from the scene of action, more reticent in giving their opinion of the disaster in store for the Army of the Tennessee. For example Marat Halstead, editor of the *Cincinnati Commercial*, addressed his friend the Secretary of the Treasury on the matter: "You do once in a while, don't you, say a word to the President, or Stanton, or Halleck, about the conduct of the war? Well now, for God's sake say that Genl Grant, entrusted with our greatest army, is a jackass in the original package. He is a poor drunken imbecile. He is a poor stick sober, and he is most of the time more than half drunk, and much of the time idiotically drunk. . . . Grant will fail miserably, hopelessly, eternally. You may look for and calculate his failures, in every position in which he may be placed, as a perfect certainty. Don't say I am grumbling. Alas! I know too well I am but feebly outlining the truth." Alarmed, Chase passed the letter on to Lincoln with the reminder that the *Commercial* was an influential paper, and the indorsement: "Reports concerning General Grant similar to the statements made by Mr Halstead are too common to be safely or even prudently disregarded." Lincoln read it with a sigh. "I think Grant has hardly a friend left, except myself," he told his secretary, and when a delegation came to protest Grant's alleged insobriety he put these civilians off with the remark, "If I knew what brand of whiskey he drinks I would send a barrel or so to some other generals." About this time a Nebraska brigadier, in Washington on leave from Vicksburg, called on the President and the two men got to talking. "What I want, and what the people want, is generals who will fight battles and win victories," Lincoln said. "Grant has done this, and I propose to stand by him."

The evidence was conflicting. Some said the general never touched a drop; others declared that he was seldom sober; while still others had him pegged as a spree drinker. "He tries to let liquor alone but he cannot resist the temptation always," a Wisconsin brigadier wrote home. "When he came to Memphis he left his wife at LaGrange, and for several days after getting here was beastly drunk, utterly incapable of doing anything. Quinby and I took him in charge, watching him day and night and keeping liquor away from him." According to this witness, the bender was only brought to an end when "we telegraphed to his wife and brought her on to take care of him." On the other hand, Mary Livermore — later famous as a suffragette — led a Sanitary Commission delegation down to Young's Point to investigate the rumors, and it was her opinion that the general's "clear eye, clean skin, firm flesh, and steady nerves . . . gave the lie to the universal calumnies then current concerning his intemperate habits." Still unsatisfied, Stanton sent the former Brook Farm colonist and Greeley journalist Charles Dana down the Mississippi, ostensibly as an inspector of the pay service, but actually as a spy for the War Department. He arrived in early April, became in effect a member of the general's military family, and soon was filing reports that glowed with praise not only of Grant but also of Sherman and McPherson, declaring that in their "unpretending simplicity" the three Ohioans were "as alike as three peas." McClernand did not fare so well in these dispatches; for if Dana acquired a fondness for the army commander's friends, he also developed a dislike for his enemies. Later he summed up his findings by describing Grant as "the most modest, the most disinterested, and the most honest man I ever knew, with a temper that nothing could disturb and a judgment that was judicial in its comprehensiveness and wisdom. Not a great man except morally; not an original or brilliant man, but sincere, thoughtful, deep, and gifted with courage that never faltered."

Aside from the rhetoric here included, practically all of the general's soldiers would have agreed with this assessment of his character and abilities, even though it was delivered in the wake of seven failures. "Everything that Grant directs is right," one declared. "His soldiers believe in him. In our private talks among ourselves I never heard a single soldier speak in doubt of Grant." According to a New York reporter, this was not only because of "his energy and disposition to do something," it was also because he had "the remarkable tact of never spoiling any mysterious and vague notions which [might] be entertained in

the minds of the privates as to the qualities of the commander-in-chief. He confines himself to saying and doing as little as possible before his men." Another
described him as "a man who could be silent in several languages," and it was remarked that, on the march, he was more inclined to talk of "Illinois horses, hogs,
cattle, and farming, than of the business actually at hand." In general he went
about his job, as one observer had stated at the outset, "with so little friction and
noise that it required a second look to be sure he was doing anything at all." One
of his staff officers got the impression that he was "half a dozen men condensed
into one," while a journalist, finding him puzzling in the extreme because he
seemed to amount to a good deal more than the sum of all his parts, came up
with the word "unpronounceable" as the one that described him best. Grant, he
wrote, "has none of the soldier's bearing about him, but is a man whom one
would take for a country merchant or a village lawyer. He had no distinctive fea-
ture; there are a thousand like him in personal appearance in the ranks. . . . A
plain, unpretending face, with a comely, brownish-red beard and a square forehead, of short stature and thick-set. He is we would say a good liver, and altogether an unpronounceable man; he is so like hundreds of others as to be only
described in general terms." The soldiers appreciated the lack of "superfluous

*General Grant's
liquor chest suggests that
he did drink, but how
much and when was the
subject of hot debate
among his supporters
and detractors.*

flummery" as he moved among them, "turning and chewing restlessly the end of his unlighted cigar." They almost never cheered him, and they did not often salute him formally; rather, they watched him, as one said, "with a certain sort of familiar reverence." Present discouragements were mutual; so, someday, would be the glory. Somehow he was more partner than boss; they were in this thing together. "Good morning, General," "Pleasant day, General," were the usual salutations, more fitting than cheers or hat-tossing exhibitions; "A pleasant salute to, and a good-natured nod from him in return, seems more appropriate." All these things were said of him, and this: "Here was no McClellan, begging the boys to allow him to light his cigar on theirs, or inquiring to what regiment that exceedingly fine-marching company belonged. . . . There was no nonsense, no sentiment; only a plain business man of the republic, there for the one single purpose of getting that command over the river in the shortest time possible."

Yet the fact remained that he and they were into their third month of camping almost within the shadow of the Vicksburg bluff, and all they had accomplished so far was the addition of five to their previous two failures; they were still not "over the river." However, as the flood waters receded, defining the banks of the bayous and even the network of greasy-looking roads hub-deep in mud, there were rumors that Grant was evolving an entirely new approach to the old problem. "As one after another of his schemes fail," Congressman Washburne heard from his brigadier brother — who had dropped the final euphonious "e" from his surname, presumably as superfluous baggage for a soldier — "I hear that he says he has a plan of his own which is yet to be tried [but] in which he has great confidence." Just what this was Grant would not say, either to subordinates or superiors, but his staff observed that he spent long hours in the former ladies' cabin of his headquarters boat the *Magnolia,* blueing the air with cigar smoke as he pored over maps and tentative orders, not so much inaccessible ("I aint got no business with you, General," they heard one caller tell him; "I just wanted to have a little talk with you, because folks will ask me if I did") as removed, withdrawn behind a barrier of intense preoccupation.

After several days of this, McPherson came into the cabin one evening, glass in hand, and stood facing Grant across the work-littered desk. "General, this won't do," he said. "You are injuring yourself. Join us in a few toasts, and throw this burden off your mind." Mrs Livermore, for one, would have been horrified, but what followed would have quickly reassured her. Grant looked up, smiled, and replied that whiskey was not the answer; if McPherson really wanted to help him, he said, he could give him a dozen cigars and leave him alone. McPherson did so, and Grant returned to brooding over his papers, still seeking a way to come to grips with the Confederates in their hilltop citadel.

★　★　★

Epilogue

—⟋⟍—

Much had happened during the winter and spring of 1862–1863, but it seemed that only on the home fronts could real changes be felt. In the North the war meant a booming economy as crafty entrepreneurs and expanding industries furnished food and equipment to the army and manufactured goods, grain, and wool for overseas markets. In the South the war meant an eroding economy. The Federal blockade and the lack of Confederate manufacturing led to a scarcity of many necessities. Rampant inflation and poor transportation and distribution systems resulted in widespread frustration: so much frustration, indeed, that beginning Easter week a series of protest rallies across the South erupted into full-fledged riots, with looters helping themselves to anything they could grab. And things were made worse when a risky bond issue floated by French bankers proved to benefit those bankers more than it did the Confederacy.

On the military front little seemed to have changed. General Ambrose Burnside had been driven twice from Fredericksburg, Virginia — once by galling Confederate resistance led by Robert E. Lee and once by heavy winter storms. Braxton Bragg had met William S. Rosecrans along Stones River near Murfreesboro, Tennessee, where the bloody two-day battle ended in a stalemate, but in a reprise of Antietam some months before, the Yankee Rosecrans remained in control of the field when Bragg withdrew south. Confederate cavalry raids by Morgan, Van Dorn, and Forrest had ravaged Federal supply depots and communications lines in Kentucky, Mississippi, and Tennessee, but these were quickly rebuilt and functioning again. John Magruder's men had recaptured Galveston from Federal control and had held on, but Hindman's rebels were stymied by Union forces at Prairie Grove, Arkansas. William Tecumseh Sherman had moved against the Confederate defenses north of Vicksburg but had been repulsed at Walnut Hills by Stephen D. Lee. Sherman had then gone with John McClernand to capture Fort Hindman on the Arkansas River, but its loss was of little consequence to the Confederacy. Federal Abel D. Streight had launched a mule-mounted infantry raid deep into rebel-held territory with the intention of severing the enemy's supply lines between Chattanooga and Atlanta, only to be captured by horse-mounted rebels under the leadership of Forrest. Admiral David Glasgow Farragut had managed to power his way upstream past the guns of Port Hudson and thus deprive the Confederacy of the use of the Mississippi between there and Vicksburg, but the heavily gunned bastions, mounted high on imposing cliffs at Port Hudson and Vicksburg, still kept the Father of Waters closed to Yankee trade. And then Ulysses S. Grant had attempted a series of expeditions to by-pass or incircle Vicksburg. Canals were dug, levees cut, and bayous dredged — to no avail. The fickle Mississippi — sometimes too high and other times too low — and the overgrown, insect-ridden terrain of the bayous thwarted each and every effort. Much had happened, but little had been accomplished, and the two sides would continue to grapple for an advantage.

Admiral Samuel F. Du Pont would attempt to strengthen the Union blockade by capturing Charleston, South Carolina, but Confederate general Pierre Gustave Toutant Beauregard, who had commanded the forces that took Fort Sumter at the beginning of the war, had strengthened the defenses of the port city and driven off Du Pont. While maneuvering for position around Fredericksburg, Federal cavalrymen, for the first time, began to prove themselves the equals of their southern counterparts. James Longstreet, detached from Robert E. Lee's main force near the Rappahannock to forage for supplies and harass the Unionists in Southside Virginia, was called to rejoin Lee when word came that Federal general Joseph Hooker was crossing the Rappahannock and marching south. Hooker's bluecoats met Robert E. Lee's graybacks in clamorous battle near Chancellorsville. Although a clear Confederate victory, the South lost one of its greatest assets when Stonewall Jackson was mortally wounded by his own men.

Out West, Grant's failed experiments had in fact yielded some important lessons. Farragut and Porter had proved that vessels could successfully steam beneath the guns of Vicksburg. Much had been learned of the terrain, and combined naval and infantry operations had provided valuable experience in working together. Grant was ready to move.

Grant sent troops overland south along the west bank of the river and directed the navy downstream, past the Vicksburg bluffs to a rendezvous below the city, beyond the reach of her guns. The sailors would then ferry the army to the east bank, where it would begin a drive inland, first to take Jackson, the Mississippi capital, and then backtrack west to besiege Vicksburg. It appeared that real changes were beginning.

★ ★ ★

Picture Credits

The sources for the illustrations in this book appear below. Credits from left to right are separated by semicolons, from top to bottom by dashes.

Dust jacket: Front, Library of Congress, Neg. No. LC-B8171-677; **rear,** Library of Congress, Neg. No. B8184-10006; **flap,** Larry Shirkey. **8-10**: From *The Photographic History of the Civil War in Ten Volumes,* Vol. 7, ed. by Francis Trevelyan Miller, Review of Reviews Company, New York, 1912. **13**: Collection of Old Capitol Museum of Mississippi History, Jackson. **17**: From *The Photographic History of the Civil War in Ten Volumes,* Vol. 2, ed. by Francis Trevelyan Miller, Review of Reviews Company, New York, 1912. **21**: Larry Sherer, courtesy Confederate Memorial Association, Washington, D.C. **27**: From *The Photographic History of the Civil War in Ten Volumes,* Vol. 7, ed. by Francis Trevelyan Miller, Review of Reviews Company, New York, 1912. **30-32**: Anne S. K. Brown Military Collection, Brown University Library, Providence. **36, 37**: Library of Congress, Waud #486. **39**: Massachusetts Commandery Military Order of the Loyal Legion and the U.S. Army Military History Institute (MASS-MOLLUS/USAMHI), copied by A. Pierce Bounds. **42**: Library of Congress, Waud #326. **45**: Library of Congress, Lumley #12. **48**: Map by Walter W. Roberts. **50**: From *The Long Arm of Lee,* Vol. 2, by Jennings Cropper Wise, J. P. Bell Company, Inc., Lynchburg, Va., 1915, courtesy Kirk Denkler. **53**: MASS-MOLLUS/USAMHI, copied by A. Pierce Bounds. **55**: Museum of the Confederacy, Richmond, Va. **58**: Color lithograph after a painting by Henry A. Ogden, Rochester Museum & Science Center, Rochester, N.Y. **61**: Library of Congress, Lumley #10. **64-66**: From *Battles and Leaders of the Civil War,* Vol. 3, ed. by Robert Underwood Johnson and Clarence Clough Buel, Century Company, New York, 1887. **69**: National Archives Neg. No. 111-B-1789. **73**: Arkansas History Commission, Little Rock. **77**: Alabama Department of Archives and History, Montgomery. **82**: Drawing by Frank Schell, Prints Collection, Miriam and Ira D. Wallach Division of Arts, Prints and Photographs, The New York Public Library, Astor, Lenox and Tilden Foundations. **84-86**: Frank and Marie-Thérèse Wood Print Collections, Alexandria, Va. **91**: L. M. Strayer Collection, Dayton. **95**: Painting by Nichole Marschall, Tennessee State Museum, copied by Bill La-Fevor. **100**: Collection of Old Capitol Museum of Mississippi History, Jackson, from *Van Dorn: The Life and Times of a Confederate General,* by Robert G. Hartje, Vanderbilt University Press, Nashville, 1967. **105**: Division of Naval History, National Museum of American History (NMAH), Smithso-

nian Institution. **108**: Karl Sundstrom Collection, copied by Richard A. Baumgartner. **110-112**: From *The Photographic History of the Civil War in Ten Volumes,* Vol. 2, ed. by Francis Trevelyan Miller, Review of Reviews Company, New York, 1912. **115**: Courtesy Chris Nelson. **119**: Courtesy Mrs. Robert J. Warner. **121**: Map by William L. Hezlep. **124**: Painting by William Travis, Division of Armed Forces History, NMAH, Smithsonian Institution. **126, 127**: Drawing by Henry Lovie, Print Collection, Miriam and Ira D. Wallach Division of Art, Prints and Photographs, The New York Public Library, Astor, Lenox and Tilden Foundations. **132**: Painting by William Travis, Division of Armed Forces History, NMAH, Smithsonian Institution. **135**: Map by William L. Hezlep. **137**: Valentine Museum, Richmond, Va. **140, 141**: Library of Congress, Neg. No. 262-13178. **146-148**: West Point Museum, U.S. Military Academy, copied by Henry Groskinsky. **150**: Trimble Family Papers, Ohio Historical Society, Columbus. **153, 157**: Frank and Marie-Thérèse Wood Print Collections, Alexandria, Va. **162**: Vermont Historical Society, Montpelier. **167**: Library of Congress, Neg. No. LC-B8171-677. **170**: Frank and Marie-Thérèse Wood Print Collections, Alexandria, Va. **175**: Library of Congress, Waud #718. **177, 182**: MASS-MOLLUS/USAMHI, copied by A. Pierce Bounds. **184, 186**: Library of Congress. **191**: From *Battles and Leaders of the Civil War,* Vol. 3, ed. by Robert Underwood Johnson and Clarence Clough Buel, Century Company, New York, 1887. **193**: Library of Congress, Neg. No. 8277 B811-2345. **196**: Chicago Historical Society, ICHi-10503. **200-202**: From Pennsylvania Historical & Museum Commission, Drake Well Museum Collection, Titusville, Pa. **207**: Courtesy Meserve-Kunhardt Collection, Mount Kisco, N.Y. **210**: Library of Congress, Neg. No. B8171-7719. **213, 215**: Frank and Marie-Thérèse Wood Print Collections, Alexandria, Va. **218-219**: Library of Congress, Neg. No. B8184-10869. **222**: Courtesy Meserve-Kunhardt Collection, Mount Kisco, N.Y. **225**: Frank and Marie-Thérèse Wood Print Collections, Alexandria Va. **228-230**: From *The Photographic History of the Civil War in Ten Volumes,* Vol. 2, ed. by Francis Trevelyan Miller, Review of Reviews Company, New York, 1912. **234, 235**: Courtesy E. Burns Apfeld Collection, Oshkosh, Wis., photographed by Bill Krueger. **239**: Confederate Memorial Hall, New Orleans—Museum of Mobile, photographed by Larry Cantrell. **242**: Library of Congress, Neg. No. B8172 1974. **244**: Museum of the Confederacy, Richmond, Va., photographed by Larry Sherer. **247**: National

Archives, Neg. No. 111-B-2748. **252:** From *The Photographic History of the Civil War in Ten Volumes*, Vol. 7, ed. by Francis Trevelyan Miller, Review of Reviews Company, New York, 1912. **254-256:** Frank and Marie-Thérèse Wood Print Collections, Alexandria, Va. **261:** Map by R. R. Donnelley & Sons Co., Cartographic Services. **265:** Ohio Historical Society, Columbus. **268:** Courtesy Mississippi Department of Archives and History, Jackson. **273:** Frank and Marie-Thérèse Wood Print Collections, Alexandria, Va. **277:** MASS-MOLLUS/USAMHI, copied by Robert Walch. **282:** Frank and Marie-Thérèse Wood Print Collections, Alexandria, Va. **286:** National Archives. **288:** From *The Photographic History of the Civil War in Ten Volumes*, Vol. 6, ed. by Francis Trevelyan Miller, Review of Reviews Company, New York, 1912. **294:** Chicago Historical Society, No. 1941.212.

Index

Numerals in italics indicate an illustration of the subject mentioned.

A

Alabama: 170-171, 172
Albatross: 291
Alexandria, Louisiana: 76, 195, 269
Alexandria, Tennessee: 118
Anderson, William C.: 192, 193
Arkansas: 20, 75, 103, 197, 267
Arkansas Post expedition: 184-187, 272
Arkansas River: 21, 68, 74, 184, 185, 191
Army of Mississippi: Davis's visit to, 15
Army of Northern Virginia: effective strength, 14, 35
Army of Tennessee: Davis's visit to, 15, 17; effective strength, 241, 243; Washington Light Artillery, 5th Company, *110-111*
Army of the Cumberland: cavalry, *8-9;* discipline in, *234-235;* effective strength, 243; infantry, *228-229*
Army of the Frontier: 68, 192
Army of the Mississippi: designation of, 184
Army of the Potomac: effective strength, 14, 34-35, 232; morale, 159-160, 161-162, 176
Army of the Tennessee: designation of, 92; morale, 262-263; regard for Grant, 293-295
Army of the Trans-Mississippi: Arkansas volunteers, *73*
Atchafalaya: 285, 286
Atlanta, Georgia: 19, 28, 245; bread riots in, 224-225

B

Banks, Nathaniel P.: 20, 27, 28, 75, 76-79, 80, 83, 149, 171, 188, 189, 190-191, 195, 197, 264, 285, 286, 292
Banks Ford: 174
Barksdale, William: 41, 43
Bates, Edward: 152, 156
Bateville, Arkansas: 191
Baton Rouge, Louisiana: 28, 189; Federal reoccupation of, 20, 75, 78
Bayou Baxter: 264, 266, 274
Bayou City: 81
Bayou Teche: 76, 79, 189; Confederate gunboat in, *190*
Beatty, Samuel: 134, 137, 138
Beauregard, P. G. T.: 297
Benjamin, Judah P.: 214, 216, 222-223

Benton: 104-*105*
Black Bayou: 279, 280, 283, 284
Black Hawk: 185, 271, 279
Black River: 264
Blockade: 7, 20, 80, 169, 296, 297
Blockade-runners: 28
Blue Wing: 184
Blunt, James G.: *69,* 70, 71, 72, 73, 74, 191
Boston Mountains: 68, 69, 194
Bragg, Braxton: 6, 15, 16, 17, 18, 27, 93, 94, 113, 114, 116-119, 143, 169, 195, 235, *239,* 242, 243, 244, 245, 248, 253, 296; criticism of, 232, 236-241; and Murfreesboro, 28, 29, 120-122, 125, 128-131, 133-142; sword of, *239*
Breckinridge, John C.: 121, 122, 129, 130, 134, 135, 136, *137,* 138-139, 232, 237
Brentwood, Tennessee: 116, 243
Brierfield (plantation): 26, 270
Brooklyn: 83, 169-170, 171
Brown, George: 269-270, 271
Brown, Isaac N.: 20, 103, 107
Brown, John: 69, 194
Browning, Orville: 155, 164
Brownson, Orestes: 150-151
Bucklin, McDonough: 205-206
Buell, Don Carlos: 113, 114, 123
Burnside, Ambrose E.: 6, 7, 14, 18, 149, 159, 160, 161, 163, 165-166, 172, 296; dismissal of, 176-178; and Fredericksburg, 34-35, 36, 37-39, 40, 42, 44, 52, 54, 56, *58,* 59-60, 61, 62, 63; headquarters of, *167;* and Mud March, 148, 173-176
Butler, Benjamin F.: 20, 77, 78, 144, 189, 197

C

Cairo: 20, 29, 103, 231, 272
Cameron, Simon: 157
Campbellsville, Tennessee: 118, 133
Cane Hill, Arkansas: 70, 71
Cary, Constance: 244
Chancellorsville, Battle of: 297
Charleston, South Carolina: 219, 297
Chase, Salmon P.: 152, 153, 156-*157,* 158-159, 292
Chattanooga, Tennessee: 15, 16, 17, 18, 19, 27, 28, 29, 107, 113, 130, 233, 235, 239, 245

Cheatham, Benjamin: 124, 125, 128, 129, 139, 236, 237
Chickasaw Bayou: 106
Chickasaw Bluffs: 19, 90; Battle of, 26-27, *84-85*, 104-109, 183, 231, 263
Chillicothe: 277, 278
Chimborazo Hospital: *218-219*
Christmas Raid: 118-119
Cincinnati: 185, 186
Cleburne, Patrick R.: 121, 122-123, 125, 129, 237
Clifton: 81, 82
Clifton, Tennessee: 93, 96, 97
Cobb, Thomas R. R.: 51, *55*
Cochrane, John: 160-161, 162, 177
Coffeeville, Mississippi: 89, 187, 189
Coldwater River: 274, 275, 276, 277, 278
Colors (Confederate): 14th Mississippi Infantry, detail from, *13;* Van Dorn's personal flag, *244*
Columbia, Tennessee: 93, 118, 241, 242, 243, 244
Columbus, Kentucky: 93, 96, 101
Confederacy: bread riots in, 7, 223-224, *225*, 226, 296; Congress, 221-222, 226; conscription in, 68, 221; economy, erosion of, 7, 218-220, 296; foreign recognition, hopes for, 6, 24, 211-212; money used in, 218-219; morale in, 13-14, 15, 24-25, 29, 231; social transformations in, 216-217; territory lost by, 13; war strategy of, 6
Corinth, Mississippi: 96, 97, 168, 246, 253
Cotton: 190
Crittenden, T. L.: 114, 116, 119, 120, 125, 126, 127-128, 134, 135, 137, 232-233, 235
Cumberland River: 16, 17, 115, 118, 241, 245, 246
Curtis, Samuel: 192, 193, 197

D

Dana, Charles: 293
Davis, Jefferson: 6, 7, *13,* 57, 67, 74, 75, 98, 116, 118, 132, 194, 214, 223, 270; addresses welcoming crowd in Richmond, 143-145; address to Mississippi legislature, 22-25; and Bragg, 238, 239-240; and civilian morale, 226-227; and defense of Vicksburg, 18, 19-22, 26-27; and Johnston, 16, 26; and Lee, 14; and Richmond bread riot, 223-224; strain on, 12; western theater of operations, visit to, 11-29
Davis, Jefferson, C.: 123
Davis, Joseph: 26
Davis, Varina: 143, 223
Davis Bend: 26, 270
Day's Gap: 247, 248
Deer Creek: 279, 280
De Kalb: 185, 277, 278
DeSoto: 267, 268
Dodge, Grenville M.: 246, *247,* 248, 253
Duck River: 28, 141, 142, 195, 236, 241
Du Pont, Samuel F.: 297

E

Early, Jubal: 46, 52
Eastport Mississippi: 246

Elizabethtown, Tennessee: 118
Elkhorn Tavern: 71, 98
Ellet, A. W.: 267, 291
Ellet, Charles, Jr.: 267
Ellet, Charles R.: 107, 267, 268, 269, 270, 275, 291
Ellet, J. A.: 291
Emancipation Proclamation: 144, 153, 164-165, 168, 213
England: *See* Great Britain
Era No. 5: 267, 268, 269
Erlanger et Cie: 214-215

F

Falmouth, Virginia: 162, 166, 176
Farragut, David G.: 20, 27, 78, 80, 90, 260, 276, 285, *286,* 291, 296, 297
Fayetteville, Arkansas: 69, 71, 74, 191, 192
Fessenden, William Pitt: 151, 155, 157
Florida: 171-172
Foote, Henry S.: 221-*222*
Forrest, Nathan Bedford: 10, 26, 28, 29, 92-94, *95,* 96-98, 99, 101, 109, 115, 116, 119, 133, 242, 243, 296; and Streight's raid, 245, 248-253
Fort Henry: 96, 97, 246, 276
Fort Hindman: 184, 196, 296; attack on, 185-*186,* 187
Fort Pemberton: 276-278
Fox, G. A.: 272, 280
France: and Confederate recognition, 115, 211-212; financial speculation by, 7, 214-216, 296
Franklin, Tennessee: 243, 244
Franklin, William B.: 40, 52, 54, 56, 60, 176, 177, 178
Fredericksburg, Battle of: 19, 24, *30-31,* 33, 34-47, *map* 48, 49-63, 231, 232; casualties, *61,* 62-63, 139
Fredericksburg, Virginia: 14, 33-34, *36-37,* 38, 148, 166; artillery fire on, 43; Federal looting of, 44-*45,* 63, 144

G

Gadsden, Alabama: 250, 253
Galveston, Texas: 169, 171; Confederate recapture of, 6, 28, 66, 80-83, 169
Garesché, Julius P.: *126-127*
Grand Gulf, Mississippi: 260, 264, 270, 290
Grand Junction, Tennessee: 88, 101, 187
Granger, Gordon: 293
Grant, Ulysses S.: 6, 7, 15, 20, 22, 26, 27, 29, 149, 182, 183, 185, 187, 191, 195, *196,* 199, 233, 234, 235, 257-258, 261, 277, 286, 291, 295, 297; allegations of insobriety, 293, 294; liquor chest of, *294;* and McClernand, 87-88, 89, 92, 188-189, 195-198, 258-259; soldiers' regard for, 293-295; Vicksburg, operations to by-pass, 256, 259-262, 263, 264, 266, 272, 274-275, 278-279, 280, 285, 291-292, 297; Vicksburg, overland offensive on, 88-92, 93, 96, 97, 98, 101-102, 107, 109, 133
Great Britain: and American cotton, 212; antislavery sentiment in, 213; and Confederate recognition, 115, 212-213; munitions exports by, 212; Northern grain shipments to, 206, 216; political cartoons, *213*
Greeley, Horace: 203

Grenada, Mississippi: 21, 88, 90, 99, 101, 107, 109

H

Haines Bluff: 103, 107, 274, 279, 292
Halleck, Henry W.: 88, 89, 92, 113, 114, 142-143, 166, 167-168, 173, 178, 188, 197, 198, 233, 235, 243, 259, 262, 264
Hamilton, Andrew Jackson: 79-80, 83
Hamilton's Crossing, Virginia: 35, 46, 50
Hardee, William J.: 117, 120, 121, 122, 129, 140, 141, 237, 239, 241
Harpers Ferry, Virginia: 6, 34
Harpeth Shoals, Tennessee: 241
Harriet Lane: Confederate capture of, *64-65*, 81
Hartford: 287, 290, 291
Hatteras: 170-171
Hay, John: 209
Helena, Arkansas: 68, 74, 83, 91, 102, 259, 275
Herron, Francis J.: 69, 70-71, 72, 73-74, 191
Hill, Ambrose P.: 46, 52
Hill, Daniel H.: 46
Hindman, Thomas C.: 6, 20, 68, 69-70, 71-72, 73, 74, 191, 194, 195, 296
Holly Springs, Mississippi: 26, 88, 93, 99, 101, 102, 107, 133, 187
Holmes, Theophilus H.: 20, 21, 67-68, 69, 72, 74, 75, 83, 194, 195
Hood, John Bell: 46
Hooker, Joseph: 40, 54, 57, *58*, 60, 176, *177*, 297; appointed to command Army of the Potomac, 178
Humphreys, Andrew: 57-58
Hunt, Henry: 42-43
Huntingdon, Tennessee: 97
Hurlbut, S. A.: 96, 262
Hurricane, the (plantation): 26

I

Illinois Creek: 71, 72
Indianola: 269-271, 273-274, 287, 290
Ingersoll, Robert G.: 93-94

J

Jackson, Mississippi: 26, 297; Davis in, 11, 12-13, 19, 21, 22
Jackson, Tennessee: 93, 94
Jackson, Thomas Jonathan: 35, 36, 37, 39, 42, 44, 46, 47-49, 50, 52, 54, 55-56, 63, 77, 297
Johnson's Farm: 104, 105
Johnston, Albert Sidney: 136
Johnston, Joseph E.: 15, 17, 19, *21*, 25, 67, 74; and Bragg, 238-241; and coördination of defense in Mississippi and Tennessee, 18, 20, 21, 22, 25-26, 242; and Davis, 16

L

LaGrange, Tennessee: 101, 187, 189, 198
Lake Providence: 264, *265*, 274, 275
Lancaster: 291

La Vergne, Tennessee: 116, 119
Lee, Mary Custis: 34
Lee, Robert E.: 6, 14, 19, 24, 132, 163, 168, 194, 240, 296, 297; and Fredericksburg, 34, 35, 36, 37, 38, 40, 41, 42, 43, 44, 46-49, 50, 51, 52, 54, 59, 63, 232
Lee, Stephen D.: 6, *108*, 109, 296
Lee's Hill: 46, 49, 54, 59
Letcher, John: 223-224
Lincoln, Abraham: 34, 87, 88, 114, 142, 149-150, 160, 161, 162-163, 165-167, 172-173, 176, 183, 188, 192, 193, 196, 197, 198, 205, 209, 234, 259; and Burnside, dismissal of, 177-178; and Chase, 152; criticism of, 150-152; and Emancipation Proclamation, 6, 163-165, 168, 213; and Grant, 292-293; and Halleck, 168-169; and Hooker, 178-179; and radical Republican intrigues, 153-159
Little Rock, Arkansas: 21, 67, 69, 74, 195
London *Times:* 212
Longstreet, James: 35, 36, 37, 42, 43, 44, 46, 47, 48-49, 51, 54, 59, 63, 297
Loring, W. W.: 276, 278
Louisville: 185
Louisville & Nashville Railroad: 118, 245
Lyons, Nathaniel: 70

M

McClellan, George B.: 6, 14, 34, 35, 38, 40, 60, 163, 165, 168, 275
McClernand, John: 87-88, 89, 92, 102, 108, 109, 149-150, 182, *184*, 195, 258-259, 262, 292, 293, 296; and Arkansas Post expedition, 183-187, 188, 189, 195-196
McCook, Alexander: 114, 116, 119, 120-121, 123, *124*, 125, 131, 140
McCown, John: 117, 120, 122, 123, 129
McDowell, Irvin: 163
McLaws, Lafayette: 46
McMinnville, Tennessee: 241, 242
McPherson, J. B.: 88, 187, 189, 198, 262, 264-266, 274, 275, 292, 293, 295
Maffitt, John N.: 171
Magnolia: 295
Magruder, John B.: 68, 132, 172, 194; Galveston recaptured by, 28, 80-81, 83, 169, 296
Marmaduke, John S.: 191, 192
Marye's Heights: *36-37*, 49; attacks at, *30-31*, 50-51, 54-55, 56-58, 160
Mason, James M.: 215, 216
Massaponax Creek: 35, 46
Meade, George G.: 52, 54
Memphis, Tennessee: 13, 27, 79, 88, 89, 91, 92, 96, 101, 133, 187, 189, 197, 198, 257, 259, 262
Memphis & Charleston Railroad: 15, 19, 101
Mendenhall, John: 137-138
Meredith, Minerva: 223
Milliken's Bend: 104, 109, 183, 185, 197
Mississippi: 287, 289-290
Mississippi Central Railroad: 88, 90, 100, 263
Mississippi River: 15, 18, 20, 24, 67, 68, 75, 77, 80,

83, 88, 89, 92, 104, 184, 189, 194, 198, 256, 257, 262, 264, 274, 275, 280, 285, 286, 290, 291, 296; 297; Federal transports on, *180-181*

Missouri: Confederate hopes for recovery of, 68; guerilla activity in, 192, 193-194

Mobile, Alabama: 19, 27-28, 77, 83, 107, 169, 171, 225, 238, 239, 240

Mobile & Ohio Railroad: 94

Monitor: 169, *170*

Monongahela: 287, *288-289*

Montgomery, Alabama: 11, 19, 28, 253

Moore, Absalom B.: 17

Morgan, George W.: 105, 106, 184, 186, 187

Morgan, John Hunt: 6, 10, 16-17, 20, *27,* 28, 29, 115, 116, 118, *119,* 123, 133, 242, 296; Christmas Raid, 118-119

Morgan, Mattie Ready: 118, *119*

Morgan, W. H.: 99-100, 101

Morning Light: 172

Mount Hope, Alabama: 247, 248

Mud March: *146-147,* 173-174, *175,* 176

Murfreesboro, Battle of, 28, 29, 120, *map* 121, 122-123, *124,* 125, *126-127,* 129-134, *map* 135, 136-140, 232; casualties, 139

Murfreesboro, Tennessee: 16, 116, 117-118, 120, 130, 169, 233, 243; courthouse at, *17;* Federal troops entering, *140-141*

N

Napoleon, Arkansas: 189, 195, 197, 199

Napoleon III: 212, 214, 215-216

Nashville, Tennessee: 13, 15, 28, 116, 117, 130, 131, 134, 243, 245

Nashville & Chattanooga Railroad: 116, 117, 245

Nashville & Northwestern Railroad: 95

Negley, J. S.: 125, 128

Neptune: 81

New Albany, Mississippi: 99

New Carthage, Louisiana: 270, 292

New England: cotton shortages in textile mills of, 79

New Orleans, Louisiana: 13, 20, 24, 76, 77, 78, 83, 188, 189, 218, 266, 276, 286; cotton speculation in, 78-79, 149

Newspapers: political cartoons, *213*

Newton, John: 160-161, *162,* 177

New York, New York: merchant ships in, *207*

North: conscription, 209, 260; election results, 260; Great Lakes trade with Gulf, 264; immigration, 208; industrial growth in, 7, 202, 206-208, 296; morale, 260; oils fields in, *200-201,* 206-208; paper money, value of, 204; profiteering on government contracts, 203-204; trade-union movement, 205; universities, 208

North Carolina: Federal operations in, 18-19

O

Obion River: 95, 97

Oostanaula River: 251, 253

Owasco: 81, 82

Oxford, Mississippi: 88, 90, 99, 101, 102

P

Palmer, John: 126, 136

Palmerston, Lord: 212, 213-214, *215,* 216

Parker's Crossroads, Battle of: 28, 97, 133

Pelham, John: 49-*50,* 52, 54

Pemberton, John C.: 15, 18, 21-22, 67, 75, 88-89, 91, 93, 98, 99, 101, 102, 109, 116, 194, 195, 235, 242

Pettus, J. J.: 13, 15, 22

Phelan, James: 13-14, 15, 22, 24, 98

Philadelphia, Pennsylvania: 206

Pickett, George: 46

Polk, James K.: 150

Polk, Leonidas: 117, 118, 120, 122, 124, 129, 133-134, 136, 139, 140, 141, 236, 237, 238, 239, 241

Pope, John: 38, 163, 168

Porter, David: 27, 91, 103-104, 107, 108, 185, 186, 187, 195, 197, 199, 266-267, 269, 270, 271, 272, *277,* 278, 292, 297; fake gunboat employed by, 272, *273,* 274; and Steele Bayou expedition, 279-285, 290

Port Hudson, Louisiana: 20, 27, 28, 75, 78, 79, 188, 189, 191, 195, 264, 266, 285, 286, 296; Farragut's fleet runs batteries at, 287-290, 291

Port Royal, Virginia: 35, 44, 46

Prairie Grove, Arkansas: 71; Battle of, 7, 20, 71-73, 192

Preston, William: 136-137

Price, Sterling: 194, 195

Q

Quantrill, William C.: 192, 194

Queen of the West: 267, *268,* 269, 270-271, 272, *273,* 275, 286-287, 290

R

Rappahannock River: 14, 15, 18, 19, 34, 35, *36-37,* 40, *map* 48, 59, 159, 161, 166, 173; pontoon bridges laid across, 41, *42,* 43

Ready, Mattie: 118

Red River: 21, 77, 80, 195, 264, 266, 267, 269, 270, 285, 286, 290, 291

Rhode Island: 170

Richmond, Fredericksburg & Potomac Railroad: 35

Richmond, Virginia: 14, 18, 24, 29, 34; bread riots in, 7, 223-224, *225,* 226; fortifications at, 217; hospitals in, *218-219;* life in, 217-221

Richmond: 287, 289

Rolling Fork: 279, 283, 284

Rome, Georgia: 248, 251, 253

Rosecrans, William S.: 6, 15, 18, 27, 113-114, *115,* 116, 117, 118, *132,* 149, 169, 197, 232, 233, 241, 242, 243, 245-246, 296; in camp, *234-235;* and Murfreesboro, 28, 120-122, 125-128, 130, 131-132, 133, 134, *142-143*

Round Forest: 134, 135; fighting in, 128-130

Rousseau, Lovell: 128

S

Sachem: 81, 82
Sanson, Emma: 250
Schofield, John M.: 68-69, 73-74, 191, 192, 193-194
Scott, Winfield: 163
Seddon, James A.: 240, 241
Selfridge, T. O., Jr.: 103
Semmes, Raphael: 171
Seward, William H.: 152, *153,* 154, 155, 157, 158, 159, 161, 164, 212, 216
Shelby, J. O.: 191
Shelbyville, Tennessee: 140, 241
Sheridan, Philip: 123, 124, 125, 128, 130, 230, 243
Sherman, John: 198, 199, 263
Sherman, William T.: 6, 88, *91,* 92, 96, 102, 103, 183, 184, 185, 186, 187, 189, 195, 196, 197, 198-199, 262, 263, 264, 265, 266, 267, 274, 293; and Chickasaw Bluffs, 26-27, 86, 106-109, 133, 296; and Grant, 89-90, 91; and Steele Bayou expedition, 280, 283, 284, 285
Sill, Joshua: 125
Skinker's Neck: 35, 38, 40, 44
Slidell, John: 214, 216
Smith, A. J.: 105
Smith, C. A.: 78
Smith, Edmund Kirby: 6, 15-16, 194-195
Smith, J. B.: 143
Smith, Martin L.: 109
Smith, Morgan L.: 105
Smith, W. F.: 60, 177
Smith, Watson: 277, 278
Smithville, Tennessee: 118
Springfield, Missouri: 69, 70, 191
Spring Hill, Tennessee: 243, 244, 248
Stafford Heights: 43, 44, 46, 48, 49, 54, 56
Stanton, Edwin M.: 87, 88, 142, 143, 152, 157, 158, 166, 167, 168, 178, 183, 184, 233, 293
Star of the West: 276
Steele, Frederick: 105, 106, 107
Steele Bayou: expedition, 279-285; Federal transports in, *282*
Stones River: 116, 117, 120, 122, 125, 134, 137, 141, 142, 169
Streight, Abel D.: 245-251, *252,* 253, 296
Stuart, J. E. B.: 46, 47, 50, 52
Sullivan, Jeremiah: 94, 96, 97
Sumner, Edwin V.: 40, 52, 54, 57, 60, 178, 192, *193;* and staff, *39*
Sunflower River: 279, 284
Sunken road: 51, *53,* 55
Switzerland: 291

T

Taliaferro, William: 46
Tallahatchie River: 88, 274, 275, 277
Taylor, Richard: 68, 75-76, *77,* 79, 190, 194, 195
Tennessee River: 93, 96, 97, 246, 247, 248
Texas: operations in, 79-83
Thomas, George: 114, 116, 120, 125, 128, 131

Tigress: 180-181, 183, 187
Tilghman, Lloyd: 276, 278
Toombs, Robert: 227
Transmississippi: and defense of Vicksburg, 18, 20-21, 67, 74-75, 83, 194; movement of supplies from, 266, 291; operations in, 67-76, 194-195
Trent affair: 214
Tullahoma, Tennessee: 28, 140, 141, 143, 236, 240
Tuscumbia, Alabama: 247, 253

V

Vallandigham, Clement L.: *150*
Van Buren, Arkansas: 68, 70, 74, 191
Van Cleve, Horatio: 126, 129, 134, 136, 137, 138
Van Dorn, Earl: 6, 22, 26, 28, 68, 71, 98-99, *100,* 101, 109, 133, 194, 242-244, 253, 276, 296; personal flag of, *244*
Velocity: 172
Vicksburg, Mississippi: 7, 15, 18, 19, 26, 27, 29, 74, 75, 77, 78, 83, 184, 188, 194, 195, 197, 198, 233, 235, 257, 260, 266, 286, 290, 291; Federal operations to bypass, *map* 261, 263-266, 274-285, 291-292; Federal overland offensive on, 88-92, 102-109; fortifications and batteries at, 19-20, 264, 273, 292, 296-297
Vicksburg Point: canal cut at, *254-255,* 263-264, 266, 273, 274, 291-292

W

Wade, Ben: 154, 155, 156
Wallace, Lew: 74
Walnut Hills: 6, 19, 90, 105, 107
Warrenton, Mississippi: 19, 260, 264, 267, 273, 292
Wartrace, Tennessee: 141, 241
Washburn, Cadwallader: 292
Washburne, Elihu B.: 275, 292, 295
Washington, D.C.: 88, 207; defenses at, 14, 34; life in, 209-*210,* 211
Weitzel, Godfrey: 189, 190
Welles, Gideon: 152, 157, 158, 172, 199, 267
Western & Atlantic Railroad: 245, 248
Westfield: 81, *82*
West Virginia: admission of, 152-153
Wheeler, Joseph: 10, 117, 119-120, 134, 241, *242,* 243, 245
White River: 185, 191, 196
William H. Webb: 269, 270-271, 273, 290
Wilmington, North Carolina: 28, 29
Wilson, James H.: 274-276, 278-279
Withers, J. M.: 124, 128, 129, 139, 236, 237
Worsham, Johnny: 217, 223

Y

Yalobusha River: 22, 89, 91, 98, 99, 107, 260, 274, 276
Yancey, William L.: 221
Yazoo Pass expedition: 274-279
Yazoo River: 19, 20, 29, 90, 91, 103, 104, 105, 107, 109, 133, 183, 185, 274, 277, 279, 280, 285, 292
Young's Point: 257, 260, 264, 279, 280, 293

SHELBY FOOTE, THE CIVIL WAR, A NARRATIVE
VOLUME 5 FREDERICKSBURG TO STEELE BAYOU

Text Copyright © 1963 by Shelby Foote
Copyright renewed 1986 by Shelby Foote
Prologue and Epilogue © 1999 by Shelby Foote
All rights reserved.

Originally published in 1963 by Random House, Inc., New York, as part of Volume II of *The Civil War, A Narrative: Fredericksburg to Meridian* by Shelby Foote.

This Time-Life edition is published by arrangement with Random House, Inc.
Cover, text design, captions, and this adaptation © 1999 Time Life Inc.

This volume is one of a series entitled *Shelby Foote, The Civil War, A Narrative.*

First printing. Printed in U.S.A.
School and library distribution by Time-Life Education, P.O. Box 85026, Richmond, Virginia 23285-5026.

TIME-LIFE is a trademark of Time Warner Inc. U.S.A.

Library of Congress Cataloging-in-Publication Data
Foote, Shelby.
  [Civil War, a narrative]
  Shelby Foote, the Civil War, a narrative / by Shelby Foote and the editors of Time-Life Books. — 40th Anniversary ed.
    p. cm.
    Originally published: The Civil War, a narrative.
New York: Random House, 1958-1974, in 3 v.
    Includes illustrations and indexes.
    Contents: v. 5 Fredericksburg to Steele Bayou
    1.United States—History—Civil War, 1861-1865.
I. Time-Life Books. II. Title.
E468.F7 1999   99-13486
973.7—dc21   CIP
ISBN 0-7835-0104-8

For information on and a full description of any of the Time-Life Books series listed at right, please call 1-800-621-7026 or write:
Reader Information
Time-Life Customer Service
P.O. Box C-32068
Richmond, Virginia 23261-2068

Time-Life Books is a division of Time Life Inc.

TIME LIFE INC.
PRESIDENT and CEO: George Artandi

TIME-LIFE BOOKS
PUBLISHER/MANAGING EDITOR: Neil Kagan
SENIOR VICE PRESIDENT,
MARKETING: Joseph A. Kuna
VICE PRESIDENT, NEW PRODUCT
DEVELOPMENT: Amy Golden
DIRECTOR OF MARKETING: Pamela R. Farrell

EDITOR: Philip Brandt George
DIRECTOR, NEW PRODUCT
DEVELOPMENT: Elizabeth D. Ward
Art Director: Ellen L. Pattisall
Marketing Manager: Peter Tardif
Senior Copyeditor: Judith Klein
Photo Coordinator: Susan L. Finken
Editorial Assistant: Patricia D. Whiteford

Special Contributors: Patricia Spayd Bray, John Drummond, Jennifer A. Gearhart, Kimberly Grandcolas, Belen Price (design and production); Roy Nanovic (index).

Correspondent: Christina Lieberman (New York).

Director of Finance: Christopher Hearing
Directors of Book Production: Marjann Caldwell, Patricia Pascale
Director of Publishing Technology: Betsi McGrath
Director of Photography and Research:
John Conrad Weiser
Director of Editorial Administration: Barbara Levitt
Manager, Technical Services: Anne Topp
Senior Production Manager: Ken Sabol
Quality Assurance Manager: James King
Chief Librarian: Louise D. Forstall

OTHER TIME-LIFE HISTORY PUBLICATIONS

Our American Century
What Life Was Like
The American Story
Voices of the Civil War
The American Indians
Lost Civilizations
Time Frame
The Civil War
Cultural Atlas
World War II
Echoes of Glory